D0987014

🌿 🌿 🌿   THE ENCHANTED AMAZON RAIN FOREST

NIGEL J. H. SMITH

THE ENCHANTED

Amazon RAIN FOREST

Stories from a Vanishing World

UNIVERSITY PRESS OF FLORIDA
GAINESVILLE
TALLAHASSEE
TAMPA
BOCA RATON
PENSACOLA
ORLANDO
MIAMI
JACKSONVILLE

HALF HOLLOW HILLS
COMMUNITY LIBRARY

Copyright 1996 by the Board of Regents of the State of Florida
Printed in the United States of America on acid-free paper
All rights reserved

01   00   99   98   97   96   6   5   4   3   2   1

Library of Congress Cataloging-in-Publication Data

Smith, Nigel J. H., 1949-
The enchanted Amazon rain forest: stories from a vanishing world / Nigel J. H. Smith.
p. cm.
Includes bibliographical references and index.
ISBN 0-8130-1377-1
1. Folklore—Amazon River Region. 2. Indians of South America—Amazon River
Region—Folklore. 3. Man—Influence on nature—Amazon River Region. I. Title.
GR133.A43S65 1996
398'.0981'1—dc20   95-45626

The University Press of Florida is the scholarly publishing agency for the State
University System of Florida, comprised of Florida A & M University, Florida Atlantic
University, Florida International University, Florida State University, University of
Central Florida, University of Florida, University of North Florida, University of South
Florida, and University of West Florida.

University Press of Florida
15 Northwest 15th Street
Gainesville, FL 32611

To Lisa, Arianne, Hillary, and Noel

✺   ✺   ✺   C O N T E N T S

The Amazon basin encompasses the world's largest remaining wilderness, but it is being developed at an accelerating pace. Bulldozers, dam builders, cattle ranchers, and mining operators are irreversibly altering the landscape and the ways of life of people inhabiting the most extensive tropical rain forest in the world. For centuries the region has lingered as a cultural and economic backwater, ignored by the main currents of economic development. A few boom-and-bust cycles, such as that of rubber, have come and gone, leaving little lasting impact on the economy of the region; some became millionaires, but after each cycle collapsed, most people remained poor and returned to traditional activities. The isolation of Amazonia from the mainstream of national life in the several countries that share the basin—Brazil, Bolivia, Peru, Ecuador, Colombia, and Venezuela—has served to foster a sense of awe and mystery about the seven-million-square-kilometer jungle.

The relatively quiet isolation of Amazonia has been ruptured forever over the last thirty years. Pioneer roads have sliced across broad sections of the basin, bringing in their wake hordes of land-hungry peasants, ranchers, speculators, and gold miners. Imposing dams have transformed several river systems and have drowned extensive tracts of forest. Mining operations are tearing gaping holes in the earth to extract iron ore, manganese, cassiterite, and other minerals.

The aspirations of governments and people living in and around the Amazon basin to tap the region's natural resources are understandable. No one would expect the governments of Brazil, Colombia, Peru, or other countries with territories in Amazonia to leave the region intact as a zoo or museum for foreigners to visit in a relatively "pristine" state. Nevertheless, the manner in which resources are being tapped, and in many cases abused, has fomented often-heated debate both in the region and abroad.

The unprecedented scale of development and ecological change in Amazonia has stirred widespread concern about the fate of the forest and indigenous people. The assassination of Chico Mendes, an organizer of rubber tappers, in 1988 brought many of the issues surrounding competition for land and resources to a head. In the past, debate about the struggle for space and natural resources in Amazonia tended to be cast in rather simplistic terms: the "good" (downtrodden peasants and indigenous groups) versus the "bad" (large landholders and multinational corporations). The actual picture is much more complicated, comprising a wide spectrum of actors with varying perceptions and abilities to inflict drastic changes on the environment.

The purpose of this book is not to explore the complex socioeconomic and ecological issues surrounding development in Amazonia. Rather, it is hoped that by highlighting some of the "subliminal" messages about conservation and respect for nature inherent in Amazonia lore, some lessons may be drawn for more rational use of the region's resources. It would be foolish to suggest that superstition and belief in myths should substitute for a sounder scientific understanding of the region's ecosystems and ways in which people interact with them. Yet some of the stories told of spirits that protect fish, game, and certain economic plants could be more widely taught in schools as examples of a more caring attitude toward nature. The roots of the environmental problems in Amazonia, as elsewhere, are as much ethical and moral as they are economic.

ꙮ　ꙮ　ꙮ

A number of institutions and organizations provided support for my fieldwork in the Amazon during the 1976–94 period, when I collected stories and legends from rural folk. While I was a researcher at the National Institute for Amazonian Research (INPA—Instituto Nacional de Pesquisas da Amazônia), I lived in Itacoatiara for most of 1977, during which time I visited fishing grounds and communities on the Amazon floodplain. I am very grateful to

INPA for the privilege of spending several years in a fascinating region. INPA provided me with a supportive environment in which to learn about the Amazon's biodiversity and rich culture.

In 1988, I was able to gather more stories on lore while collecting data on plant genetic resources for the Secretariat of the Consultative Group on International Agricultural Research (CGIAR), World Bank. As a participant in the Critical Environmental Zones Project led by Roger Kasperson, Jeanne Kasperson, and Bill Turner II at Clark University, I had the opportunity to visit the Amazon several times during the 1991–93 period. This project was supported with funds from the National Science Foundation and the United Nations University in Tokyo. Additional tales and legends were garnered during several consulting missions for Cali-based CIAT (Centro Internacional de Agricultura Tropical) and for the Latin America–Environment (LATEN) division of the World Bank from 1992 to 1994. I do not wish to imply, however, that any institution or organization endorses this study.

I am greatly indebted to the late Charles Wagley for the inspiration and encouragement to explore the significance of folklore among rural inhabitants in Amazonia for conservation and development. I am not an anthropologist, and I remain in awe of Wagley's grand vision of culture and environment in Amazonia and his receptivity to other disciplines working in anthropology's turf. My appreciation for Amazonian culture was also greatly enhanced by discussions with the late Eduardo Galvão while I was a student conducting fieldwork in the Brazilian Amazon in the early 1970s. Without Hilgard Sternberg's early support and guidance during my training as a geographer, I would never have embarked on a course of Amazonian studies. I will always be grateful to these "Masters" for their intellectual rigor, questioning of assumptions, emphasis on fieldwork, and openness to new avenues of inquiry. I am also indebted to Michael Goulding and Dennis Mahar for sharpening my thinking about the culture of rural folk in Amazonia and the complex issues surrounding the conservation of biodiversity.

Richard Evans Schultes and Wade Davis made helpful comments on the book manuscript. Candace Slater kindly took the trouble to comment on parts of chapter 5. I do not wish to imply that any of the above individuals necessarily agrees with my research approach or findings. Views and conclusions expressed herein are those of the author. I am also most grateful to Walda Metcalf, Editor in Chief at the University Press of Florida, for her enthusiasm and assistance during the process of turning a raw manuscript into a book. Michael Senecal and Karin Kaufman provided valuable assistance during copyediting. Jeff Lower drew the two maps depicting rivers, highways, and urban centers and the location of indigenous groups mentioned in the text.

Finally, I am indebted to my family, and most especially to Lisa, for their patience and forbearance during my many and sometimes prolonged absences from home to undertake fieldwork in Amazonia. I have thought of them often in my hammock during warm, starlight nights on the Amazon floodplain, thousands of miles from home.

Lore and Land in Transition

When Europeans first arrived in Amazonia at the beginning of the sixteenth century, the region was densely inhabited, particularly along the rivers. In spite of the relatively dense settlement, substantial tracts of forest at various stages of succession remained, and many animals and plants important for subsistence were abundant. How indigenous people managed their resources so well remains largely a mystery. But lore, or more specifically, the belief in spirit protectors of game, fish, and sacred and haunted places, undoubtedly played a role in protecting the natural resources of the region.

Soon after the Europeans first explored the Amazon River and a few of its tributaries, the region's culture and environment changed dramatically. Introduced diseases decimated most indigenous groups, and many areas devoted to crops and recovering forest were abandoned. The population of Amazonia in the seventeenth, eighteenth, and nineteenth centuries was sparse, with major urban centers containing fewer than 100,000 inhabitants. Even the rubber boom from the 1870s to about 1915 had little overall impact on population densities. Rubber tappers poured into the region, particularly from the Brazilian Northeast, but more indigenous people succumbed to disease and conflict. The economy of the Amazon for some four hundred years after contact was largely extractive, with little farming or ranching. Deforestation was thus minimal. Although the forest returned in many areas, some natural resources, such as turtles, were heavily plundered.

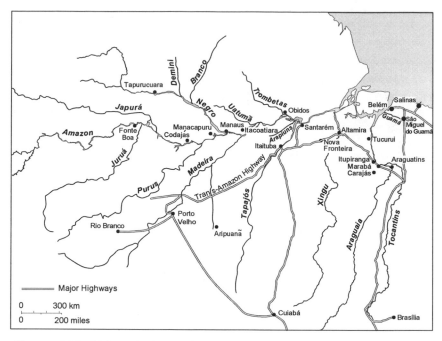

Figure 1.1. Major highways in the Brazilian Amazon.

Only in the last three decades have governments taken serious steps to integrate the Amazon frontier with the rest of their countries. In 1964, for example, the Brazilians bulldozed a dirt highway from Brasília on the savanna plateau of central Brazil to Belém, an ancient port at the mouth of the Amazon (figure 1.1). A decade later, private construction companies and the military cut a three-thousand-kilometer swath—the Transamazon colonization scheme—from the parched backlands of the Northeast to the moist jungles near the Peruvian border. The opening of the Cuiabá–Porto Velho and Cuiabá-Santarém Highways in the early 1970s, and the penetration of new roads into the lowland forests of Bolivia, Peru, and Ecuador, have spurred an unprecedented land rush to Amazonia.

Brazilians alone have recently slashed fifteen thousand kilometers of roads across the vast ocean of forest to foster agricultural development and to place an indelible stamp of sovereignty on the region. Furthermore, several large companies are unlocking vast mineral deposits, such as bauxite in the Trombetas watershed and iron ore and manganese at Serra dos Carajás. A string of hydroelectric dams was built in the Amazon during the 1970s and 1980s, in some cases flooding more than two thousand square kilometers of forest.

This tidal wave of land-hungry settlers and developers of mineral and energy resources has alarmed those concerned with the fragility of the forest and aquatic environments. Highway construction typically leads to landscapes dominated by cattle pasture (figure 1.2). The actual and potential ecological impact of the various development projects in the Amazon basin has ignited a heated debate in the academic world as well as in the popular press. The dangers of allowing the forest cover to shrink drastically, particularly with respect to loss of biodiversity, disruption of rainfall, increased soil erosion, and the worsen-

Figure 1.2. A ten-year-old pasture in former rain forest. The pasture is planted to an African grass that formed after a crop of manioc was harvested. Artificial pastures often dominate the landscapes of rural areas in Amazonia after highway construction. Fazenda Bom Futuro, km 33 of the Obidos–Monte Alegre road, Pará, 25 June 1994.

ing of floods, are frequently emphasized. Loss of forest cover in Amazonia and other tropical regions is eliminating species that might improve agriculture and increase our arsenal of drugs for fighting disease.

The plight of Indian groups in the face of ambitious development schemes and hordes of incoming colonists has also stirred up considerable discussion. Few tribes benefit from contact with civilization; most succumb to disease before they can assimilate with national society. The loss of aboriginal cultural diversity in Amazonia is at least as serious as the hemorrhaging of plant and animal species. Each indigenous group has acquired a wisdom accumulated over generations of daily interaction with its environment. The knowledge these groups possess about the location of wild plant resources, especially those with therapeutic value, and unusual crops and varieties could well profit modern medicine and farming (figure 1.3).

The assassination of Chico Mendes in 1988 galvanized media attention in Brazil and abroad on the demise of forests and people who depend on them for a living. Chico Mendes was helping to organize rubber tappers in Acre to protect forest tracts from bulldozers and chain saws sent by ranchers when he was gunned down. As a result of political pressure from nongovernment organizations in Brazil and in some industrial countries, several extractive reserves have been set aside for families who have traditionally tapped rubber, gathered Brazil nuts, and harvested other products from the forest. Rubber tappers, though, constitute only a small fraction of the rural inhabitants of Amazonia.

With so much attention focused on the ecological repercussions of development and its impact on Indian groups and rubber tappers, the effects of such schemes on small farmers and fisherfolk who also engage in extractive activities has been largely overlooked. Concern for the future of the world's richest biome and the remaining aboriginal inhabitants and extractivists is certainly warranted, but another dimension to the problem of threatened cultures needs to be explored: the erosion of knowledge of the vast majority of peasants in the region. For the purposes of this study, peasants are defined as nontribal Indians and those of mixed ethnic background who engage in small-scale farming, sharecropping, fishing, hunting, gathering, and itinerant mining or who work as ranch hands. In the Amazonian context, peasants are an extremely heterogeneous group.

Peasants account for most of the region's population, and their lifestyles and beliefs are changing rapidly with the influx of settlers from different re-

Figure 1.3. Middle-class shoppers at a market stall specializing in medicinal plant and animal products. Many of the plants are collected in forest environments. Mosqueiro, Pará, 12 June 1994.

gions. In the case of the Brazilian Amazon, for example, many settlers are coming from the South, particularly from Paraná, Rio Grande do Sul, and São Paulo, a temperate zone with traditions different from that of the North. In the jungle regions of Bolivia, Peru, and Ecuador, pioneers frequently come from the densely settled higher valleys and basins of the Andes. Newcomers to the Amazon inevitably bring with them different customs and beliefs, and by interacting with local peasants change the latter's perception of the world.

Widespread development projects, ranging from oil exploration in the western portion of the region to tin mining in Rondônia, are also affecting the culture of peasants in Amazonia. Rural folk are often attracted to such schemes by the opportunities to earn cash; some learn new skills and attain a higher material standard of living. The establishment of light industries around the major Amazonian towns, such as Manaus and Belém, has acted like a magnet drawing people in from rural areas in search of wage labor. Radio, television, magazines, giant road graders, and even jet aircraft are now penetrating areas that until recently had been essentially cut off from the outside world. Instead of being perceived as a backward area and a burden to national treasuries,

Amazonia is increasingly seen as a huge stock of natural resources to be exploited.

It is not within the scope of this book to analyze the various development strategies of the Amazon region, nor to explore all their myriad environmental and societal repercussions. Nevertheless, a brief overview of the extent of such changes will provide a useful backdrop to the discussion of regional folklore. I do not wish to sound overly pessimistic about the future of Amazonia; development must come in one form or another, and no culture remains static for long. Nor do I wish to imply that the folklore of the region will be entirely erased by the onrush of development, for peasant culture in the Amazon basin is remarkably resilient. A major aim of this book, then, is to unfurl the rich tapestry of rural lore so that it may be appreciated for its unusual imagination and for its environmental message. Folklore provides insights into people's perceptions about their environment, both ecological and social. Particular attention will be paid to lore dealing with the management of natural resources.

Myths and legends incorporate many spiritual and moral values present in a culture and often pinpoint tensions and temptations faced by individuals in their everyday life. Whereas folktales in industrial nations are now essentially relegated to children's books, they form an integral part of the life of rural folk in developing regions. Stories about the supernatural frequently influence the behavior of aborigines and peasants by discouraging behavior deemed abnormal and by suppressing greed. Amazonian folklore represents far more than a collection of nursery rhymes or bedtime horror stories: it shapes the attitudes and actions of millions of people.

Myths, legends, and folktales are prose narratives but can be distinguished by certain characteristics. Folktales are regarded as fiction and are not to be taken seriously. None of the tales recounted in this book fall under this category. Myths, on the other hand, are considered to be truthful in the society in which they are told. Generally depicting events in the distant past, myths are usually sacred and are accepted on faith. They are often associated with ritual and involve animals, deities, or culture heroes who lived in an earlier world, different from that of today, or in another world, such as in the sky or beneath the earth. Myths usually account for the origin of the world, of humankind, for death, and for geographical features such as prominent hills and natural phenomena such as fire. Legends are also regarded as true but are set in a less remote period and portray events that occurred in a world much like the world that exists today. Legends recount stories about past heroes, leaders, treasure, ghosts, fairies, and saints, and their principal characters are generally human.

Most of the lore in this book can best be described as myth-legends. Aboriginal mythologies have contributed ideas and characters in the lore recounted by rural folk in the basin today. Some of the lore describes events that reportedly occurred very recently, and much of it is concerned with animal-like creatures. A small portion of the lore discussed here can be regarded as anecdotes rather than myth-legends. Anecdotes tend to be humorous accounts spotlighting human foibles, but they also emphasize the power of the supernatural.

Folklore influences the way in which natural resources are tapped and used in the Amazon and helps to preserve the productivity of game, fish, and wild plants of economic value. Fear of supernatural reprisal for abusing nature's providence, for example, underlies much of the lore of hunters, fishermen, and gatherers. Peasants derive appreciable amounts of food and income from wild animals and plants, and their preoccupation with the availability of these natural resources is clearly revealed in the lore. Many legends were conceived in order to entertain audiences with colorful and inspiring stories; indirectly, though, they also serve to relieve some of the pressure on animal and plant life.

Lore dealing with the consumption of game and fish is explored with particular attention paid to its role in helping to protect people's health. Minerals and precious stones are also the subject of some unusual beliefs and tales. Ideas about spirit mothers protecting game and plants also apply to physical objects of esteem and commercial value. Several stories about minerals have arisen since colonial times and are particularly interesting in the light of the quickening tempo of mineral exploitation in the region.

Spirits and ghosts also spill into the dark streets and passageways of village life, and most of them are concerned with moral issues. Many stories reveal the unfortunate supernatural destiny of those who fail to abide by societal norms of conduct. Pugnacious black sows, giant white dogs, three-legged cows, and bothersome nocturnal birds all attest to the fate of transgressors, particularly those involved in illicit sex. Even tales that deal with hunting and fishing highlight expectations about cooperation and sharing. Amazonian peasants are thus concerned about proper behavior between people as well as human relationships with nature.

My interest in lore stems from research on the use of plant and animal resources by rural folk in the Brazilian Amazon. My approach to lore thus stems from the cultural-ecology tradition in geography and anthropology. It was only after spending several years with fishermen and farmers that I became increasingly intrigued by a spiritual or supernatural dimension to their livelihoods. My focus is on the significance of lore for the conservation of natural resources. For those more interested in the symbolism and structural elements of prose-narratives, I hope the texts will provide fertile ground for other levels of analysis.

For some time, natural history has been disparaged as rather old fashioned, and even unscientific. I reject this notion. Some of the best writing on the ethnobotany and ecology of the region was written in the eighteenth and nineteenth centuries. My natural history approach incorporates more modern concerns about the carrying capacity of the region for supporting human populations, the impact of widespread environmental destruction on culture, and the relevance of folklore for environmental education.

A fair amount of literature about Amazonian lore exists, but it is widely scattered and deals mostly with specific Indian groups. The numerous ethnologies of Amazonian aborigines have proved extremely helpful in attempting to trace the origins of many legends recounted by peasants. Books and articles that treat the lore of nontribal people in Amazonia are mostly in Portuguese and generally do not explore the origins or meanings of myths, nor do they provide information about informants or locations of interviews. Much of the folklore of peasants in Amazonia is based on secondary material and is poorly documented. Outstanding accounts of lore of rural folk in the region can be found in the writings of Charles Wagley and Eduardo Galvão. Wagley and Galvão sojourned with peasants and indigenous groups, and their works on the cosmology of peasants are based on stays at a small town near the estuary of the Amazon. These studies conducted at a single urban center are valuable because the authors took care to identify informants, to describe the locality of the lore, and to explore its significance.

Tales recounted here were collected from widely scattered locations in the Brazilian Amazon. Rural folk were interviewed at various places along the one-thousand-kilometer Marabá-Itaituba stretch of the Transamazon Highway and in the villages of Tapurucuara on the upper Rio Negro and Aripuanã in northern Mato Grosso. Farmers and fishermen were canvassed for stories in their homes on the Amazon floodplain in the vicinities of Itacoatiara and Manacapuru in Amazonas State, and Obidos and Santarém in Pará. Other individuals were interviewed along the lower Arapiuns and middle Tocantins Rivers in Pará (figure 1.1).

Stories were obtained from individuals during several field research projects, ranging from settlement issues along the Transamazon Highway, fishing methods and yields along the middle Amazon, the extent and distribution of anthropogenic black earth sites, to recent attempts to intensify agricultural production on upland and floodplain sites. Fieldwork for this book was conducted intermittently from 1977 to 1994, although some of the photographs date back to the early 1970s, when I initiated fieldwork in the Amazon. Interviews were conducted with approximately 250 individuals. Brazilians have a lively sense of humor, so no group interviews were attempted. Occasionally, however, families were jointly canvassed for their experiences or knowledge of the supernatural.

Some of the stories presented are well known in the region, such as the legend of the giant water snake, *cobra grande,* whereas others are introduced to the literature for the first time. Even for widespread myth-legends, though, new twists to old stories are told and supernatural creatures may appear in novel settings or behave in strange ways. My study is thus not a dictionary of Amazon lore, nor an account of every ghost, spirit, or monster reported from Amazonia.

Stories recounted here were gathered personally, without the services of an interpreter. Although the core of the book consists of tales gathered firsthand, I attempt to trace the possible genesis of some concepts, to ascertain their distribution, and to contrast various versions and interpretations of the meaning of myth-legends.

Individuals or family groups were never confronted directly with questions about the supernatural or food avoidances. Rather, a conversation was initiated about some other topic, such as crop yields or planting patterns, before queries were raised about ghosts, goblins, and monsters. Instead of asking, "Do you believe in such-and-such a creature?" I would pose the question by saying that I had heard something about a giant snake, for example, and then I would solicit the interviewee for any information about the beast. People were generally mildly embarrassed about discussing such matters because of a fear of being ridiculed; a direct question would probably not have elicited much useful information. Sometimes I got the impression that the events being described actually happened to the informant, but he or she was ascribing them to someone else. In this manner, they could play it safe in the event that I frowned in disbelief or, worse, burst out laughing.

Stories were cross-checked with other interviewees whenever possible. When confirming the appearance of a spirit or other supernatural phenomenon with other individuals, I frequently noted that certain details were omitted or the creature or apparition was embellished in some way. There is nothing unusual about discrepancies concerning legends in cultures where oral histories predominate. Anthropologists often come across variations of a myth in a single aboriginal group, a culture that is far more homogeneous than peasant society. Story tellers alter aspects of lore due to forgetfulness or to create the most awe among their listeners. The essential elements of a story, though, remain intact for a considerable time.

For each tale presented I identify the informant and the place where the interview was conducted, indicate his or her age, and give the location where the event is purported to have taken place. Peasants sometimes migrate, so a brief history of the interviewee is sketched where appropriate. Only people who were born or who have resided for several years in Amazonia were canvassed for this study. Most of the informants have lived their entire lives in the region. The bulk of the study is thus based on folk who have a long and intimate association with nature and culture in Amazonia. I include a few stories recounted by recent arrivals to the North to illustrate the process of cultural adaptation. Pioneers from other regions soon acquire knowledge about their new environment from locals.

Lore is separated into sections dealing with hunters, fishermen, gatherers of forest products, miners, and the mores of village dwellers. Some supernatural beasts are occupational hazards to one activity, such as hunting, whereas others plague woodsmen, fishermen, and women and children working in fields or drawing water from streams. Many hunters live in villages and go into the forest on occasion to acquire fresh meat. They may also farm part of the year on a riverbank, so hunters are often familiar with a wide range of tales.

It is customary for peasants in the region to change occupations several times during the year. A fisherman along the Tocantins, for example, may abandon his main livelihood for several months during the flood season, when catches are generally disappointing, to collect Brazil nuts[1] in the forest; there he might encounter jungle demons, or at least learn of their haunts and habits from fellow workers. Although a peasant is likely to be familiar with a large cast of ghosts, spirits, and other supernatural creatures, no individual is likely to have heard of all the beasts discussed here. Occupational activities provide useful hitching posts around which folktales can be grouped, but I do not wish to imply that the occupations discussed, or their associated lore, are mutually exclusive.

Whenever appropriate, I speculate on the possible role lore may have in

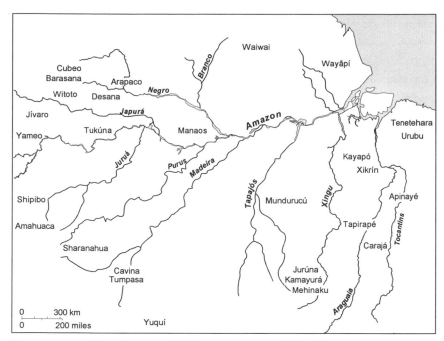

Figure 1.4. Approximate locations of indigenous groups with shared beliefs in supernatural entities recognized by rural folk in the Brazilian Amazon.

helping to conserve natural resources or reinforce division of labor. Some tales are clearly designed to uphold generally accepted moral values. The origins of legendary beasts and folkloric ideas are traced whenever possible. Not surprisingly, indigenous cultures from widely scattered locations across the Amazon basin are the crucibles for many of the supernatural creatures that roam the forests or lie submerged in lakes, streams, and rivers (figure 1.4).

Before discussing peasant lore in Amazonia, the biophysical setting of the region is provided so that myth-legends can be better understood in the context of the natural world in which they have evolved. Then the socioeconomic environment of Amazonian peasants is described; their ethnic origins, religious beliefs, and linkages with regional and extraregional markets. The following chapter discusses supernatural creatures of the hunter's world and lore surrounding that important subsistence activity.

From forays into the realm of forest spirits the text turns to fishermen and their supernatural concerns. Waters as well as the jungle are suffused with an extraordinary selection of ghosts and monsters. A chapter on lore surrounding *panema,* a hex that makes a person unable to catch fish or game, explores how hunters and gatherers attempt to avoid this condition and measures taken to cure it. The subsequent chapter on food avoidances unfurls a rich lore on consumption of fish and game and discusses how such notions help protect people's health. Another chapter dealing with lore and health focuses on the baneful influence of the evil eye.

Legends surrounding the extraction of forest products and gold are explored next to illustrate the broad spectrum of regional lore that spans the living world as well as inanimate objects. As in the case of hunting and fishing, lore that deals with gathering plant products in the forest underscores a preoccupation with their productivity and a concern for the abuse of nature's providence. The chapter on haunted streets examines ghosts and supernatural creatures that are encountered in villages; such tales usually incorporate a strong moral message. The book ends with an overview of regional lore, brings together several themes that thread through the diversity of tales, and assesses the future of folklore in the Amazon in view of the accelerated pace of development.

🌿 🌿 🌿 C H A P T E R 2

Forests, Rivers, and Minerals

The Amazon rain forest straddles the equator and blankets millions of square kilometers of flat to undulating terrain. The vast carpet of trees stretches from the trade wind–buffeted coast of Pará and Amapá in Brazil to the moisture-laden cloud forests curling up the eastern slopes of the Andes in Bolivia, Peru, Ecuador, and Colombia. Amazonia's forest is unrivaled in size and diversity: it covers more than half the area of the continental United States and contains several times as many plant species as grow in the United States and Canada combined. One can fly in a propeller-driven plane over the region for several hours without seeing a house, road, or field. The cauliflower-textured canopy of the forest may only be broken now and then by a sinuous river glinting from below or a patch of grassland with gnarled and stunted trees. Often the only landmarks are occasional crowns of purple or yellow blooms that stand out conspicuously against the dark green of the forest.

This profusion of trees, vines, orchids, ferns, and shrubs contains numerous plants of subsistence, medicinal, and commercial value. Fruits, nuts, latex, fibers, and essential oils provide an important supplement to the diet and income of millions of rural folk dispersed along the rivers, creeks, and roads that pierce the exuberant forest. Economically important plants, such as rubber trees and towering Brazil nut trees, usually have patchy distributions in the jungle. Accordingly, lengthy trips into the woods are often necessary in order to gather the scattered products. Most plants that belong to a single species are widely separated in order to reduce damage from pests and diseases. In a clump of trees of the same species, insects, pathogenic bacteria, and certain disease-causing fungi can easily spread through the tightly packed population and cause extensive damage. Zones of mixed species provide buffers against pest attack, especially important considering that no cold season checks insects and pathogens in the region. Extended sorties into the jungle to gather the milky sap of rubber trees, the pods of Brazil nut trees, fruits, and construction materials (figure 2.1) provide plenty of opportunities to reinforce the awe of being in such a huge wilderness.

The dissipated arrangement of plant species in the Amazon basin is mirrored in the patchy distribution of animals. Whereas the rain forest teems with millions of animal species, mostly insects, the population density of any sizable mammal desired as food is often low. Plants and animals have co-evolved in tropical forests for hundreds of millions of years, so they have had ample time to fine tune their interdependence. Because game animals depend on plant products for food, they are also thinly dispersed throughout the forest; hunters frequently have to range far in order to locate suitable prey. Hunters, just as gatherers, often spend considerable time in the forest searching for desirable quarry such as tapir,[1] white-lipped peccary, white-collared peccary, or brocket deer.

A hunter usually leaves home at daybreak after drinking some thick, heavily sugared coffee and eating some leftovers from the previous night's supper. He may bring along a small bag of granular manioc flour to stave off hunger and some shotgun shells carefully wrapped in plastic so that they are protected from sweat and rain. A sixteen- or twenty-gauge shotgun is the principal weapon; rifles are outlawed in Brazil because they can be used effectively in guerrilla campaigns. Once the hunter has slipped into the forest, he treads quietly and constantly listens for the sounds of game, such as the telltale chatter of monkeys or the shrill whistle of a tapir. The hunter also scans the ground for animal tracks, especially along moist stream banks. He may walk all day without spotting any quarry, or he may be lucky enough to encounter a slumbering two-hundred-kilogram tapir within an hour of leaving home. Only rarely, though, will a hunter searching for meat spend more than a day in the forest.

Sometimes a hunter teams up with neighbors for a trip into the forest. Groups are particularly common when a hunt is planned for several days; hunters feel safer in a party, either from surprise attack by Indians, snake bites, or accidental injury. Men also appreciate company in the forest, even if they can-

Figure 2.1. Houses (on right) thatched with fronds of curuá palm. The stacked curuá palm fronds had recently been cut from surrounding upland forest to repair a roof and extend an eave. Alenquer, Pará, 19 March 1993.

not talk much during the day because they might scare off game. A pause along the trail to roll and smoke a cigarette and to discuss strategy provides welcome relief from hours of hacking through tangled vegetation and trudging over crumpled terrain. Some men are endowed with exceptional hearing, whereas others are better able to discern spoor on the leafy forest floor, a further advantage in joining ranks when hunting. Kills are usually divided equally among participants, regardless of who dispatched the animal. Extra hands are especially useful when a tapir is slaughtered because the carcass can be brought back immediately. When a lone hunter makes a big kill, he has to return home to fetch help, leaving it vulnerable to predators and vultures.

When a man leaves for a day's hunt, either alone or in a group, he often brings along several dogs. Canine companions fan out into the forest and cover a much larger area than that traversed by a man. Dogs chase nine-banded armadillo, paca, agouti, and white-collared peccary down burrows or into hollow logs and keep them there until their master arrives. Well-trained dogs outpace game such as deer and chase them toward their owner, where the quarry can be shot. Dogs are particularly helpful when a hunter surprises a band of white-lipped peccary; instead of fleeing, some of the piglike creatures turn to fend off the harassing dogs. While they are thus engaged, a hunter can dispatch several individuals in the rear-guard brigade before they disperse. Hunters of spotted cats find dogs useful because they tree ocelot, margay cat, and jaguar, thereby allowing the hunter to catch up and shoot down his prey. The ability of dogs to locate and trap game explains why they are included in the lore of hunters.

Another important hunting method involves waiting in the forest by night for game to come to a bait tree. Cat hunters tie a dead monkey or bird to the base of a tree and erect a small log platform nearby and wait for a jaguar or an ocelot to approach. When the spotted cat tears into the attached bait, the hunter clicks on his flashlight and shoots at the momentarily mesmerized animal. Trees with falling fruit, nuts, or flowers that are favored by game provide further nocturnal opportunities for hunters. During the day, a hunter will often spot tracks around the base of a fruiting tree indicating that game is nearby. A hunter returns to the promising tree in the late afternoon, clears away some of the underbrush so that he has a clear shot, then attaches his hammock or makes a platform in some trees. Hunters employ the waiting method during the dry season, when the rustle of crisp leaves betrays animal movement and because they are less likely to be soaked by torrential downpours.

The burden of combing huge areas of the forest in order to garner sufficient rewards is not the only onerous dimension to subsistence activities. Peasants must also deal with the seasonality of the forest fruits and game movements. The roller-coaster flow of nuts and fruits, as well as the wet-season migration of white-lipped peccary herds, dictates a varied diet and requires a range of subsistence skills. Most forest fruits and nuts, for example, fall in the rainy season. The wet season varies in different parts of the basin; south of the equator, for example, the rains begin in earnest around November or December and last until May. Most jungle trees drop their fruits in the wet season because the seeds are generally viable for only a short time and must germinate quickly. Brazil nut gatherers, for example, collect the fallen nuts from December to March; thereafter, they must seek other employment, such as panning for gold or diamonds or clearing forest for a rancher.

Rubber tappers draw off most of the sticky white latex from wild trees within a few months during the dry season. The pulsating rhythm of forest production thus necessitates absences from home lasting several months and travel over great distances in search of rubber trees, Brazil nuts, or palm fiber. The itinerant nature of rural life in Amazonia is partly responsible for the wide distribution of many of the mythical creatures and frightening ghosts that weave through the region's cultural fabric.

The dispersed distribution and ephemeral availability of so many forest products important for income and food is a source of concern for peasants. In some years, abundant harvests of forest products are gathered, whereas in others, the pickings are meager. A preoccupation with the supply of natural goods underlies several of the stories about game animals and trees. Some of the lore suggests that people are tempted to destroy a resource for quick gain, such as by gashing rubber trees too deeply in order to boost the supply of latex. To check such greed, spirit protectors stand ready to punish those who try to take more than nature is willing to give. A hunter may be in a position to kill half a dozen or more cornered white-lipped peccaries, but he may refrain from so doing because of fear of reprisal by the father of game.

Many parallels can be drawn between the lives and lore of fishermen and hunters. As in the case of forest animals, a bewildering assortment of fish swim the waters of the region, but the population density of desirable species is often low. At least two thousand species of fish cruise the watercourses of Amazonia, ranging from the smooth-skinned piraíba, a 120-kilogram catfish that lurks on the bottom of major rivers, to tiny and brightly colored aquarium fishes that dart through the warm waters of the Rio Negro and its tributaries. Amazonia contains four times as many kinds of fishes as the Congo and about eight times as many as the Mississippi. Several hundred species of fish are consumed in Amazonia. Within just a sixty-kilometer radius of Itacoatiara, a town along the middle Amazon, approximately one hundred species of fish are caught for food, about the same number of freshwater fish species as in all of Argentina. It is not uncommon to see a fisherman returning from a day's work with twenty or thirty fish belonging to a dozen species in his canoe.

The great diversity of water types partly accounts for the unusual number of fishes in Amazonia. Some rivers, such as the Rio Negro, flow like dark tea from bleached sands, where a buildup of humus stains the water. Other watercourses, such as the Tapajós, are relatively clear because they drain the highly leached mantles of the Brazilian and Guianan shields, where few nutrients or suspended sediments are being released. Turbid rivers, such as the Purus, Juruá, and the headwaters of the Amazon, tumble off the Andes in the far western portion of the basin. The backbone mountain chain of South America contains young and fertile soils, especially volcanics, that account for the relatively high nutrient content of these "white-water" rivers. Rivers with headwaters clawing into the Andes pick up a great deal of sediment, particularly clays and silt, as they plunge down the deep mountain gorges. The fine particles in suspension produce the characteristic creamed-coffee color of "white-water" rivers, and the sediments are deposited and constantly reworked by the often meandering rivers downstream.

The abundance of habitats in Amazonian waters is another reason for the proliferation of fish species. In addition to the main river channel, for example, the Amazon floodplain contains thousands of lakes and side channels as well as forests that are seasonally flooded. The floodplain dilates for fifty kilometers along certain stretches, thereby offering an extensive and varied habitat for fish. Some rivers are interrupted by majestic waterfalls, such as the Aripuanã, or turbulent rapids, such as the clear-water Xingu.

Many fish are restricted to particular habitats, so peasants adapt their fishing methods to the environment in which the desirable species occurs. In rapids, for example, fishermen employ gaffs to snag certain catfish as they migrate upstream. In lakes and placid side channels, bows and arrows are used effectively to shoot medium-sized fish, such as the peacock bass. Bottom trotlines baited with fish are extended some fifty meters into the main channel of the Amazon and other large rivers to catch bottom-dwelling catfish such as the gray piraíba and the olive-skinned jaú. To haul in a bottom trotline, one man paddles at the rear of the canoe while the other, seated at the bow, pulls up the line. If a large catfish has swallowed the bait, a struggle usually ensues. A careless fisherman is sometimes snagged by one of the half-dozen hooks, similar to the size used to hang beef carcasses, and drowns when the powerful fish dives.

Fishing methods also vary according to season. About a month after the rains begin, the Amazon and its southern affluents swell and soon pour through side channels into backswamps and lakes. At the height of the flood stage, the rivers spill over their banks and one can paddle for hours across the Amazon floodplain without being able to set foot on dry ground. Ephemeral lakes fill again, and permanent lagoons enlarge several times. The surge of fresh water recharges the lakes with nutrients, and as the flood subsides, sediments decant, allowing sunlight to penetrate the water and promote plant and animal life. Floating plants, algae, and phytoplankton flourish, thereby providing the foundation for myriad food webs. As the water creeps daily up riverbanks, fish gain access to new food resources: the fruits, nuts, flowers, leaves, and falling insects from floodplain forests. Fishermen attach suspended trotlines between poles or trees in flooded forests to capture fish that move into the seasonably available habitat to feed and breed. The hooks, normally four to eight to a trotline, are baited with fruits or nuts to capture frugivores, such as the dark green and gold tambaqui (figure 2.2), or frogs to catch silvery arawana. The surface-cruising arawana occasionally finds its way into the aquarium trade, where it sells for hundreds of times more than it fetches in markets in the Amazon. Swamp woods are important fishing grounds during high water and provide the setting for a large selection of supernatural stories, far more interesting and frightening than those typically found in Hollywood productions such as *Creature from the Black Lagoon*.

When river levels drop, fishermen tailor their fishing methods to the changing environment. As the waters retreat from floodplain forests, fish are concentrated in lakes and channels; now cast nets can be employed effectively. At low water, gillnet catches increase because fish are crowded and because fishermen can slap the water with their paddles and chase their quarry into nets placed at an angle to the shore of a lake. Harpoons come into play in shrunken

Figure 2.2. Tambaqui, one of the premier food fishes of the Amazon, eats fruits and nuts that fall from the canopy of floodplain forest. Surubim-Açu, vicinity of Santarém, Pará, 1 September 1993.

lakes to pierce the pink and silver pirarucu, which becomes vulnerable when it surfaces for air. To capture pirarucu, which can reach two meters long and weigh close to one hundred kilograms, a fisherman squats on the front bench of his canoe and gently propels his canoe with paddle in one hand. The harpoon with attached line is held in his other hand; when the torpedo-shaped fish breaks the surface to gulp air, the lance is hurled in the direction the fisherman thinks the pirarucu is headed. After the carnivorous fish is struck, it customarily rushes under a mat of floating vegetation, tugging the lead line and attached buoy with it. An hour may pass before the creature tires sufficiently to be clubbed and hauled safely aboard. Pirarucu are also captured in floodplain lakes at low water by encircling a floating meadow with a gillnet and scaring the fish into the net by slapping the aquatic vegetation with poles.

The high value and savory taste of pirarucu, combined with its useful byproducts, are major reasons why the fish figures so prominently in riverine lore. The delicate, pink flesh is largely unencumbered with bones and rivals the esteemed trout in taste. Once salted and sun-dried, strips of the carcass can be stored for months. The fifteen-centimeter-long tongue is bony and makes a handy grater for the kitchen, and the stiff scales approach the size of a credit card and serve as nail files or as "sandpaper" for bows and other woodwork. Pirarucu fisheries were once a major economic activity along the Amazon during the dry season. Peasants made temporary camps along the margins of lakes, where they salted and sun-dried their catches for market. Unfortunately, pirarucu populations have dwindled in many areas due to heavy pressure from the growing ranks of commercial fishermen and the rapid adoption of gillnets that trap sexually immature specimens.

The rewards of fishing, as in the case of hunting, are highly variable. The unpredictable nature of the resource supply is one reason that so much lore surrounds this important subsistence and commercial activity. Catches are generally low when the water is rising because fish disperse across the extensive floodplains. With the widespread adoption of seines in the mid-twentieth century, and the installation of ice factories in many smaller towns, large catches are now made as the water level drops and huge schools of fish, especially jaraqui and sardinha, abandon the floodplains of white-water rivers after breeding. As the schools of fish migrate upstream in search of suitable tributaries, they are encircled by seines let out by canoes. In areas where seines are prohibited, such as around Obidos and Santarém, fishermen use gillnets and cast nets to capture migrating fish. In some years, though, the annual fish runs are disappointing because of fluctuations in the amplitude of high and low water, among other factors.

Minerals and precious stones are another natural, albeit nonrenewable, resource exploited extensively by old-timers and recent migrants to Amazonia. Gold, aluminum ore (bauxite), iron ore, tin ore (cassiterite), and manganese mining are currently major economic enterprises in the region. Before significant tin deposits are taken over by large companies, they are often pioneered by hordes of itinerant miners (*garimpeiros*). In Rondônia, for example, thousands of migrants worked gravel along streams in search of cassiterite until the federal government outlawed that allegedly wasteful practice in 1970. Tin mining operations in Rondônia are now handled by corporations based in São Paulo.

Independent miners are still responsible for most of the diamonds and gold mined in Amazonia. The precious stones have been sifted from the alluvial gravel of the clear-water Tocantins for about a century. Diamonds are washed from the ancient Brazilian shield and are deposited along the sandy shores of the Tocantins, where they are found in the dry season. Intrepid garimpeiros also pan for diamonds in the rivers and streams that cascade off the Guianan shield and eventually flow into the Rio Branco in Roraima. Diamond mining is thus concentrated in two portions of Amazonia and provides seasonal employment for thousands of rural and urban folk.

Gold mining emerged as a significant economic activity more recently. In the 1950s, several promising strikes were reported in the Tapajós valley, and a flood of prospective miners soon descended on Itaituba, a fishing village and rubber port on the left bank of the clear-water river. Dozens of mining camps quickly sprung up on the western flank of the Tapajós watershed. Some of these camps are still operating, and many new ones have formed. To reach a gold mining area (*garimpo*), a miner buys passage on an air taxi or rents the plane with companions. Upon reaching the field, the miner buys additional goods at highly inflated prices from the single store run by the owner of the garimpo, and heads for the forest to stake out an individual claim. Miners work alone or in small groups, creating plenty of opportunities for imaginative interpretations of strange sounds and sights in the jungle. Camp life can also be short; disputes are frequently settled by shotgun, revolver, or machete. Gold is sold to the camp boss or to buyers in town, and the earnings are frequently squandered on alcohol and prostitutes. Few garimpeiros ever become wealthy. Profits accrue mainly to the airstrip barons, gold dealers, mining supply stores, and owners of air taxis. Most of the gold from the Tapajós valley is flown to São Paulo.

Gold is currently mined in numerous locations in the Brazilian Amazon. A second gold rush to Amazonia, far outpacing that to the Tapajós, occurred immediately after the uncovering of a seven-kilogram chunk of gold at Serra Pelada, a formerly forest-clad hill near Marabá, in 1980. In September of that year, at least one and a half tons of gold were extracted from the hill, now reduced to an excavated pit. Several more hills in southern Pará were honeycombed by itinerant miners in the early 1980s.

Significant gold strikes in Amazonia coincided with unusually high prices for the precious metal on world markets, and Brazil was soon among the leading producers of gold. In addition to panning for gold in streams and washing away forest earth with hydraulic hoses, some gold miners have turned their attention to stretches of the Madeira and Negro Rivers, where floating barges equipped with hoses suck up large quantities of riverbed sediment. Although gold prices slipped somewhat in the 1990s, several hundred thousand gold miners are still combing forests and dredging river bottoms in search of fortunes. Gold and diamonds have clearly ignited the passions of people in Amazonia, so it is not surprising that precious metals and stones have infiltrated the lore of the region.

People and Place

Rural folk in Amazonia subscribe to various religious beliefs, are of diverse racial heritage, and engage in a range of subsistence tasks and jobs throughout the year. Although their ethnic origins and occupations differ, peasants in the Brazilian Amazon are referred to as *caboclos*. The term can be used in a demeaning manner, much as country folk in the southern United States are occasionally called "rednecks." In the Brazilian Amazon, a person can be reminded of his humble origins by calling him a caboclo. Urban residents, even those belonging to the lowest economic strata, derive satisfaction from the fact that they no longer toil in fields or trudge through trackless jungle. On the other hand, a male friend may be called caboclo, a sign of affection, whereas a female may be referred to endearingly as cabocla. Many words in Brazilian Portuguese have two or more meanings.

Caboclos typically live in isolated huts or in hamlets, are barely literate, nominally Catholic, and are acutely aware of their low ranking in the social order. Caboclos may be subservient, but they are generally ambitious. Peasants, like most of us, are keenly interested in bettering their lot. Caboclos are not conservative in the sense that they shun change. On the contrary, they will seize any opportunity to accumulate goods. The chances for upward mobility for poor people are generally better in Amazonian towns and cities, hence the pronounced rural-urban migration in the region. In the countryside, the options open to caboclos are generally more restricted, so they are still heavily steeped in tradition. When development projects, such as mineral operations, take root in a rural area, peasants flock to such activities in search of employment. Peasant society is thus far from static. Poles of dynamic economic activity are multiplying, such as the mineral complex at Carajás, and are changing people's perspectives on nature. Development often results in rising incomes, a flux of newcomers, and improved schooling opportunities. The amoebalike growth of such large-scale enterprises inevitably provokes environmental and cultural change.

To understand better the rapidly changing face of the region's rural society, the historical origins of caboclo culture need to be examined. First, the racial makeup of the Amazonian population will be discussed to provide an idea of the appearance of caboclos. Then the religious beliefs of peasants will be explored because they are important in understanding the lore of the region. The educational experience of caboclos is also examined to underscore the caboclos' close ties with nature and the informal quality of their instruction. Finally, the socioeconomic milieu of peasants is introduced to highlight the relationship of peasants to middlemen and consumers and so that exploitation of forest products can be linked to regional and world markets.

Most caboclos are to some degree Indian in ancestry (figure 3.1). In many cases, peasants are of pure Indian extraction, although a generation may have passed since they lived in a tribal setting. In most instances caboclos of Indian heritage no longer speak their native tongue and the groups that their ancestors belonged to have long since disappeared. Almost half of the indigenous groups in Brazil that have brushed against civilization in this century became extinct within fifty years. Unlike aborigines in Latin American countries such as Mexico, Guatemala, and Peru, Brazilian Indians often lose their distinctive culture when touched by civilization. Only in the Rio Negro drainage do significant numbers of nontribal Indians still speak their languages as well as *língua geral,* a lingua franca spoken by Indians and Portuguese during the colonial period. But even along the Negro, many acculturated Indians have adopted western clothing and live in houses similar to caboclos throughout Amazonia.

The switch from communal life, often with many families occupying a large long house or *maloca,* to isolated homesteads is one reason that indigenous people discard so many of their unique cultural attributes. Ceremonial parties with ritualized dancing and singing no longer have any meaning, or cannot be conveniently arranged, when families are strung along rivers and streams. Missionaries encourage Indians to live as nuclear families in separate houses, to

Figure 3.1. Children of mixed ethnic background with a mother of predominately indigenous heritage and a father of Italian descent from southern Brazil. Some of the children are holding pieces of Indian pottery found in their back yard, attesting to the antiquity of human settlement in many areas of Amazonia. Cachimbo district of Juriti, Pará, 24 June 1994.

wear clothes, and to abandon customs related to their animistic religions. Aborigines are taught the gospel, Portuguese or Spanish, and sometimes technical skills such as carpentry, so that they can function more effectively in national society. Those not under the charge of missionaries pick up Portuguese or Spanish, sometimes both, in border areas with Brazil, through traders and by working with peasants. Caboclos of Indian extraction do not generally look back on their ancestry with pride; European culture is regarded as superior, even as it wreaks havoc with their ancestral lifeways and the environment.

Upon meeting a caboclo of obviously pure Indian background it is virtually impossible to tell from which tribe he or she may be descended. The woman will likely wear a simple cotton dress with a printed design purchased in a store or made from material bought in a *kilo* shop, where fabric is sold by weight. The man will likely wear a Seiko or Citizen watch from Manaus and be clad in a t-shirt, shorts, and plastic sandals. He may go much of the time bare-chested and while in the field wear a straw hat with a broad, slightly down-curving rim to shade his face from the fierce tropical sun and pelting rain. Baseball caps, often advertising major construction companies and stores, are more prestigious than straw hats, even though they offer less protection from the sun. Gone are the distinctive body paint or colorful bird feathers. The practice in some cultures of deforming the body by shaping heads, scarring females to enhance their beauty, or shaving men's facial hair, has ceased.

The two other main racial ingredients in caboclo culture stem from Europe and Africa. The Portuguese quickly mingled with the natives to produce a mestizo population in Amazonia and throughout Brazil. European women were scarce during the early years of colonization of the New World in the sixteenth century. Far from discouraging interracial marriage, authorities in Brazil encouraged it. Indian women excited the passions of Portuguese settlers because of their smooth, well-rounded features unencumbered by clothes, and their sleek, black hair. Sexual liaisons were quickly initiated. In Amazonia, the European genetic influence has been strongest in the large towns. The Portuguese engaged mostly in commerce and the management of sugarcane plantations and cacao extraction near urban centers. Slave raiders and riverine traders were mainly responsible for miscegenation in rural areas during the early colonial period. Few Portuguese settled the land as small-scale farmers; racial mixing occurred on plantations, on sporadic trips to the interior to obtain spices, dyes, and wood for construction, and in towns. Belém, Amazonia's major city with more than a million inhabitants, was established in 1616 and soon acquired a mestizo population.

The Spanish erected missions and trading posts in the forests of western Amazonia in the sixteenth and seventeenth centuries. Miscegenation was also rapid and widespread in that portion of the basin. Dutch, French, and English traded with natives of the lower Amazon for close to two centuries after the discovery of the New World until they were routed by the Portuguese and their Indian allies. Small groups of Flemish, English, and Irish even settled among tribes of the lower Amazon during the seventeenth century. Dutch and English adventurers planted sugarcane along the lower reaches of the Tocantins and Xingu between 1580 and 1640 while Portugal fell under the Spanish crown.

Genes from several European nations thus found their way into the regional population soon after contact.

The Portuguese were delighted to find numerous tribes in Brazil in the sixteenth century. They thought that the natives would be useful in extracting forest products and would serve as a labor pool for plantations. Although the Indians generally traded if they were well treated, they abhorred the strenuous and regulated life of a plantation. Introduced diseases such as influenza and smallpox soon took a devastating toll among indigenous groups. The Portuguese then turned to Africa for workers. From approximately the middle of the sixteenth century until the nineteenth century, millions of Africans from such groups as the Bantu, Minas, Yorubas, Gêges, and Haussás were imported into Brazil to toil on sugar, cacao, and tobacco plantations from Pará to São Paulo.

The precise dimension of the black slave trade to Brazil is disputed, but at least three million Africans lost their freedom to produce sugar, molasses, alcohol, and rolled tobacco and collect cacao beans in Brazil. The imprint of African culture is strongest along the Atlantic coast, especially in Bahia, where slaves were put to work on sugar plantations. In the eighteenth century, substantial numbers of slaves were sent to Minas Gerais to mine gold, but few Africans were shipped to the North because most settlers could not afford them. By one account, 50,910 Africans were imported into Amazonia between 1755 and 1815, but most authorities put the figure much lower. Slaves were imported to Belém beginning in 1690, but because of mismanagement of the trading company charged with organizing the slave traffic and settlers' financial difficulties, only a few thousand Africans had been forcibly sent to Pará by 1750. Between 1757 and 1800, a total of 23,884 slaves were landed at Belém. It is probably safe to assert that no more than 30,000 Africans were taken to the Brazilian Amazon.

Although the volume of slave traffic to the Amazon basin was small compared to other parts of Brazil and the New World, the slaves' cultural imprint has been appreciable. The indigenous and European population remained small during the approximately 150 years Africans were being imported to the Brazilian Amazon. Thus, although their numbers were modest, the imported slaves' ethnic contributions have been far from negligible. Furthermore, the ancestry of many of the rubber tappers who poured into the Amazon basin during the late 1800s and early twentieth century can be traced in part to Africa. African

Brazilians account for less than 10 percent of the region's population, but their cultural impact is felt, particularly in eastern Amazonia and in towns and cities. Most of the slaves ended up in Pará, and some descendants of former slaves even set up small settlements, called *quilombos,* such as in the Trombetas watershed. In the Santarém area, inhabitants of quilombos in the forest of the Trombetas are reputed to have discovered plants that are efficacious in treating snake bites.

The tempo of racial blending picked up in the nineteenth century when the rubber boom drew thousands of fortune seekers, particularly from the drought-plagued Northeast, into the humid valleys of Amazonia (figure 3.2). In 1878 alone, some 50,000 drought victims fled Ceará to tap rubber trees in the jungles of the North. From 1850 to 1915, between 200,000 and 350,000 northeasterners, mostly of mixed ethnic background, poured into the region. When the Japanese cut off rubber supplies from plantations in Southeast Asia during the Second World War, a brief boom attracted an additional 15,000 *Nordestinos* to the Amazon to collect the milky latex of wild rubber trees. Those Amazonian Indians that did not flee deeper into the forest or die from gunfire or introduced diseases, frequently joined the rubber collecting economy and settled down with outsiders.

Caboclos thus vary in physical appearance from swarthy European to black or Indian, with many combinations along the broad physiognomic spectrum. Brazil is a racial melting pot and ethnic segregation is weakly developed. Except for a handful of descendants of quilombo settlements along the Trombetas, black caboclos do not live in isolated villages and they freely intermarry with other peasants. It is true that African Brazilians rarely hold prominent positions of power, but they do not live in ghettoes. In the Brazilian Amazon, black caboclos are sometimes affectionately nicknamed *preto* (black) or *pretão* (big black) without incurring their wrath. Such nicknames are not intended as racial slurs. In neither the countryside nor urban areas is there any stigma attached to having a black neighbor. Although it would be naïve to suggest that racial discrimination does not exist in Brazil, it is fair to say that racial tensions are negligible, at least in the Amazon.

Although the racial heritage of Amazonian peasants varies, the indigenous element predominates. A caboclo, then, is more likely to have bronzed skin, high cheekbones set in a rounded face, and straight, black hair. Gray or white hair generally only manifests itself in the very late years: "premature" gray hair is virtually unheard of among caboclos and a source of some puzzlement to

Figure 3.2. "India-rubber manufacture on the banks of the Madeira" in the late 1860s. The rubber boom in the Amazon in the latter part of the nineteenth century and early twentieth century drew hundreds of thousands of fortune seekers into the region. From F. Keller, *The Amazon and Madeira Rivers: Sketches and Descriptions from the Note-Book of an Explorer* (London: Chapman and Hall, 1874), 101.

them when they see visiting scientists in their forties with a complete head of white hair. Peasants are also generally short and muscular. Their sturdy build reflects a well-rounded diet and an active, outdoor lifestyle. Hunting, fishing, and farming consume far more calories than sitting behind a keyboard. Obesity is rare among Amazonian peasants, and a generous girth is associated with prosperity and well-being, the opposite of the modern urban perception that being overweight is ugly and a symptom of a person who is unhappy and no longer in control of his or her life.

Many religions have been grafted into caboclo culture, producing a fascinating array of interpretations of the supernatural. The intricate cosmologies of indigenous peoples that existed prior to contact with Europeans compose the basic stock of religious beliefs, particularly as they relate to lore. The precise number of tribes that thrived in Amazonia at the time of contact with the white man in the early sixteenth century is not known, but it must have totaled several hundred. As late as 1957, even after three hundred years of decimating slave raids and successive epidemics of introduced diseases, some ninety-four indigenous groups remained in the Brazilian Amazon alone. The numerous tribes belonged to many different linguistic families, such as Tupi, Carib, Aruak, Gê, and Tukano, and each group had its unique repertoire of myths and spiritual ideas.

Although rain-forest cultures share many religious attributes, and some themes are common to the mythology of widely separated tribes, the religious life of these diverse groups differed considerably, as it does today. The role of images, incantations, hallucinogenic drugs, and the cast of characters in the supernatural order vary among indigenous groups. Different interpretations on the origin and purpose of humankind and people's relationships with the spirit world have greatly enriched the flavor of Amazonian lore. Many tribes have slid into oblivion, but some of their cosmological notions and tales have survived, albeit in altered form, and are still recounted by caboclos.

The complex mosaic of Indian cultures in Amazonia has resulted in a vast array of religious beliefs and practices, but certain common elements can be distilled from these colorful cosmologies. The spiritual plane, for example, intrudes on the lives of humans in a number of ways. Souls of those slain in battle trouble enemy warriors, and the spirits of those who have died at home plague villagers. Ceremonies are often prescribed to ward off angry or dissatisfied souls, and the location of a house may be shifted to escape unwelcome visits by the departed. Game, fish, and certain trees also harbor spirits that need to be respected if the flow of forest and aquatic products is to continue. People are not free to exploit animals and plants at whim; they do not belong to humans. Excessive greed during hunts, for example, is likely to be punished by supernatural game wardens. Such notions regarding the dangerous attributes of the souls of those who have died violently and ideas about spirit protectors of plants and animals are an integral part of caboclo lore.

Intermediaries between the physical and ethereal worlds occupy prominent positions in tribal societies of Amazonia, as is the case among aboriginal groups throughout the world. Shamans are responsible for deciphering the causes of sickness and curing patients, and they are expected to pinpoint propitious times for launching attacks on enemies. Shamans, of which there may be several in an Indian group, take drugs to contact spirits for information and advice. Hunters, for example, consult shamans for suggestions as to the most likely place to find game and fish. Caboclos also seek mediums for help, though the latter do not usually imbibe or inhale hallucinogenic compounds in their trade. A folk curer can be male or female and is known variously as a *pajé, curador, curandeiro,* or *curandeira.* Strictly speaking, a pajé is an Indian shaman operating in a tribal setting. But peasants call some curers pajés even if they practice in urban settings. A pajé would, however, be expected to use more rituals and ingredients from indigenous medicine, whereas a curandeiro employs a blend of indigenous and African and European folk medicines. A more modest curer who relies on prayers, rather than on tobacco smoke and various herbal remedies, is referred to as a *rezador* or *benzedor* (blesser). Distinctions between such healers are not sharp, particularly in rural and village life in today's fast-changing Amazon. Accordingly, terms for curers are used more or less interchangeably.

Rural and urban folk consult pajés for advice in matters of love and finance and for the treatment of conditions attributed to evil influences. Curandeiras or curandeiros may be married or single and may reside in towns or in the countryside. If the fame of a curer grows, he or she may move to a town to facilitate their access to a larger clientele. Only the most famous pajés ply their trade full time; most farm, fish, and hunt if they are men, or gather forest products, work on farms, and run households if they are women. Peasant shamans dress in an undistinguished manner. One cannot tell simply by looking at a caboclo whether he or she is a medium.

Pajés act as brokers between the land of the living and the next world. They relay messages between the dead and those still on earth, seek the help of spirits in changing the fortunes of their customers, and are well acquainted with the vast number of plants deemed to contain properties that ward off evil and cure the sick. Unlike shamans in some aboriginal cultures, however, caboclo curers are not feared. Sorcery is not the art of curandeiros; they are healers, using their divinely bestowed powers in the service of humankind. Pajés are respected and generally admired by peasants and urban folk and normally receive a modest payment for their efforts, in the form of either cash or produce. It is considered inappropriate to set fees in advance or to demand payment, because the medium's power is thought to be a gift from above that should not be exploited for profit.

Pajés provide a striking example of the meshing of native religions and Christianity. Many tribes subscribed to monotheism when they first met priests in the sixteenth century. Tupan, for example, was the supreme celestial being of the now-extinct Tupinambá tribe. The Christian idea of a conflict between God and Lucifer, the fallen angel who became the devil, is mirrored in aboriginal myths about heavenly twins, often the sun and the moon, who sometimes fight. Most caboclos recognize Christ as the supreme power of good in the universe. Roman Catholic saints and the Virgin Mary work in tandem with various Indian spirits in the eyes of most peasants; all are called upon by curers for help. The divine hierarchy of Catholicism is superimposed on the animated world of the Indians, but saints have not replaced the culture heroes and spirits that manipulate the fortunes of people.

Several aspects of native religions and Christianity coincide, but they are not entirely compatible. The meeting of religions produced conflicts as well as syncretism. The early explorers, such as Orellana and Cabral, were often accompanied by priests or friars. Evangelism and the search for new riches went hand in hand. One of the first tasks of Portuguese and Spanish adventurers upon arriving at a native village was to erect a tall wooden cross. Various Roman Catholic orders, particularly the Jesuits, Franciscans, Capuchins, Carmelites, and Mercedarians, established missions in the Amazon between the sixteenth and nineteenth centuries. Missionary orders differed with respect to style and color of their habits, the order and duration of services, and the language of instruction. But they all had a similar impact on native cultures. Indians were brought into new settlements, preferably clustered near the church or chapel. The consumption of alcoholic beverages, made traditionally by fermenting manioc or maize, was discouraged. Nudity or parsimonious clothing and the reverence of pagan images were anathema to the new religious leaders. Nevertheless, congregational singing and the sprinkling of saintly images in chapels echoed some of the attributes of native religions.

Missionaries inevitably suffered great hardships and setbacks. Sometimes people rose up against the priests and killed or expelled them. Friars often succumbed to fevers and other diseases in pioneer areas where medical care was rudimentary even by colonial standards. In spite of the many obstacles, priests penetrated deep into Amazonia along the meandering water courses. Their impact on native cultures was profound and far-reaching.

Although aboriginal societies were forever altered when they were baptized by missionaries, it is not fair to pin all of the blame for the rapid deculturation of Indian groups after contact on priests. In many cases, missionaries acted as buffers between the appetite of Portuguese plantation owners for slaves and the desire of the fathers to keep their villages intact so that the gospel could be preached more effectively. Jesuits, in particular, often resisted the efforts of slave raiders to siphon off Indians. The Marquis of Pombal successfully urged King José of Portugal to expel the Jesuits from Brazil in 1759 because they were obstructing the efforts of plantation owners to obtain free labor.

The relentless spread of the Christian faith has continued to the present. Along the Rio Negro, for example, Salesians provide biblical and primary school instruction to Indian children who board in missions located in Barcelos, Tapurucuara, and Sao Gabriel da Cachocira. Priests from other Italian-based orders and from the Brazilian Catholic church make periodic visits to remote headwaters to administer to Indians and peasants. More recently, various Protestant sects have made impressive numbers of converts in Amazon towns and in the countryside. The New Tribes Mission and the Summer Institute of Linguistics have been active among Indians, and the Assemblies of God, Baptists, Lutherans, Presbyterians, Methodists, and Adventists have been busy establishing churches among caboclos.

Most peasants in Amazonia are still nominally Catholic, but the overlay of fundamental Christian sects is gradually changing the flavor of caboclo culture. The doctrines of Pentecostal groups are far less compatible with Indian concepts of spirituality than the teachings of the Vatican. Evangelical Christians look askance at images, whether of the Virgin Mary or sacred flutes, as well as at smoking. Many Pentecostal Christians do not regard Catholics as brothers in Christ, and the Pope is the devil incarnate to some. Respect for saints' days is thus ridiculed by Baptists, for example, and Adventists toil on Sundays to the shock of Catholics. In a small village it is not uncommon now to find a Catholic chapel and several gospel halls built by various fundamental Protestant sects all vying for worshippers on Sundays. Open animosity between Catholics and Protestants is rare in Amazonia, but the nature of peasant culture is certainly being changed by the inroads made by aggressive revivalist groups.

Whereas the impact of Christianity on the religious life of Amazonia has been enormous, the influence of African cosmologies has been less marked, particularly in the countryside. African Brazilian cults in Brazil are strongest in Bahia, Rio de Janeiro and São Paulo; in Amazonia, they are evident mainly in the larger towns and cities. In urban areas, the gods of African slaves have left a strong imprint on the regional culture; witness, for example, the huge throngs of people from all social levels that gather on the Ponta Negra beach on the outskirts of Manaus on New Year's Eve. Men and women, clad in white, dance to the syncopated rhythm of tambourines and bongo drums until many fall into trances. Dolls representing *Iemanjá,* the goddess of water, are placed on model boats and launched on the murky surface of the Negro. African gods are often reconciled with Catholic icons; for example, Iemanjá (figure 3.3) is associated with the Virgin Mary. Fair-skinned and tall images of Iemenjá adorn *umbanda* stores, which specialize in charms and herbal remedies. Graceful Iemenjá echoes aboriginal concepts of water nymphs in Amazonia as well as European ideas on mermaids. All three supernatural aquatic females have found niches in the regional lore.

The most widespread African Brazilian cult in Amazonia is *batuque.* Sessions are held at night in simple, open-air huts in urban areas where people sing, dance, and slip into trances. Mediums call upon African deities to help customers tackle their day-to-day problems. In rural areas, curers may also invoke African spiritual forces as well as those belonging to aboriginal religions and Christianity. Batuque mediums are often elderly black women who pray to Catholic saints and communicate with Old and New World spirits.

In practice, considerable variation is noted among African Brazilian religious cults in Amazonia and elsewhere. Practitioners of African Brazilian religions call their groups by various names, in part a reflection of the diverse spiritual traditions of the ancestors of black Brazilians. In Macapá, for example, the leader of one African Brazilian "church" (*terreira*) was born in Belém but received her training in São Luis, Maranhão. Mãe Dulce (figure 3.4) has presided over Terreira Santa Barbara in Macapá, the capital of Amapá territory, for more than a decade and attends to clients from rural areas as well. Terreira

Figure 3.3. Figure of *Iemanjá* next to a framed print of Saint George slaying a dragon in an umbanda store. African Brazilian religious cults are good examples of syncretism between various religious traditions. Avenida João Coelho, Manaus, Amazonas, January 1980.

Santa Barbara is a simple brick addition to the medium's home where the congregation gathers and where Mãe Dulce has a private consultation room. The terreira contains life-sized statues of several black, Indian, and Caucasian spirits as well as an altar crowded with various images, including Saint George, Saint Sebastian, and Iemanjá. Mãe Dulce treats the supernatural afflictions of hunters and fishermen, indicating that she has acquired a blend of indigenous, African, and Christian approaches to healing.

One evening in 1979, I watched an African Brazilian medium enter a trance in the Tocantins river town of Marabá. She was an old woman of modest means who left her farm along the Tocantins when her husband died. In Marabá, the

Figure 3.4. Mãe Dulce next to a statue of Pena Verde, an Indian spirit. Hunters and fishermen from the interior are among the individuals who seek out Mother Dulce for treatment of problems associated with the supernatural. Macapá, Amapá, 14 December 1994.

gentle, soft-spoken lady with grizzled hair and wrinkled face was known to be adept at contacting the spirit world. Although I was only able to decipher a few verses spoken by the medium while in a trance in the living room of a friend's house, the message uttered by two spirits indicate a blending of African and Indian notions about the supernatural. A dolphin spirit spoke thus:

> *I come from Maracá*
> *I am a little girl dolphin*
> *I have come to play*

Two species of dolphins are common in the lakes and rivers of the region, with the larger pink dolphin occurring in a wider range of habitats. Known locally as *boto,* the pink dolphin figures prominently in peasant lore because it allegedly transforms into human form. Pink dolphins can be malevolent and impregnate unsuspecting young ladies. The smaller gray dolphin, called *tucuxi,* is considered a friend, and stories are told of the social animals nudging people to shore to prevent them from drowning.

The next spirit to speak up claimed to be a man:

> *I come from the middle of the ocean*
> *I am José Tupinambá*
> *I am a caboclo*
> *I am from the middle of the ocean*
> *There is a rock that does not reach the bottom*

Evidently the spirit dwells on a rock in the Atlantic that is not attached to the ocean floor. The second verse illustrates the mixing of Indian and African spiritualism as well as the stamp of Christianity. Oceans figure prominently in the spiritual life of African Brazilians, a reflection of the longing of slaves to return to their homeland from which they were so rudely torn. José is Portuguese for Joseph, a biblical name, and Tupinambá is the name of a now-vanished tribe that lived along the coast of Brazil.

Umbanda shops visited by both rural and urban folk typify the hybrid nature of Amazonian religious life. Figures of Indians resplendent with multihued feathers, elderly black men, blond nymphs, and hand-painted Catholic saints adorn the shelves of such stores and compete for the attention of customers. People from all walks of life enter umbanda shops to purchase powders, lotions, and assorted herbal and animal-based remedies designed to purge the body of evil influences, provide a tonic, or kindle the passions of a desired partner. Folk curers may prescribe commercially produced concoctions for their patients; these packaged items are made mainly in Belém from roots, flowers, bark, leaves, essential oils, and various other ingredients. Many of the lotions contain alcohol; the powerful smell of this ingredient is thought to be helpful in warding off evil. The juxtaposition of vivid symbols and paraphernalia from various religions is not at all incongruous to locals. In peasant society the similarities, rather than differences, between spiritual beliefs are emphasized. Indian, African, and Christian notions about the realm beyond the five senses are perceived as variations of a theme. Roles in the supernatural play are interchangeable.

Another major reason the Amazon region is such a rich depository of folk-lore is that most of the population has had a limited formal education. Wherever people are largely illiterate and still rural, the importance of storytelling remains strong. Most peasants have had no more than one or two years of primary school instruction. Many cannot read or write. Schools in the interior are scattered sparingly and function sporadically. Most rural schools consist simply of a thatch roof with open sides, a blackboard, and a few wooden benches without back supports. Teachers are poorly and irregularly paid, so absenteeism among instructors is nearly as chronic as it is among pupils. On the floodplains of major rivers, schools shut down for several months at high water because they become partially submerged. A desire to improve the educational opportunities of children is one of the main propelling forces behind rural-urban migration in the region. Peasants realize that literacy is vital if their offspring are to have a better standard of living.

Amazonian peasants are by and large illiterate, but they possess the skills to make a living from the land and waters. Instruction by parents in hunting, fishing, and farming techniques begins at an early age. Boys are usually fishing with a handline when they are five years old, and by the time they reach their teens, they are likely to be proficient in several other fishing methods, such as the bow and arrow, the pole, and gillnets. Preteen girls help their mothers in farming chores, such as weeding vegetable nurseries, or in preparing manioc flour, a basic staple. The hut where starchy manioc roots are peeled, grated, and sifted and where the dough is agitated over a large, hot griddle provides a convenient setting for gossip and discussions about unusual events, such as ghostly apparitions. Daily contact with untamed waters and forest, rather than the classroom, accounts for the keen interest in the supernatural.

Historically, settlement and cultural interaction in Amazonia have been especially intense along rivers that provide easy avenues for dispersal and trade. Rivers provide protein from fish, turtles, and the succulent flesh of the capybara, the world's largest rodent. The generous floodplains of silt-laden rivers are fertile ground for annual and tree crops. Maize, beans, vegetables, sweet potato, and manioc are planted at low water and harvested when the rivers swell. Bush and tree crops are cultivated on the higher parts of the floodplain and in upland areas for both subsistence and cash income. Indian populations were especially dense along the margins of rivers. After contact many died out, while survivors fled into the forest or remained to participate in the emerging economic system. The new economic order was based mainly on plant and animal products collected in the wild and the growing of food for urban centers.

De-tribalized Indians and mestizos soon fell under the control of traders who sold goods to customers at inflated prices in return for natural products. This arrangement, known as the *aviamento* system, prevails in the more isolated parts of the region to this day. Clients are practically locked into perpetual debt to their patron, known as *patrão* in the Brazilian Amazon. Traders claim that substantial price markups on manufactured goods they carry are warranted because of high transportation costs. In former times, clients who attempted to flee an area before settling their accounts were persecuted and even killed.

The trader operates either from a makeshift hut in upland areas or from a boat or a general store erected on a raft of logs. The raft is usually moored at the confluence of two water courses, or at the entrance to a lake, to take advantage of river traffic. A small warehouse on the raft is used to store rubber, hides, and dried fish as well as kerosene and diesel oil. Caboclos complain about the high prices charged for goods such as coffee, sugar, and powdered milk, but there is little point in moving to a different river where another patrão eagerly awaits new customers. The trader travels periodically to cities, such as Manaus, Santarém, or Belém, to negotiate deals with wholesalers interested in forest products.

Pioneer highways that slice across Amazonia have opened up fresh opportunities for entrepreneurs. Although the grip of the aviamento system eases along the new roads because of the increased competition between merchants, the same cycle of indebtedness often takes root. Some store owners along pioneer highways do not wish to play the traditional role of a patrão and post a sign explaining: *Fiado, só amanhã* (credit, only tomorrow). Cooperatives, which promise to liberate peasants from the clutches of patrons, rarely work, because few small farmers or extractivists have managerial experience and most are too poor to join and maintain them. In areas where credit has been made available to small-scale farmers, such as along the Transamazon Highway, peasants frequently fall into arrears with banks. The aviamento system may seem harsh, but financial institutions are no less kind to defaulters than river barons. Talk of foreclosure and letters from irate bankers that are illegible to the recipient are at least as threatening as an admonishment from a patrão weary of listening to excuses.

Before proceeding to an examination of the regional lore, a few words are

Figure 3.5. Farmer harvesting cabbage from raised vegetable bed on the Amazon floodplain at high water. Paraná Cachoeri, near Oriximiná, Pará, 20 June 1994.

in order about the rural economy. On the floodplain, people plant crops as the waters recede, usually beginning in June along the Amazon and its southern tributaries. Fish catches are highest at low water because the fish are more concentrated in lakes and channels. The drier months are thus the season of plenty. When river levels rise, annual crops must be harvested promptly. At high water, which lasts roughly from February to May or June along the Amazon, catches are modest because the fish are dispersed across the broad floodplains. The diet of peasants on the floodplain is also relatively poor in fresh food, except for fruits harvested from home gardens and gathered in forests and vegetables grown in raised beds (figure 3.5).

Those small farmers who also raise cattle on the Amazon floodplain have three options when the waters rise: rent pasture on upland sites; build a floating corral (*maromba*); or, if they live along the border between uplands and floodplain, construct a small corral (*caiçara*) for their livestock by the water's edge. The latter two options require the gathering of floating grasses twice a day for the restricted animals. Marombas and waterline corrals are the traditional approach to managing small cattle herds. Wealthier individuals on the Amazon floodplain generally concentrate on cattle production and typically own artificial pastures on uplands.

The agricultural calendar for the uplands, or *terra firme,* differs from the farming cycle on floodplains. While people plant crops in alluvial soils of the Amazon and its southern tributaries in July and August, farmers on the uplands generally clear forest or second growth for burning. When caboclos gather their harvests on floodplains from December to March, peasants on the uplands are planting their crops in the ash-enriched soils of slash-and-burn fields. Whether on the floodplain or uplands, the settlement pattern is usually dispersed. Although some parts of the Amazon basin are experiencing rapid population growth, such as Rondônia and southeastern Pará, the overall population density of the region is still low. Extensive stands of forest and endless lakes and side channels are a propitious setting for a rich collection of lore.

CHAPTER   4

Goblins, Ghosts, and Hunters

A visitor to the Amazon rain forest is soon impressed by the teeming wildlife. Buzzes, sharp whistles, flutelike calls, and resonating croaks attest to the rich diversity of insects, birds, mammals, and amphibians in the evergreen jungle. A naturalist is at once fascinated and humbled in the midst of this, the most species-rich environment on earth. Peasants, though, are less concerned with the biotic diversity of the forest; their aims are more practical, such as putting meat on the table. Although caboclos are clearly interested in satisfying material needs when they enter the jungle, they nevertheless regard the forest with awe. Peasants perceive another dimension to the world seen by the curious scientist. Rural folk are aware of the many noisy and colorful animals that dwell in the damp forest, many of which are still unstudied, but they also believe in a large cast of supernatural creatures that make their home deep in the dimly lit woods.

Most of the ghosts, goblins, and spirits that drift through the forest are of concern primarily to hunters. Because they never hunt, women do not normally stray far into the jungle, although they make short forays into the woods to collect fruits and firewood. Most fuel wood is gathered in slash-and-burn fields. Men are thus most likely to provoke the ire of supernatural keepers of game when they comb the forest in search of prey. Although some of the lore helps to check overexploitation of game, the supernatural protectors of game are not symptomatic of a shortage of protein in the regional diet.

Of the many supernatural characters of the Amazon forest, none is better known than *curupira*, also called *caipira, caipora*, or *caapora*. The latter is a Tupi word meaning inhabitant (*pora*) of the woods (*caá*). Curupira changes shape and employs various antics to confuse and sometimes destroy hunters. The creature can appear as a young boy or an old man and range in height from that of a circus midget to the proportions of a professional basketball player. Typically, though, curupira appears as a boylike figure. Curupira taunts hunters by occasionally assuming animal form, such as a brocket deer, paca, or frog.

Descriptions of curupira vary, but two characteristics are usually noted when the creature surprises hunters in humanoid form. First, curupira's feet are turned backward. This twisted piece of anatomy enables the cunning forest spirit to trick hunters into thinking they are fleeing the creature, when they are really following the malevolent goblin deeper into the woods and farther from familiar territory. Second, curupira is usually hairy and extremely ugly.

People who remain close to home need not fear curupira. The creature does not wander into gardens, back yards, or streets; it prefers the deep shade of tall jungle, far from the bustle of towns and villages. Headwater forests are the favored haunts of this legendary creature; there curupira strolls freely among wild animals, especially white-lipped peccaries and brocket deer. Sometimes curupira rides on peccaries or deer, and he treats them when they are sick. The hairy runt sleeps curled up among buttress roots of forest giants, particularly the majestic kapok tree.

As a custodian of game animals, curupira is on the lookout for those who abuse nature's providence. The father of game is especially concerned for the welfare of white-lipped peccaries, and several caboclos asserted that it is unwise to kill more than five of the piglike animals on one hunt. If this limit is exceeded, curupira may resort to several ploys to punish the transgressor. Curupira can summon a hunter by his name; intrigued, the man follows the sound, imagining it to be the voice of a friend or relative. Soon the hunter is lost, and curupira, having accomplished his mission, disappears. Sometimes the father of game dispatches his victims quickly. Curupira's shrill, high-pitched whistle is sufficient to floor a man. When husbands or sons fail to return from a hunt, a jaguar, Indians, or curupira are often blamed for their demise.

A story told by a Rio Negro peasant of pure Indian extraction illustrates the rage of curupira when hunters kill more animals than they need. The informant, a man in his sixties, has spent his entire life in the Negro region and was

Figure 4.1. Tapurucuara, the site of a Salesian mission, on the upper Rio Negro, Amazonas, 14 January 1979.

interviewed in 1979 in the sleepy riverside town of Tapurucuara (figure 4.1), about a week's boat trip upriver from Manaus.

Some fifty years ago, a party of forty men was making its way up the Demini, a left-bank affluent of the Negro, in search of the fibrous piaçava palm. Most of the piaçava cutters had recently migrated from northeastern Brazil, and some were accompanied by their wives. About halfway up the Demini, the party decided to camp for a while to stock up on game meat because animals are scarce in sandy piaçava groves. Hunting was good in those uninhabited parts, and quite a few of the men had killed more than six peccaries each. The butchered carcasses were placed on pole platforms over fires to dry.

That evening around ten o'clock, a stranger suddenly appeared at the forest campsite. The tall man was dressed in a monk's habit with a wide, floppy hood. He had light skin, long hair, and a prominent potbelly. A glass-encased lantern carried by the priestly figure cast an erratic, eerie glow that accentuated his rotund features. "The old man sends word that those who have killed five or more peccaries should give one to him," the friar announced in a firm voice.

Many in the party were from the faraway state of Ceará and remained unimpressed by the unexpected visitor. "Why should we surrender any game to this stranger?" they muttered to one another. Finally, a *Cearense* stood up and addressed the priestly apparition: "Tell the old man to go and hunt his own game." The wife of one of the men grew alarmed at the brewing confrontation. She was a native of Amazonas state and had heard about the father of game. She explained anxiously to the group that the stranger had appeared out of the blue in a deserted forest and that it would be foolish to deny his request. The husband of the woman, also an *Amazonense,* had killed only one white-lipped peccary, but he nevertheless offered a hind leg from his kill to the father. The portly monk whispered to the generous couple that the old man would come at midnight, but they were not to worry because he would not harm them. If they became scared, the friar advised them to climb into a canoe and paddle into the middle of the river. The messenger then shuffled back into the somber forest.

Close to midnight, a deep boom thundered from a distant hill.[1] It sounded like a bomb exploding, and the drowsy men all groaned in their hammocks. The party, except for the generous couple from Amazonas, had suddenly lost their souls. The shadowless men slouched in their hammocks as if in a coma. The thunder drew closer, and each time it rumbled the hapless men moaned in unison. The old man finally arrived. He first tapped the drying peccary carcasses with a stake, and they immediately sprang to life. At least one hundred peccaries jumped down from makeshift platforms over smoky fires and assembled on the ground. The old man then walked over to the hammocks and kneaded the disrespectful men to the consistency of dough. When the corpses were as mushy as ripe avocado, he sucked out the pulpy flesh from the top of their heads. Curupira then tossed the crinkled and empty skins back into the hammocks. The unharmed couple from Amazonas cowered in the understory brush at the edge of the camp and watched in awe. They heard the father of game grumbling that white-lipped peccaries are his children and that no one should kill more than he needs. The old man then melted into the forest followed by the reborn peccaries.

The old man first stole the shadows (*assombrar*) of his victims before dispatching them. Belief in shadow or soul loss is shared by many tribal groups in Amazonia, such as the Mehinaku of the upper Xingu, the Urubu of the Gurupi River, and the Apinayé, who inhabit transitional rain forest between the Tocantins and Araguaia Rivers. A person who has been stripped of his or her shadow is disoriented and, unless treated, dies.

A man in his mid-fifties who lives at kilometer sixty-six of the Marabá-Altamira stretch of the Transamazon Highway recounted a story about a hunter who was *assombrado* by the father of game but managed to survive. The lucky man was in the forest fringe of eastern Amazonia, near Presidente Dutra in Maranhão, with his dogs when they flushed an armadillo. The armor-plated mammal, as is customary when under attack, sought refuge down a burrow. The hunter widened the entrance to the hole with his machete and then stopped for a short rest. One of the dogs eagerly took over the digging and soon disappeared down the burrow. No sooner had the dog slipped out of sight than it started whining and yelping and frantically backed out of the hole. An old man, only two feet high, followed the terrified dog out of the narrow burrow. He had white hair and sported an unruly beard. Without saying a word, the curupira strode into the forest. The astonished hunter returned home and soon fell ill. The father of game had drawn away his shadow. The sick man was successfully treated by a curador, but he never ventured into the woods to hunt again.

On occasion the father of game warns hunters that they are not welcome without harming them. A Transamazon settler who was born in Maranhão remembered a close call he had with the father of game one evening some seventy kilometers northwest of Marabá. Raimundo was waiting in his hammock by a gameleira tree when a large deer arrived to feed on the golf ball–sized yellow fruits scattered on the forest floor. Raimundo fired at close range and the deer collapsed instantly. The informant was about to climb down from his hammock when another fully grown deer approached the strangling fig tree. This deer, though, had a curupira mounted on its back. Raimundo froze. Curupira rode up to the prostrate deer and whipped the mortally wounded animal with a section of pliable vine. "Get up," instructed the father of game. "You should not be lying down." Thus castigated, the fallen deer leapt to its feet and trotted briskly away. Raimundo folded up his hammock and returned home.

Sometimes curupira sends a signal to trespassers that they must depart by focusing his wrath on their dogs. When the excited yelps of dogs in pursuit of game turn to howls of pain and the hunter arrives to find no quarry, it is safe to assume that the father of game has struck. If a person comes across a young palm tree in the forest with the emergent fronds tied together, he or she should return home immediately, for the father of game lives nearby. Curupiras reveal their whereabouts by striking the wall-like buttress roots of certain trees; the forceful thud is especially likely to be heard when a storm is heralded by a strong gust of wind.

A colonist from the Transamazon, Rosimar, recalled hearing the characteristic drumbeat of a curupira one night near the Xingu river. He was perched on a pole platform in the forest close to a graceful piquiá tree. Several animals, such as the spotted paca, relish the juicy fruits of piquiá, and Rosimar had noted game tracks leading to the tree earlier that day. After sitting uneventfully for some time, Rosimar was abruptly aroused by two sharp knocks coming from a nearby tree. The informant shone his flashlight in the direction of the sound, but could see nothing unusual. Puzzled, Rosimar turned off the light and resumed his watch. Shortly he heard two more loud raps against wood, only this time they were farther away. And after a brief pause, the increasingly distant sound was heard again. Although the unnatural tapping was receding, Rosimar decided to leave at once. Father of game was lurking in the vicinity.

Curupira will sometimes shake or push over a tree to ward off people. The son of a Transamazon settler had a close encounter with a curupira one evening some twenty kilometers northeast of Altamira. The son and a companion, both in their early twenties, had erected a narrow platform by day between two slender trees within shotgun range of a massive gameleira. As the hunters waited that night on their recently constructed perch, flashlights and guns at the ready, something shook vigorously one of the trees supporting their lookout post. The tree trembled twice in rapid succession. The forest had been still that evening, so the young men grew alarmed. A rash of goose bumps erupted all over their bodies. Without further ado, the frightened hunting partners jumped down from their platform and left for home. Instead of shaking a tree to scare hunters, the father of game may shove one down close to the intruder. When the hunter notes that the fallen tree is not rotten and the air is calm, a hasty retreat is the wisest course.

Curupira customarily appears in humanoid shape, though he also approaches hunters in the guise of an animal. A Transamazon colonist, José Ferreira, was waiting one night in his hammock slung near a towering Brazil nut tree close to the Xingu river. The curled, marble-sized flowers of Brazil nut trees attract deer, which feed on them during the day and after sundown. The informant, a native of Pará, had spotted fresh deer tracks around the base of the Brazil nut tree earlier in the day, so he was confident that his quarry would return to feed. Conditions were nearly perfect. No wind or rain disguised the sound of animal movements, and a new moon cast a faint light on the vigil. After lying in his hammock for a few hours, the forty-year-old colonist heard the crunch of crisp leaves below. Imagining that a deer had arrived, he hastily pressed the button on his flashlight. But no creature was to be seen. Not even a rat scurried for cover. José surmised that curupira was playing tricks with him, so he left empty-handed for home.

The father of game can transform himself into other game animals and disappear at will, thereby confusing both hunters and dogs. A sixty-year-old Transamazon settler from Maranhão had taken this dogs into the jungle one day some fifty kilometers northwest of Marabá. After walking for a few hours, the dogs started barking and running after a small animal. Probably an armadillo or an agouti, surmised Manuel Bizerra. Experienced hunters who know their dogs can judge fairly accurately the identity of the game that their helpers have flushed by the pitch and frequency of yelps and barks. The elderly informant ran hard to catch up with his now stationary, but still barking, dogs. The quarry must have slipped down a burrow. When Manuel drew alongside the circle of dogs, he saw that they were barking at a hole that would scarcely fit a lizard. Manuel called off his frustrated dogs. It would be useless to hunt any more that day.

A similar incident occurred to an old-timer who lives as a sharecropper on a small farm near the community of Lastancia, in the municipality of Itupiranga. Felipe has had an itinerant life in the rural parts of eastern Amazonia. Born in dry Piaui state, Felipe grew up mostly in Maranhão, in the forest fringe of eastern Amazonia, and moved to Pará in 1982. In 1988, he was hunting with a friend along the course of Grota do Dedinho, about twelve kilometers from Igaparapé Vermelho. Dedinho stream is not far from where he currently lives, an area only penetrated by settlers in the last few decades. The morning's hunt had been uneventful until the dogs suddenly took off in front. The hunters ran to keep up with the dogs. When they finally caught up with them, they were circling and barking excitedly around a hole in the ground. The hunters inspected the small hole; about the only game animal that would fit down it would be an agouti. But no sound or sign of an agouti could be deciphered. The hunters waited for an hour, to no avail. They figured that caapora was playing tricks on them, so they called it a day.

Some hunters try to placate the father of game by leaving tobacco as a gift on fallen logs or on the tops of stumps.[2] The use of tobacco in dealings with the supernatural is ancient. Many South American tribes use tobacco in magico-religious ceremonies, and the leafy herb was domesticated by the continent's aborigines for its supernatural properties. Shamans puff tobacco smoke over the sick to ward off evil, and in some cultures they sip green tobacco juice to help induce a narcotic state so that they can communicate with spirits.

The father of game is fond of smoking and is thus normally pleased with offerings of tobacco. If the father of game asks a hunter for tobacco and is refused, trouble will likely ensue. An eighty-year-old farmer (figure 4.2) on Combu Island opposite Belém provided an illustration of curupira's anger when denied tobacco. Bocinha, as the elderly gentleman is nicknamed, recalled an incident that happened to a friend of his many years ago on Combu Island. His friend was walking along a trail in the floodplain forest on his way to tap rubber trees. Suddenly, he came upon a small black man who immediately asked for a cigarette. The rubber tapper claimed that he did not have any. Appar-

Figure 4.2. Bocinha, an eighty-year-old storyteller, by a vat of fermenting cacao beans. Combu Island, Amazon estuary, near Belém, Pará, 15 December 1994.

ently unsatisfied, the curupira hit the rubber tapper with his hand. Each time he tried to get up, the rubber tapper was knocked down, even though he could no longer see the diminutive figure. After being knocked over several times, the rubber tapper was able to get up. A voice told him to go away.

To deter curupira from beating dogs, hunters sometimes rub garlic on the heads of their canine companions. Garlic, a domesticate of the Old World, has long been used to protect people from malevolent forces, and it has found a similar use in a new context. If a hunter suspects that a curupira is following him, he may tie some vines into a ball and leave it on the trail. When the creature comes upon the tangled mass on the ground, he stops to inspect it. While the father of game is thus distracted, the hunter has a chance to slip away. If that ploy fails, the persecuted individual can tear a termite nest from a tree and burn it. The pungent smoke makes curupira cringe. A caboclo may also rub himself with a garlic clove or powdered cow horn if he suspects that the father of game is prowling nearby. Some peasants contend that it is useless to pray for deliverance from curupira. The creature is believed to be derived from a human, usually an old Indian man, and is also capable of communicating with God.

After a successful kill, a hunter can reduce the chances of upsetting the father of game by observing certain precautions. An elderly caboclo who lives along the Rio Negro emphasized the importance of taking a bath before eating game. It is disrespectful to sit down to a meal of wild meat with a sweaty body. This attention to cleanliness undoubtedly has hygienic value, but concern for washing stems more from the fear of arousing the ire of the father of game. Respect for the carcass of the game animal is also prudent. Sebastião considers it risky to singe the hair from quarry in a fire because curupira might detect the acrid smell of scorched fur. Hair can be safely removed by pouring boiling water over the slain animal and then scraping the skin with a sharp knife. More commonly, the quarry is skinned before cooking. Cooking the meat also requires care. Should the pot boil over and steam rise from the embers, the odor of scalding animal stew could waft in the direction of a nearby father of game and stir his anger. Loud noises, bragging, or undue haste also attract the attention of curupira and are imprudent after a hunt.

A number of actions are thus taken to avoid curupira. It is wise to resist killing more animals than one needs and to observe proper conduct after the kill. The father of game can also be kept at bay with gifts of tobacco, the burning of termite nests, by rubbing one's body with garlic or powdered cow horn, or by placing a liana ball on the trail. Rural people still steeped in tradition take curupira seriously because brushes with the waif often trigger illness. A person who has lost his or her shadow at the hands of the father of game seeks the services of a folk curer. One reputedly effective method of retrieving a stolen shadow is to fan the victim with the aromatic smoke produced by burning the ruby red resin of the caraña tree.[3]

The concept of the father of game is not unique to peasants of the Amazon. The notion of a spirit protector of game is widely held by aborigines in the Americas. Indians inhabiting the forests of eastern Canada were wary of killing too many animals because of fear of reprisal by game "bosses." The idea of supernatural game wardens most likely penetrated the New World during the Pleistocene, when hunters and gatherers immigrated in various waves across the Bering land bridge.

The father of game was well ensconced in the forests of Amazonia by the time Europeans arrived. The master of animals among the now-extinct Pauserna-Guarasug'we' of the Bolivian Amazon, for example, would allegedly make transgressors ill, or kill them. *Kaapoaré* would become upset if tribal members killed more than two peccaries on a hunt. The Urubu of the Gurupi River in eastern Amazonia believe in two supernatural creatures that are connected with game: *curupir* has its feet turned backward, and *timakanã* reprimands those who kill more animals than they need. The Tenetehara who also inhabit the jungles of eastern Amazonia believe that the owner of the forest, *maranaüwa,* is especially watchful over white-lipped peccaries and that it punishes those who wantonly kill the species. Farther to the west, along the upper reaches of the Tapajós, the Mundurucú claim that the mother of game, *putcha ši,* robs the souls of those who break hunting taboos. In northwest Amazonia, the Tukano also believe that the master of animals can make people ill. Peasants have thus acquired their belief in curupira from indigenous cultures.

The main task of curupira is to protect game from human abuse. The father of game is associated particularly with the white-lipped peccary and to a lesser extent with the white-collared peccary. Several informants said that they had tried unsuccessfully to shoot the lead peccary in a band of white-lippeds and that they now avoid trying to kill the front-runner. The large male peccary at the head of the herd is variously believed to be a curupira in disguise, to be under the watchful eye of the father of game, or to be the father of game's mount. Some hunters thus refrain from shooting the lead peccary as a precautionary measure. Observers in the Peruvian Amazon have noted that bands of white-lipped peccaries are generally flanked by males, at least while they are traveling. If hunters consistently spare the leading male, they help preserve the genetic vigor of peccary populations by allowing the larger, stronger, and more aggressive individuals to live.

The concept of the father of game helps sustain the productivity of game in other ways. Numerous no-hunting zones created by the fear of curupira are scattered throughout the Amazon forest. Such no-man's-lands have amorphous boundaries and are ephemeral. While one patch of forest is once again penetrated because no curupira has been spotted or heard recently in the vicinity, another tract of jungle becomes off limits because someone reports a scary encounter with the father of game. No-hunting areas are reported from several indigenous groups. Among the Carajá of the Araguaia, for example, sections of the forest and certain pools are avoided because they are inhabited by dangerous monsters. The Mehinaku of the upper Xingu shun parts of the jungle because they are reputed to harbor fearsome spirits. The Desana of northwest Amazonia avoid certain hills because they are the dwelling places of *vái-mahsë*, the master of animals. Such supernatural territories may not be inviolate, but they surely reduce hunting pressure.

Several other humanoid chimeras haunt the world of hunters. *Pai da mata* (father of the forest) and *cabokinha* (little girl of the forest) are probably versions of curupira, because descriptions of the creatures are similar. A Transamazon settler and a companion, both from the state of Minas Gerais in central Brazil, came within a few feet of pai da mata while hunting in the forest some eighty kilometers west of Altamira. Antonio and his friend were following the fresh tracks of a sizable band of white-lipped peccary when they heard a fine whistle, quite unlike any bird or mammal they had heard before. The men could not pinpoint the source of the plaintive sound. Then a black man only four feet high suddenly strode out from behind a tree. The startled hunters could only catch a glimpse of the midget before it slipped back into the forest maze.

The father of the forest wore shorts, but no shirt, and had dark, shiny hair that cascaded halfway down his back. The runt did not look at the hunters, nor did he speak. After pai da mata disappeared, the men attempted to resume the hunt. But they could no longer locate the peccary tracks they had been following, even though the sharp-hoofed animals leave a broad swath of upturned leaves and chopped earth in their wake. It was as if pai da mata had wiped the slate clean so that the peccaries could escape. Antonio and his companion shortly became disoriented. They tramped through the forest for the rest of the day trying to find their way home. As night fell they finally broke out of the jungle into a field along the Transamazon Highway, some eight kilometers from where they thought they would exit.

Cabokinha is a small, hairy girl according to one informant, though another claimed that the creature is a boy. Besouro, a Transamazon colonist from the northeastern state of Paraíba do Norte, came across an ugly girl in the forest one day near the Nova Fronteira settlement, not far from the above-mentioned incident with the father of the forest. Besouro was hunting with his dogs when cabokinha ambushed them. She struck the dogs viciously, and they raced around in circles as if possessed. Besouro called his dogs away and immediately left for home. It would be useless, indeed dangerous, to continue hunting that day.

One of the most feared supernatural beasts of the jungle is wolf's cape (capé-lobo). Wolf's cape is said to derive from an old Indian who leaves his village to live his last days alone in the forest. Instead of dying, however, he gradually transforms into a foul-smelling hairy ape armed with long, canine fangs and a single eye protruding from his forehead. The terrestrial creature walks upright and leaves rounded footprints in the soil, similar to those left if one presses the bottom of a bottle into the ground. The scream of capé-lobo can be heard for up to ten leagues, and the blast is sufficient to buckle the knees of even the most robust hunter. Wolf's cape employs its awesome teeth to tear into dogs and goats, its favorite prey, but people are also incorporated into its carnivorous diet.

A Transamazon colonist recounted a frightening experience he had with wolf's cape near Barra de Corda in his native state of Maranhão. Nilton and a friend were lying in hammocks one night by a forest tree with falling fruit. The evening was calm, and no game had come to feed at the bait tree. Finally, around four o'clock in the morning, some large animal stirred the brittle leaves below. Nilton clicked on his flashlight and fired at the red eyes glowing in the bright beam. Although Nilton was confident that he had got off a good shot, he was amazed to find no quarry on the ground when the blue-gray haze cleared. Not even a trail of blood could be seen leading off into the forest. Then a wolf's cape came to investigate. The grotesque brute shuffled around their hammocks, letting out deep, dry grunts. Nilton hastily tossed some tobacco to the ground. Fortunately, capé-lobo accepted the gift and withdrew. The hunters wanted to return home immediately, but they decided it would be safer to negotiate the shadowy path back at daybreak. No more animals came near them that night.

A couple of Nilton's relatives were hunting with dogs in another part of the forest flanking eastern Amazonia when they had a close call with a wolf's cape. As usual, the dogs had spread out in advance of the men sniffing the ground for fresh spoor. Suddenly, the dogs started yelping and whining in pain. The hunters rushed to the distressed hounds and found them writhing on the ground in agony. A capé-lobo was hurling the animals through the air with great force, and the latter were clearly on the losing side of the fight. No sooner had the concerned hunters arrived on the scene than their nostrils were assaulted by a vile odor emanating from the wolf's cape. The gasping men promptly developed throbbing headaches and felt dizzy. The light-headed hunters managed to stumble home, but they felt ill for a month.

The arresting smell of capé-lobo is said to originate in its filthy, matted fur. The stench, high-pitched roar, and well-developed teeth of the ape-man make it a formidable adversary. Wolf's cape can only be killed by penetrating its eye; bullets and lead shot do not harm the rest of the creature's stocky body. The rumored haunts of wolf's cape are understandably given a wide berth.

A closely related legendary beast of the forest is the equally fearsome *mapinguary*. Some peasants insist that mapinguary and wolf's cape are different creatures, but descriptions are so similar that they are undoubtedly versions of the same brute. It seems that capé-lobo is the name ascribed to the creature in Pará and Maranhão, whereas in western Amazonia it is called mapinguary.

A Tukúna woman married to a caboclo in the village of Aripuanã in northern Mato Grosso claimed that mapinguary is an old Indian who leaves his village to live alone in the forest. Eventually, he turns into a long-haired beast with stubby legs, no feet, and only one eye in the center of its forehead. The piercing shriek of mapinguary can be heard over large distances, and the creature relishes the brains of humans. The ape-Indian can only be dispatched by stabbing its belly button, or by setting it afire.

The informant described a close shave that a couple of men had with a mapinguary one day in the forest near the confluence of the clear-water Aripuanã and the muddy Madeira. The men were walking in single file through the jungle when a mapinguary jumped in front of the lead man and tried to grab him. Before the creature could grasp its prey, however, the man sliced off the beast's hand with his machete. The men then chased the wounded mapinguary until it sought shelter among some rocks. The caboclos stacked some wood around the dreaded creature's hiding place and cooked it.

Not all those who meet mapinguary are so fortunate. A middle-aged lady who was born in Amazonas state and lives in the village of Itapiranga on the north bank of the Amazon some 350 kilometers downstream from its confluence with the Negro recalled a tragic encounter with mapinguary. It happened in a nearby settlement in the 1940s. It was Sunday and people were either resting, chatting at their doorways, attending chapel, or playing soccer on the small, dusty field at the edge of the cluster of huts that formed the community. One man, apparently bored, decided to go hunting. "No," his wife protested, "it's Sunday, and besides we have no need of meat today." In spite of his wife's misgivings, the man persisted with his plans. He had not been gone long when frantic shouts were heard coming from the nearby forest. A friend of the departed hunter grabbed his shotgun and a handful of shells and ran in the direction of the distress calls. When he arrived at the spot from where the screams had been coming, he was too late to be of any assistance: his lifeless neighbor sagged in the vicelike grip of a mapinguary. The gorillalike beast fed voraciously on its victim and paused for a moment to murmur, "Sunday also eats."

Apart from avoiding the reported haunts of mapinguary and resisting the temptation to hunt on Sundays, there is little a hunter or a woodsman can do to reduce the chances of encountering the creature. Unlike curupira, the awesome mapinguary does not expect hunters to limit their game take or bathe themselves thoroughly before eating their kills. It seems likely that mapinguary and capé-lobo have trickled into the reservoir of peasant folklore from one or more Indian cultures. The Desana of northwest Amazonia, for example, believe in a forest demon called *boráro* that shares several characteristics with mapinguary and wolf's cape. Boráro is a tall, naked humanoid with a hairy chest, glowing red eyes, a huge penis, and a powerful, jaguarlike roar. The evil-smelling boráro subdues its victims by urinating on them or crushing their bodies so that the flesh can be sucked out from the tops of their heads. The Cubeo, another Tukano group of the northwest Amazon, hold that a jungle fiend, *abuhuwa,* cuts a hole in its victim's head, siphons out the contents of the body, and then drapes the skin of the deceased on a branch. In aboriginal cosmologies of Amazonia, nearly all forest ogres share two attributes: they stink and they are hairy. Hairiness is thought to represent unbridled sexual energy, whereas the unpleasant odor is associated with death.

Amazonian Indians, in contrast, are fastidious when it comes to cleanliness. Men, women, and children take frequent baths in streams, lakes, and rivers. Body odor is distasteful to them, as it is in peasant society. Furthermore, aborigines in the basin shave body hair. One is unlikely to find a tribal Indian with a hairy chest or beard. Hairiness is repugnant to them. In modern, Western culture, beards are sometimes regarded as symptomatic of a subversive nature, but hirsute chests and arms are symbols of machismo. And in Brazil today, urban males will often purposefully leave the top buttons of their shirts undone in order to reveal a ruff of hairs.

Mapinguary thus stems in large part from aboriginal prejudices, but the concept has been modified by contact with European culture. The idea of the single eye, for example, may be linked to the infamous Cyclops of Greek mythology. Cyclops has one eye in the middle of its forehead, and it can knock a person over with its shattering call. In contrast to mapinguary, however, Cyclops devours its victims completely. A hint of European mythology concerning werewolves surfaces in the stories of wolf's cape. Wolves do not occur in Amazonia, although a lanky, maned wolf inhabits the savannas of central Brazil. Aspects of mapinguary morphology have probably been molded to accommodate Old World lore.

Ground sloths may have served as a model for the legendary mapinguary. David Oren, a biologist at the Goeldi Museum in Belém, suggests that a 1.8-meter-high mylodontid ground sloth may have survived until recent times in parts of Amazonia, where it could have surprised hunters and woodsmen. Early hunters in the Americas are thought to have driven cumbersome ground sloths, some of which reached the dimensions of an elephant, to extinction by about 10,000 years ago. Climate change may also have contributed to the demise of some species of ground sloths. A smaller and more secretive forest-dwelling ground sloth might have been able to hold on longer. It is possible that the creature, one of numerous species that lived in South America while the continent was isolated from North America for millions of years, may still occur in remote parts of western Amazonia. Although such an idea may seem preposterous, an "extinct" peccary was discovered living in Paraguay a couple of decades ago, and a new species of monkey from southern Brazil was found in the early 1990s. It is unlikely anyone will uncover a *Lost World* or a *Jurassic Park* full of Pleistocene megafauna or dinosaurs in the deep recesses of the Andes or lofty table mountains of the Colombian and Venezuelan Amazon, but zoological surprises surely lurk in the region.

The vanished, or possibly nearly extinct, ground sloth in question was hairy and walked with its claws turned in toward its body, thereby creating a strange footprint. The rounded "footprints" of mapinguary could be based on the tail of ground sloths used for support while foraging. The tail was probably used as a tripod for greater stability while reaching up to feed on plants, and would have left a roughly circular or oval impression in the ground. The mylodontid family of ground sloths had bony plates in the skin, and some reports of mapinguary in Acre describe the creature as apelike with scaly skin similar to that of a caiman. The notion that mapinguary can only be killed by penetrating it through the navel, mouth, or eye may be a reflection of the tough, partially armored skin and shieldlike rib cage of mylodontid ground sloths.

Ghosts, possibly guises of the father of game, also plague hunters while they search for game. A Transamazon colonist who has lived most of his life in the rain forests of Pará described an experience he had one Sunday in 1952 some fifteen kilometers east of Itupiranga, a village on a steep bank of the Tocantins. Manuel Santana and a companion were hunting in the forest when their dogs treed what Manuel thought must be a large animal, such as a puma. When the hunters arrived at the base of the tree where the dogs were barking excitedly, the men could not spot any game among the branches. Manuel was puzzled, because his trail-wise dogs were trained to chase only useful animals. The dogs were called away from the tree and the hunt resumed. The dogs shortly picked up another scent and gave chase. They soon stopped again and continued barking. Before the hunters could catch up, the excited barking turned into a cacophony of frenzied growls, snarls, and painful yelps. When Manuel and his friend reached the dogs, they were cowering and whimpering at the base of a tree. The assailant was nowhere in sight. The men called off the hunt; they should not have been working on a Sunday.

In some areas of the Amazon, certain forest patches are avoided at all times, not just on Sundays, because they are haunted by human and animal spirits. The concept of *lugares encantados,* or enchanted places, has its roots in aboriginal cultures. Several Amazonian tribes revere sacred waterfalls or prominent rocks along rivers where ancestral and other spirits dwell. Although the locations of venerated spots may change, the idea survives among peasants.

A farmer along the Transamazon reported that he came upon a lugar encantado one day near where he used to live in the vicinity of São Miguel do Guamá, in the Bragantina zone east of Belém. It was late in the afternoon, and Manuel da Cunha was on his way to an ingazeiro, a leguminous tree found in forest and old second growth. The elongated pods of ingá, also called ingazeiro, encase seeds that are surrounded by a sticky white coating, and this sweet, juicy pulp is much appreciated by both people and game animals. Earlier that day, the informant had noticed deer tracks in the vicinity of the tree.

Dusk was approaching as Manuel ducked into the cool, shadowy interior of the forest. As he walked by a small spring, gun slung over his shoulder, he heard a cock crow. Unlike their wild ancestors in the forests of Thailand and Burma, domesticated chickens normally shun the dark jungle, although they scrounge scraps and insects in fields and weedy patches. Assuming that one of his prize cocks was lost, Manuel walked around the shaded spring looking for the bird. Then a dog barked: the sound came from the water. As Manuel stared into the crystal-clear spring, voices drifted up from its depths. The chorus of village sounds continued, though no people or livestock could be seen. The place was enchanted, and it was time to leave, especially with night descending so rapidly. Manuel never hunted close to that spring again.

Lights, not necessarily associated with any particular spot, sometimes drift in front of hunters and startle them. A Transamazon settler saw a green ball of light in a forest near the Nova Fronteira settlement one evening. He was waiting for game by a fruiting tree when the puzzling glow suddenly materialized. It floated for an instant and then vanished. Another Transamazon colonist noticed a green orb of light the size of a large watermelon in the same area while he was hunting one evening. The shimmering sphere quivered in the soft breeze about a meter above the forest floor. The orb made no sound and finally dissipated, like a gas.

Mysterious lights are also reported from other parts of the Amazon basin. Near Itupiranga on the left bank of the Tocantins, for example, a hunter recalled a night he spent close to a fruiting gameleira tree in June 1953. Manuel da Cunha and a companion were perched in their hammocks with their legs dangling over the sides when a disc of light oozed out of the ground in front of them. The uncanny light was a vivid white, like bleached cotton, and spun as it rose to the level of the hammocks. Then it vanished. The men were not scared away, but no game appeared that night. Seventeen years later in the same vicinity, another man was hunting at night and had just shot a deer when a bright red light came out of the carcass. Joaquim remained on his pole platform some three meters above ground. The incandescent globe drifted aimlessly around the kill for half an hour, lighting up the forest with its intense, flarelike glow. Then the flaming globe glided back to the prostrate deer and flickered out.

Joaquim jumped down from his platform, retrieved the lifeless deer, and left for home (figure 4.3).

The unusual forest lights provoke surprise, but not fear, among rural folk. The lights do not appear when a taboo has been broken and no lore has arisen for dealing with them. Some of the sightings may be due to methane escaping from decaying vegetation; puffs of ignited methane are responsible for will-o'-the-wisps in other parts of the world. Other incandescent blobs may be triggered by lightning. Shimmering balls of light have been reported from many parts of the world, especially after lightning strikes. Such light balls lack a well-

Figure 4.3. Meat from a brocket deer drying on the roof of a farmhouse. The seated farmer killed the deer a few days earlier. Because most rural folk in Amazonia lack refrigerators, they must salt and sun-dry large kills to avoid spoilage. Sitio Santo Antonio, km 56 of the Santarém-Rurópolis Highway, Pará, 17 November 1992.

defined shape, vary from the size of a marble to a basketball, are dim or bright, and can be observed in buildings as well as outdoors.

Various theories have been spun to account for ball lightning. Some have suggested that the glow arises from electric current loops in the blob that interact with the earth's magnetic field. Other ideas advanced to explain the phenomenon include plasma vortex rings caused by the laserlike action of lightning, small-scale nuclear reactions triggered by lightning that allows the collision of air molecules and high-energy protons, micrometer-sized antimatter meteorites, and the glow of photons produced when cosmic-ray shower positrons are annihilated.

The origin of will-o'-the-wisps is not clear, but they have penetrated the lore of several regions. In the southern Himalayas, for example, such lights are called *shipa*, a category that includes the yeti and dragons, and children are warned not to throw rocks at the shimmering objects for fear that they may turn on the aggressors. In the Amazon, the Apinayé refer to such light as *ačén* and attribute them to the campfires of departed souls.

The dangers of hunting on Sunday have emerged in a number of tales, such as those concerned with mapinguary and ghosts. But it can also be risky to hunt on other holy days, especially those commemorating saints. A fifty-year-old man who was born in Pará and currently lives along the Transamazon provided an illustration of the folly of hunting on the day of São Bento de Lameu.

Some twenty years ago, two men set off with their guns into the forest inland from the Guamá River in northeastern Pará. It was daytime, and the dogs managed to flush a nocturnal paca from its resting place. The spotted rodent quickly raced down an hole. The hunters could hear the throaty snarl of the plump rodent, and judging it to be a full-grown specimen weighing some ten kilos, one of the men hurried home to fetch a hoe while the other kept vigil at the entrance to the burrow. As soon as the man came back with the implement, the companions took turns at widening the hole. They soon noticed something odd: the metal hoe was wearing down very quickly, although it was new and little gravel was encountered in the soil to abrade the cutting edge. By the time they reached the end of the burrow, the once-sharp hoe had been ground to a blunt stub. And then an even bigger surprise was in store. At the end of the hole sat a large frog staring at them. The paca had turned into an amphibian, a clear sign that they had no business hunting that day.

On another São Bento's day in the same region during the 1940s, five men and their dogs set out to hunt in the jungle. After a while, the party flushed a small band of white-lipped peccaries, but the herd escaped. A short time later, the dogs disturbed a deer and chased it toward the hunters. Although several volleys were fired, the agile creature bounded past the men apparently unscathed. Then a little farther along the trail, the party came upon a small white deer. The men were surprised, because albino deer are rare in Amazonia; albino animals are conspicuous prey against the somber background of the forest. Several hunters shot at the diminutive creature, but to no avail. The albino deer glared at them, then walked calmly away. The hunters realized that they would have no luck on that sacred day, so they turned around and went home.

A considerable number of saints reside in heaven, and more are instated from time to time. Catholics do not observe the day of every saint because it would be inconvenient. Caboclos typically honor at least a handful of holy days during the year. Which saints are selected for reverence on their respective days usually depends on individual experience. A person may become convinced that he or she should not be working on a saint's day when an accident happens or something mysterious is seen. Or if a saint has been especially helpful in obtaining favors, the person so blessed is likely to refrain from working on that saint's day.

A *Paraense* who lives on the outskirts of Itaituba on the left margin of the Tapajós told a story that illustrates the gratitude felt by people when a saint intercedes on their behalf. Several years ago, a hunter was in the forest some fifty kilometers southwest of Itaituba when a jaguar chased him up a tree. The spotted cat is an agile climber, so the terrified man knew it would not be long before he became a meal for the jungle's most powerful predator. The beleaguered hunter prayed to Saint John for help and promised to build the saint a chapel if he would deliver him from certain death. Saint John appeared immediately and scared away the hungry cat. The grateful hunter subsequently erected a wattle-and-daub chapel on the spot where the miracle had occurred. The shaded structure, slightly under two meters high, reputedly still stands in the forest. The roof is so low one has to stoop to enter.

Every year a few dozen hunters and woodsmen make their way to the forest-shrouded chapel to honor Saint John. Devotees of the saint light candles on the altar, recite prayers, make requests, and leave gifts, including gold that is mined nearby. Rumors of accumulated wealth in the shrine soon spread, and one character resolved to go and investigate. When he arrived at the chapel, he removed a solid gold chain that was draped around the image of Saint John. But when the thief tried to retrace his steps to the margin of the Tapajós, he became lost. After wandering through the jungle for several hours, the guilt-laden fellow decided it would be better to return the gift to the shrine. Only after the present had been restored to its proper place was the man able to exit the forest.

The world of hunters is thus suffused with a frightening and often unpredictable cast of paranormal creatures. Some of the apparitions from beyond the realm of the five senses probably check human pressure on game populations. A conservation role is also played by enchanted places and holy days. But these cultural checks to the overexploitation of natural resources do not spring from any conscious desire to perpetuate an ecological balance with nature. Few peasants espouse a Thoreauvian ethic that calls for respect for wild creatures because they have a right to exist on this planet. Eastern concepts about living in harmony with nature, such as Taoism, are also quite alien to caboclos. Amazonian peasants are much more interested in making a living from their environment.

CHAPTER 5

Submerged Spirits

The Amazon basin, with its myriad waterways extending from the rivers emptying into the pounding surf of the Atlantic shore in the east to icy Andean streams in the west, is home to more species of fish than any other watershed in the world. This aquatic wonderland, encompassing cool forest streams, thundering waterfalls, treacherous rapids, placid lakes, and sluggish channels, is also a propitious setting for the germination of a stunning variety of legendary beasts. Some of the mythical creatures are relatively benign, but others are dreaded by fishermen and all those who must come close to the water's edge. As in the case of hunters, many ideas about the supernatural mold the behavior of fishermen, so that they respect the providence of nature and live in harmony with their fellow man.

The most widespread and well-known supernatural denizen of Amazonian waters is cobra grande, the big snake. Cobra grande is believed to reach up to two hundred meters long, far in excess of the maximum recorded length of fourteen meters for the anaconda, Amazonia's largest snake. The origin of this legendary giant serpent is disputed among rural folk. Some feel that cobra grande is just an anaconda that has grown exceptionally large, whereas others suggest that the fearsome snake is derived from a boa constrictor. Boas, however, do not grow longer than five meters. Still, some people think that this terrestrial snake becomes a cobra grande when it grows too large and heavy to live any longer on land; it then seeks the safety and comfort of water for the remainder of its life. The boa constrictor is known in Brazil as *jibóia*, hence the other name for the giant snake: *boi-una*. The suffix *una* means "black" in língua geral. Língua geral was a lingua franca spoken by Portuguese and indigenous people in the Amazon basin during the colonial period to facilitate communication.

Even smaller snakes can be candidates for cobra grande. Some believe the mythical serpent is an overgrown surucucu, which is highly venomous, or pepéua, a shy aquatic snake. Neither surucucu nor pepéua exceed four meters in length. A few fishermen suggest that cobra grande evolves from any kind of snake, whereas others insist that the giant serpent is unique; it does not grow from any other species.

Cobra grande can also spring from humans. Along the Itacaiúnas River (figure 5.1), a tributary of the Tocantins, people attribute the creation of a menacing boi-una to a despicable human act. Dona Ruth, a resident of Marabá at the confluence of the Itacaiúnas and Tocantins, described the origin of the boi-una that reportedly overturns boats on a stretch of the river known for its productive groves of Brazil nut trees.

One day a young girl became pregnant. She grew nervous because she did not want her parents to find out what had happened; her father would be especially outraged. So she wore tight dresses that suppressed her swelling abdomen. When the time came to give birth, she retreated to a banana patch and delivered a baby girl. Ashamed of her licentious behavior and fearing the wrath of her parents, she tossed the infant into the swirling current of the Itacaiúnas. Once in the cloudy river, the baby assumed the shape of a giant snake and survives today to harass river traffic. This boi-una tale was revealed during a séance. Speaking through a medium, the Itacaiúnas boi-una said that she was the daughter of a woman living in Marabá who has kept her illegitimate act secret for all these years. The snake spirit mentioned that she wanted to be disenchanted. To break the spell, someone had to place a cup of hot milk on a bank of the river. When boi-una surfaced to drink the milk, the volunteer was to slash the serpent's head with a razor-sharp knife so that blood gushed out. Then the person must turn around and not look back under any circumstances. Evidently, no one has had the courage to disenchant this boi-una.

The curse of another human-derived cobra grande was lifted successfully by a group of men near Carolina, a town on the right bank of the Tocantins. According to Dona Ruth, the giant snake was known as Norato, and he used to leave the river at night to join parties. Norato liked to dance, and he always

Figure 5.1. The Itacaiúnas River, one of the many rivers in Amazonia that is thought to harbor *cobra grande*, a legendary giant snake. View from kilometer 9 of the Marabá-Altamira stretch of the Transamazon Highway, Pará, 10 November 1992.

wore a smart white jacket. While Norato enjoyed the festivities, his scaly skin remained at the water's edge. During the early hours of the morning, he used to slip away from dances, wriggle into his reptilian cloak, and slither back into the warm water. One evening a man happened to be standing on the bank of the Tocantins when he noticed a bow wave approaching. The man remained motionless and witnessed a snake land on the shore and turn into a man. It was Norato. He shed his crinkly skin and walked off in the direction of the party, then in full swing. The astonished man hurried to a friend, and both decided to pour some gasoline on the coiled skin of the cobra grande and burn it. When Norato returned to the riverbank several hours later, he found his mantle in ashes. Norato's fate was thus changed, and he remained a human.

The story of another boi-una emerged in an impromptu spiritualist session I witnessed in Marabá. The medium was a black, gray-haired lady in her sixties. Dona Joana wore a knee-length cotton dress printed with small, delicate flowers and a pair of loosely fitted plastic sandals. No jewelry adorned her wrinkled fingers, neck, or ear lobes. It was about eight o'clock one evening in April 1979, and several people were watching an American film from the 1930s on a small black-and-white television in the modest home of Dona Ruth. My questions to the medium about boi-una were eliciting vague, reluctant answers when Dona Joana suddenly pursed her lips and let out a prolonged, soft hissing sound. She ripped out the comb from the back of her head and threw it on the ground. Her liberated hair fluffed out, dramatically altering her appearance. Dona Joana slid down from the couch on which we were sitting and lay with her stomach to the smooth, concrete floor. She kept her extended arms pressed tightly to her sides and began slithering slowly across the sparsely furnished living room.

No one in the room was alarmed. Dona Joana had been visited by a boiuna spirit before. The television still flickered, casting a dancing, harsh glare on Dona Joana as she wiggled across the floor. After curving to the left, she stopped, rolled over on her back, and seemed to be trying to get up. But with her arms still tucked tightly under her sides, Dona Joana's sit-ups were not enough to set her on her feet again. Dona Ruth bent down and helped the possessed Dona Joana stand. The medium stumbled around the room for some fifteen seconds. She appeared dizzy and looked like she might fall at any moment. Then Dona Joana broke into a quiet song:

> *I am boi-una*
> *I am boi-una*
> *I am a snake from the deep*
> *I am a snake of everyone*
>
> *The boi-una is girl*
> *The boi-una is girl*
> *The boi-una is girl*
> *The boi-una is girl*
>
> *I am boi-una*
> *I am boi-una*
> *I am a snake from the deep*
> *I am a snake of everyone*

One of Dona Ruth's daughters asked the medium where boi-una had come from. The snake-spirit replied in a faint voice that she lives by a rock in the Arari River in the state of Amazonas. Another person asked whether she had been thrown into the river as a child. "Yes," replied Dona Joana.

Notions about cobra grande are far more than quaint superstition. Rural inhabitants from Marajó Island at the mouth of the Amazon all the way up the river and along its hundreds of tributaries firmly believe in the existence of a giant aquatic serpent. Rosinha, a teenager on Marajó, had her newborn child taken away from her and tossed into the Amazon one day in the 1940s because her father was convinced that she had been impregnated by a cobra grande while swimming. Rosinha claimed that one night she was overtaken by an urge to strip and plunge into the river. Upon the advice of a pajé, Rosinha's father hurled the baby boy into the muddy river so that the child could join its presumed father at the bottom. The father of the young lass was subsequently prosecuted in Belém and sent to jail. During the highly publicized hearings, the real father of the victim, Vicente, was uncovered. He was a young lad who had been visiting relatives near the home of the accused. Vicente disappeared when he discovered the outcome of one of his rendezvous with Rosinha.

Cobra grande lives in rivers, channels, and lakes, but it shuns rain-forest streams. The creature spends much of its time in holes excavated at the bottom of lagoons and deep rivers. Patches of smooth water are common along the Amazon and its major tributaries where upwelling currents erupt on the surface. These bulging lenses of spreading water are sometimes attributed to the vigorous movements of cobra grande as it digs an abode deep below. A related sign that the mythical snake has been at work is a sliver of land that has recently slid into the water. Upwelling currents steepen banks until portions slough off into the water. Scalloped scars along river margins indicate dangerous currents and the possible dwelling places of giant serpents.

A boatman who was born in Cametá on the Tocantins and now works on the Tucurui reservoir recalled an unusual sighting of a cobra grande in the 1940s. A large snake, the thickness of a fifty-five-gallon oil drum, surfaced one day along the Tocantins near Vizeu. The cobra grande appeared to be tussling with an electric eel. Several individuals experienced a vision in which the snake explained that the electric eel was trying to take over its deep spot in the river. The snake warned people to stay away from the area during the "underwater revolution." The origin of this giant serpent was attributed to a one-month-old baby girl called Noratinha who became lost and turned into a snake. The girl was reputedly born in the village of Cametá Tapera, a little downstream from Cametá. Eventually, the giant snake grew too big for the Tocantins, especially at low water, and moved away.

Lake-dwelling big snakes are especially conspicuous during the dry season, when the numerous lagoons along rivers such as the Amazon, Madeira, and Purus shrink. If water levels drop too much, the supernatural snakes wriggle across the alluvial landscape in search of deeper lakes or rivers. These seasonal migrations are deemed responsible for certain channels that weave across the extensive floodplains of some Amazonian rivers.

A fisherman who lives in the vicinity of Itacoatiara in Amazonas state was especially impressed by a channel he saw during the 1977 dry season. It was in the exposed, muddy bed of Lake Branco, a lagoon near Itacoatiara that is fed by the Amazon at high water. Ajenor claimed that a cobra grande had carved out the sinuous canal and had even bulldozed aside logs lying in its path. A muscular cobra grande is reputed to have gouged a one-meter-deep trough up a bank of the black-water Uatumã, a tributary of the Amazon, near the tiny settlement of Sebastião. Cobra grande thus actively shapes the ever-shifting morphology of aquatic environments in Amazonia.

Cobra grande has a frightful appearance as well as awesome power. Pointed canines protrude from its lower jaw through gaps in the roof of its cavernous mouth and jut out like horns. As in the case of some forest demons, cobra grande exudes a putrid stench, strong enough to make a victim giddy. Boi-una also utters some bizarre notes. Elizeo, a forty-five-year-old fisherman who lives near Itacoatiara, has never seen a cobra grande, but he is sure that he heard one in Lake Miwá Grande on the Amazon floodplain. The still night was suddenly shaken by a muffled explosion coming from the lake's depths. Thousands of fish jumped instantly. The giant snake represents the mother of fish, and aquatic charges respond whenever she rumbles. Silvery pirarucu and caimians, for example, slap the water surface with their tails when cobra grande growls. Explosives are used illegally to fish in the Amazon, and some of the loud, underwater sounds attributed to the giant snake may be the result of commercial fishermen tossing bombs into the water.

Several other fishermen claim to have heard the giant snake. Antonio Vitor was working alone one evening in Lake Jaraquizinho, some fifteen kilometers south of Itacoatiara, when he heard a loud din coming from the water. When Antonio saw a pair of enormous eyes beaming from the source of the racket, he hastily paddled away. Ricardo heard a cobra grande make a rumbling sound around eleven o'clock one night near Itacoatiara. He also promptly left the area in which he had been fishing. In another incident, a small party was returning home in a tiny motorboat when they encountered a huge serpent along the Paraná do Arana in the municipality of Maués. It was about midnight when a cobra grande erupted close by. The group of people could not see the snake distinctly, but its thrashing around made the water boil. The crew immediately disengaged the throbbing engine so that it would not attract the snake's attention. The terrified passengers waited for two hours before the commotion ceased. Finally, the boat continued on its way, but it proceeded with great caution. Domingos remembered the incident vividly. He felt that the snake must have been two hundred meters long.

The enormous size of cobra grande, combined with its remarkable speed and strength, make it look like a boat approaching in the distance. When the monstrous serpent swims at the surface it pushes up a huge bow wave that curls and foams, thereby creating a conspicuous V-shaped wake. A Transamazon colonist who lives at kilometer twenty-six of the Itaituba-Altamira stretch of the highway recalled a close shave he had with the legendary snake about 1935. Raimundo was handline fishing with a friend in a canoe on the Tapajós some five kilometers from the village of Itaituba, now a bustling gold-rush town. It was eleven o'clock on a clear morning when Raimundo spotted what he thought was a canoe approaching from midriver. As the object came closer, though, both fishermen saw the head of a cobra grande, its slick scales glinting in the bright sun. Raimundo and his companion immediately let go of their lines, grabbed their paddles, and made for shore. By the time they reached the sandy beach, the menacing serpent was only fifteen meters away. The men clambered out of the canoe and scurried into the low woods growing on the higher parts of the riverbank. The bow wave of the frustrated snake pitched their hastily abandoned canoe like a piece of flotsam on to the sloping beach. From the cover of the trees, the fishermen could see the huge snake cruising offshore. After waiting for about six hours, they gave up on the idea of paddling home and walked back to Itaituba.

Although cobra grande attacks by day, it more commonly disturbs people at night. Its eyes do not reflect light with a red hue as do the eyes of other nocturnal creatures. Instead, they cast penetrating beams, like flashlights. Assiz, a fisherman in his late twenties, encountered a cobra grande at the entrance to Lake Chato, which is fed by the Arari River, some thirty kilometers south of Itacoatiara. It was about one o'clock in the morning when Assiz saw what appeared to be flashlights scanning the lake surface. He thought that other fishermen were at work, so he called out. No response. When the lights drew close he noted that the water was churning, so Assiz retreated at once.

Along the Rio Pequeninho, an affluent of the Arari, a cobra grande is notorious for scaring people who venture on to the narrow river at night. The large, saucer-shaped eyes of the serpent are set a meter apart, and they cast an orange-yellow light. The color of the giant snake's eyes varies. A fisherman saw a cobra grande with eyes that cast a blue glow in Lake Miwá Grande. Barriga and a companion were checking a gillnet for fish when the cold light approached. Both men fled promptly and claim never to have fished that spot again. An old-timer, now in his late sixties, who works on a small farm on the Amazon floodplain near Santarém, reported sighting a cobra grande when he was ten years old. Manuel saw the enormous snake on the Arapiuns River, an affluent of the lower Tapajós, in the early hours of the morning. Manuel estimated the serpent to be ten meters in circumference and one hundred meters long. The giant snake's flashlight eyes cut through the darkness. The cobra grande lived in an area of upwelling currents at a place called Toronon, near the sandy beaches of Icuxi point. The snake's abode was rumored to contain a lot of fish, but people were wary of approaching the spot. It used to be a safe haven for fish, but Manuel commented that no one pays attention to that anymore.

The smoldering eyes of cobra grande strike terror in fishermen. Paca was fishing one evening with a friend in Lake Jacaré on the Amazon floodplain several hours by canoe from Itacoatiara. The men suddenly became aware of the intense, shining eyes of a cobra grande. The fishermen immediately paddled for the safety of the lake shore, where they waited by a tree until daybreak. That was the last time the men fished those parts. Similar experiences have been reported by fishermen working along Paraná do Urbano near Urucurituba, in Lake Araçá close to Itacoatiara, and on the Madeira near Nova Aripuanã. The giant serpent's eyes stab darkness like searchlights. One fisherman claimed to have seen the huge snake at night while it was still half a kilometer away.

Calm nights with a fine rain often portend of a meeting with the supernatural serpent. The mood is somber. It is useless to fish with gigs, for the surface is dancing. Fishermen huddle under plastic or palm-thatch awnings in their canoes or on a bank waiting for fish to swim into gillnets. One cannot even make coffee because of the drizzle. Mosquitoes are especially bothersome during moist nights, and even the pungent smoke from self-rolled cigarettes does little to ward them off. Some inhabitants of the green-tinted Aripuanã River are apprehensive on damp evenings. An eighty-meter-long boi-una lives in a deep pit at the base of Sumaúma Falls, and the monstrous snake is especially fond of venturing forth in search of victims when a misty rain cascades at night.

Instead of scaring people away, cobra grande sometimes immobilizes them. A young fisherman who lives in Itacoatiara recalled paddling home one night

Figure 5.2. Cast-net fishing along the Amazon River near Obidos, Pará, 25 June 1994.

when his canoe unexpectedly became stuck. Assuming the impediment to be a submerged log or branch, João attempted to back off, but to no avail. No matter how hard he paddled, the craft would not budge. Rather than jump into the cloudy water to investigate, João remained in his canoe until the cobra grande let him go some fifteen minutes later. The mythical serpent thus possesses a powerful magnetic force that it can turn on at will. In another example, a thirty-seven-horsepower motorboat was held captive by the force of a cobra grande one night near Lago do Batista, thirty-five kilometers southeast of Itacoatiara. After several hours of being locked in one position, the boat was released. In neither instance was the giant snake visible, but the fisherman and the passengers attributed their predicament to its capricious magnetism.

Cobra grande can influence events in other ways while remaining invisible. A fisherman recalled how a cobra grande killed a friend of his without him realizing what had happened. The friend was cast-net fishing (figure 5.2) along the bank of the Amazon one day near Parintins when he came close to a sub-merged cobra grande. The fisherman instantly lost his soul. He became fever-ish and returned home. Symptoms grew rapidly more alarming, and the shadowless fisherman lost control of his mental faculties. After eight days of disoriented, fitful behavior, the fisherman died. A pajé volunteered that the man had been assombrado by cobra grande.

The monstrous snake not only dispatches its victims by drawing away their shadows but also occasionally feeds on them. Cobra grande swallows people whole and will smash a canoe or overturn a boat to reach its prey. According to a Tukúna woman who lives in Aripuanã in northern Mato Grosso, a man was paddling across the clear-water Tapajós near Pimentel several decades ago when a cobra grande swamped his canoe and devoured him. In another fatal case some years ago, a man was hunting caimans in Lake Miwá on the Ama-zon floodplain when an enormous boi-una attacked him. Witnesses on the lake shore stood by helplessly as the snake, with its telltale floodlight eyes, en-gulfed its hapless victim. Cobra grande has also struck farther down the Ama-zon in Lago Grande near Parintins. Three people were traveling in a canoe on the broad lake when a huge snake smashed the dugout. No trace of the pas-sengers was found. A piece of the hull bobbing at the surface was all that re-mained of the tragic encounter.

Instead of eating its victim, cobra grande sometimes takes them below to live in an underwater world. One day, two children were playing along the banks of the Amazon on Ilha do Risco, a huge, lenticular-shaped island in the middle of the river some fifteen kilometers downstream from Itacoatiara. A cobra grande spotted the infants and enticed them into the creamed-coffee current. According to Jurundir, a twenty-four-year-old man who lives on Ilha do Risco and is training to be a pajé, the children now live as snakes at the bottom of the deep river.

The myth of a giant water snake with powers to rob the souls of people and to lead them to an aquatic afterlife was clearly born in aboriginal cultures. Snakes figure prominently in the cosmologies of several Indian groups living in the Amazon basin. The Desana, for example, think that the master of fish, *vái-bogó,* is a large aquatic snake that attempts to upset the canoes of fisher-men. The Kayapó of the Rio Fresco believe that a huge water snake, *mrü-kra-o,* kills people; victims are obliged to accompany the snake below the surface and reside there forever. The Yameo of the Peruvian Amazon claim that an evil water serpent sinks canoes and drowns people. In the middle of the seventeenth century, the Mayna believed that a mother of water in the form of a giant snake inhabited the turbulent waters of the Mansariche gorge on the Marañon River.

Although cobra grande is generally regarded as a spirit protector of fish, no guidelines to avoid stirring its ire are apparent in the region's lore. Fishermen do not limit catches to avoid provoking boi-una. Attacks by the giant serpent are unpredictable, unless one invades its known haunts. Its victims include fishermen at work, passengers on boats, and even innocent children playing by the water's edge. The malicious aspect of the giant snake also has echoes in aboriginal cultures. Among the Jívaro of the Ecuadorian Amazon, for example, anaconda attacks are attributed to the souls of people who have been murdered. And the Cocamilla of the Peruvian Amazon must perform elaborate rituals if they are to fish in certain ox-bow lakes because they are considered the haunts of deceased shamans who have transformed into large anacondas. Respect for cobra grande serves to reduce fishing pressure because its rumored haunts are generally avoided.

Cobra grande is not the only legendary water serpent that instills fear and awe among riverine folk in Amazonia. The howler monkey snake (*guariba-boia*) does not exceed six meters in length, but it is a respected foe of fishermen. Guariba-boia has the head of a howler monkey, known in the Brazilian Amazon as *guariba,* attached to the body of a serpent. One fisherman suggested that guariba-boia is a snake with the head of a sloth, whereas another man claimed that guariba-boia has the sleek, elongated body of a howler monkey and the webbed paws of an otter. Unlike cobra grande, the howler monkey snake is rarely seen. Its hollow, resonating roar coming from below water signals the creature's presence. The loud, prolonged howl of guariba-boia can be heard day or night, but one is more likely to notice it on rainy nights. Guariba-boia's call resembles the din made by a troop of howler monkeys defending its forest territory.

Although the howler monkey snake is much smaller than cobra grande and is rarely seen, the creature is considered dangerous. The needle-sharp teeth of guariba-boia contain a lethal venom. After inflicting a severe bite and injecting a quick-acting poison into its victim, the howler monkey snake feasts on its prey, often swallowing it whole. Some caboclos have allegedly suffered a painful, but mercifully quick, death in the jaws of a guariba-boia. When sufficiently hungry, the howler monkey snake will reportedly even swamp a canoe and drag the occupants below, where they are digested.

Along the Amazon, the howler monkey snake reportedly occurs from Fonte Boa near the border between Brazil and Colombia, east to the vicinity of Urucurituba in the middle Amazon. One fisherman asserted that the secretive creature also inhabits the murky lakes of the Rio Negro. Guariba-boia apparently spends most of its time in a burrow it excavates at the bottom of a lake, channel, or in a flooded forest (figure 5.3). When not resting in its hole, guariba-boia wallows in mud or hides in clumps of floating grass or in thickets of aninga (figure 5.4).

Other beasts not recognized by science harass those who venture onto lakes, rivers, and channels, particularly if they are going to fish or to hunt capybara,

Figure 5.3. Floodplain forest along the Amazon at high water, one of the haunts of the legendary howler monkey snake, *guariba-boia*. Periquito, near Santarém, Pará, 14 March 1993.

Figure 5.4. A clump of aninga with characteristic inverted heart-shaped leaves at the edge of a floodplain forest. Aninga thickets are thought to be inhabited by a number of supernatural creatures, including the howler monkey snake and the tapir nymph. Periquito, near Santarém, Pará, 14 March 1993

manati, or turtles. The tapir nymph (*tapirê-iauara*) is not feared so much because of its size, as it grows no larger than a cow, but because of its vile odor, aggressiveness, and great speed when attacking. A major distinguishing feature of the aquatic creature is its huge ears, which droop for half a meter by the sides of the beast's head. The large ears of zebu cattle may be a model for this feature: ears of the Gir breed can reach forty-two centimeters long. The characteristic loud crashing sound made by the ears as they flop on water warns fishermen that a tapirê-iauara is approaching.

Four informants who live in the vicinity of Itacoatiara, Amazonas, and along Paraná Cachoeri near Oriximiná in Pará claim to have seen the tapir nymph. João Simas saw one in Igarapé Rico, a stream that can be reached by a short canoe trip from Urucurituba. It was daybreak as João guided his canoe around a bend of the stream on his way home from a night's fishing. As he paddled out of the curve in the channel, he came upon a tapir nymph chewing a caiman in a stand of aninga. The creature was relishing its meal on a bed of twigs in the miniature aroid forest. The startled tapirê-iauara quickly dove into the stream and swam away with its zebulike ears flapping on the surface. The beast was the size of a half-grown cow and had a reddish coat.

Another fisherman spotted a tapir nymph during the day in the vicinity of Urucurituba. Domingos and two companions had just killed a pirarucu when they heard the sharp splashing of a tapir nymph's ears. The rhythmic flopping noise was coming closer, so the men paddled hastily to some trees and climbed them. The tapir nymph passed quickly by the trees, swimming with the grace of an otter. The beast had the head of a jaguar, finlike ears, and rust-colored fur. Its back feet looked like those of horse, whereas the front paws were unmistakably jaguarlike. The feline attributes of the creature are responsible for its other name: water jaguar (*onça d'água*).

A farmer who lives along Paraná Cachoeri was fishing one night in 1972 with two other companions in Lago Socorro on the Amazon floodplain. A strange sound was heard in a clump of fleshy aninga. The fishermen went to investigate and spotted a water jaguar in their flashlight beams: it was red and had a large, catlike face and long ears. The creature did not attack, but the men resolved not to fish there again. Another witness saw a water jaguar when he was working along the Orinoco River in Venezuela. It had a massive jaguarlike head bordered by a thick mane. The shiny, golden coat of the onça d'água repelled water like the waxy feathers of a duck. All those who have come close to the water jaguar report being nauseated by the beast's oily smell.

Details of water jaguar's anatomy also vary among those recounting secondhand stories. For example, two fishermen claimed that all four legs of the creature are similar to those of a jaguar, whereas another asserted that the legs resemble those of a donkey but with catlike paws instead of hooves. A farmer and fisherman along the Arapiuns River near Santarém described tapirê-iauara as a creature with the legs of a jaguar and the feet of a duck. One fisherman stated that the front legs are reminiscent of those of a donkey, whereas the back legs are like those of a jaguar. According to yet another fisherman, the water jaguar's front paws look like those belonging to an otter, only they are the size of dinner plates. Furthermore, the beast has black hair, not red or golden, with a distinctive white breast patch. The giant otter also has a creamy chest patch, but it has short ears and does not grow longer than 2.2 meters.

The water jaguar ranges from the upper Orinoco in Venezuela, down the Negro, and along the Amazon from Codajás in Amazonas to at least Santarém in Pará (figure 1.1). Tapirê-iauara is also reputed to ply the waters of the Madeira up to at least Manicoré, as well as the Arapiuns, an affluent of the lower Tapajós. The water jaguar is thus legend across a broad swath of central Amazonia but is not as well known, or as widely distributed, as the notion of cobra grande.

The habitat preference of the water jaguar is also much narrower than that of the giant water serpent. Tapirê-iauara seeks the shelter of the aninga groves that cloak the margins of sluggish streams and backswamps. Prehistoric-looking aninga also occasionally occurs as miniature-forest islands in the middle of Amazon floodplain lakes; these isolated, almost pure stands of aninga often serve as nesting sites for colonies of egrets and herons. Fear of the water jaguar appears to be breaking down in some areas, because people have been overharvesting eggs of herons and egrets to sell for food, such as in Lago Grande near Monte Alegre.

Clumps of tall, graceful buriti palm, which grow along the banks of rivers and in sandy swamps, are also favored haunts of the water jaguar. Another palm that provides shelter for the noisy creature is pupunharana. This spine-covered palm grows in nearly impenetrable thickets on the Amazon floodplain. Banks with tall, rank grass, especially bamboo, are also frequented by the tapir nymph.

The diet of the water jaguar includes caimans, capybara, fish, and people. The beast brings its scalpel-sharp teeth and formidable paws into play when dispatching prey. A man in his late sixties who has spent most of his life along the Arapiuns River near Santarém suggested that the creature also overpowers its victims by causing them to faint from its body odor. Piranhas and tambaqui are the water jaguar's favorite fish. A fisherman who lives near Manacapuru, Amazonas, claimed that water jaguar is attracted by the aroma of singed fish scales and by freshly caught piranhas placed in the bottom of canoes. The dangers inherent in scorching fish scales are echoes of the hunter's concern not to burn game hair or allow the pot to boil over for fear that the smell might attract curupira.

Fishermen with catches are especially prone to tapirê-iauara attacks. A man narrowly escaped death while trotline fishing in the Paraua River some three days' motorboat journey downstream from Fonte Boa, a town on the upper Amazon. The fisherman was removing a tambaqui from a hook when the heads of two water jaguars popped out of the water nearby. The creatures eyed the astonished fisherman for an instant, then started swimming toward him. The man immediately began paddling his tiny canoe toward the shore. Although he was briskly dipping his diamond-shaped paddle into the water, the water jaguars were closing on their intended victim. The agile tapir nymphs dived, swam under the fisherman's dugout canoe, and surfaced in front of him. The decisive moment had arrived. The fisherman grabbed his single-barreled, twelve-gauge shotgun and released a volley into the head of one of the menacing beasts. It promptly floated, lifeless. The other water jaguar fled. The fisherman cut off the gigantic paws of the dead water jaguar and later showed them to a priest.

Tapir nymphs are not always dispatched so easily. Several fishermen who live in Itacoatiara or its vicinity provided stories that illustrate the pugnacious and tough nature of tapirê-iauara. A man was paddling across the turbid Madeira one day near Nova Olinda when a water jaguar suddenly appeared and promptly gave chase. Fortunately, the fisherman had a .22 rifle on board, so he reached for the weapon lying behind him and fired at the rapidly approaching creature. It took twelve slugs to stop the persistent beast.

Another fisherman also working along the Madeira was attacked by a water jaguar, but this time the incident occurred in a flooded forest. It was broad daylight when a water jaguar surprised the fisherman and forced him to vacate his canoe. The determined tapir nymph then devoured the tambaqui left in the hastily abandoned canoe. And in an inundated wood on Ilha do Risco near Itacoatiara, a fisherman heard the unmistakable crashing sound of an approaching tapirê-iauara. He paddled quickly to a tree and had just scrambled up the trunk when the aquatic beast arrived. The creature swamped the terrified man's canoe and made off with two recently caught tambaqui.

Some thirty years ago, a fisherman working in a flooded forest near Juriti in the middle Amazon was not so fortunate. He and a companion had set out trotlines baited with fish to catch the commercially valuable pirarucu. At nightfall, they retired to their hammocks suspended above the water among some trees. They were both asleep when a tapirê-iauara launched out of the water and bit one of the hammocks, tearing it. Before the occupant had time to flee, the water jaguar reared up again and grabbed him. The terrified victim was dragged into the water and was never seen again. The other fisherman vacated his hammock and clambered up a tree.

Even if water jaguar fails to reach its victim, its putrid body odor sometimes overpowers the prey. A fisherman shimmied up a tree to escape a water jaguar once but nearly lost his grip when the combative beast's smell reached his nostrils. The man lingered at the threshold of unconsciousness for some time, but he managed to hold on to a branch. One twenty-two-year-old who lives on the right bank of the Amazon a little downstream from Itacoatiara suggested that tapir nymph's stench (*catinga*) can be potent enough to kill a victim outright. The foul odor is also sufficiently strong to steal a person's shadow; the victim becomes dizzy from the fumes because his or her soul has taken off.

Water nymph possesses other supernatural powers with which to taunt rural folk on floodplains. A man was hunting capybara one night near Itapiranga on the left bank of the middle Amazon when he came upon what he thought was a specimen of the world's largest rodent in an aningal. As he raised his shotgun barrel, though, he realized that he was staring at a water jaguar. The hunter was transfixed; tapirê-iauara had immobilized him. The mesmerizing force was described as something akin to the paralyzing magnetism of cobra grande. The man was unable to shoot. After a few seconds, the water jaguar withdrew into the water-logged aroid jungle.

Sometimes people organize posses to rid an area of water jaguars. When tapirê-iauara suspects trouble, though, it is difficult to get in a good shot. An elderly caboclo from the Rio Negro described one method of coaxing the wary creature within firing range. First, a small wooden platform is lashed together over the water close to a riverbank or lake shore. Then a piranha is lightly roasted over an open fire at sunset. The following morning, a person eats the cold, poorly cooked fish and climbs on to the pole platform. Four armed companions wait on land hidden among bushes or trees. Halitosis emanating from the person who ate the almost raw breakfast beckons water jaguar. The beast comes wanting to kill the individual who has eaten cold fish. Cold food is associated with the underworld in the cosmologies of indigenous people in Amazonia. Eating such food insults supernatural creatures because it allegedly reminds them that they pertain to the raw domain of anticulture.

Upon arriving at the platform, the water jaguar releases a skunklike stink in the direction of the offending person. The latter immediately feels faint and slumps, soulless, across the platform floor. Although the lure is in distress, he is beyond the reach of the enraged tapir nymph. At least four hunters should be ready to shoot, because the belligerent creature often comes accompanied by other water jaguars.

After slaughtering or scaring off water jaguar, the men retrieve the decoy who has been assombrado. A fire is made with twigs, leaves, and bones from the improperly cooked piranha. The shadowless man is thrust into the rising smoke so that he can regain his soul and sanity. Some fishermen take along the hardened sap from the caraña tree in their canoes to discourage tapir nymphs. Caraña resin washed into the water is especially repugnant to tapirê-iauara.

The tapir myth is a vestige of aboriginal lore, because *tapiré* derives from the Tupi word for tapir. In língua geral, *y* means "water" and *ara* signifies "lady." In Tupi, *uara* means "dweller" and *yguara* refers to "inhabitant of water." And along the Tapajós, *oyoára* is a water nymph. A caboclo from the Rio Negro said that another name for the water jaguar in língua geral is *paraná pura iuaretê*. In the eighteenth century, the South American river turtle was known in língua geral as *yuraretê*. Apparently, though, *iuaretê* could also refer to jaguar. Iuaretê is the name of an outpost served by the Brazilian Air Force on the upper Uaupés River near the border with Colombia. Paraná is a side arm or side channel of a river, but the meaning of *pura* is obscure. An approximate translation of paraná pura iuaretê is "the turtle or jaguar dweller of river side channels." Perhaps a monster turtle once roamed the minds of Amazonians and the two creatures have blended together.

A supernatural creature resembling water jaguar is reported to share the latter's habitat. *Tai-açu-iara* is a large, black, piglike beast that hunts sloughs shaded by the elephant-ear leaves of aninga. The creature is equipped with powerful jaguar paws and attacks people at night along channels and lakes. One was reportedly shot along the Amazon near Parintins one evening. Jaguars, including the black phase, were once common on the Amazon floodplain but are now rarely seen. For example, the last reported sighting of a jaguar on Ilha do Carmo, a little downstream from Obidos, was in the 1930s. No jaguar were reported on the Amazon floodplain in the vicinity of Itacoatiara in the mid-1970s; they apparently had been extinct there for several decades.

The meaning of *tai* is not known, but *açu* means "large" and *iara* is a nymph. Tai-açu-iara is most likely a version of tapirê-iauara, just as mapinguary and capé-lobo are essentially the same. The water jaguar probably played a specific role in the spirit world of some tribe that is no longer with us. Cut loose from its original mooring, tapirê-iauara cruises the mental maps of rural folk virtually at will. It is precisely this unpredictable quality of the water jaguar's behavior that makes it so feared.

The mother of fish (*mãe de peixe*) is another supernatural entity with clear ties to aboriginal lore. She plays a role similar to that of the father of game, only her charges are different. Mãe de peixe is a chimera of many guises who looks after fish populations. Among the Kamayurá, for example, the mother of fish is a caiman. The notion of the black caiman as a protector of fish appears to be ancient. The Tello obelisk, fashioned by the Chavín in the headwaters of the Amazon some three thousand years ago, depicts a deified caiman thought to represent the master of fish.

In caboclo culture, the spirit protector of fish most commonly appears as a snake, especially cobra grande. A huge boa occupies a similar role among the Shipibo, whereas the Wayãpí consider the anaconda as the master of water. As such, mãe de peixe is a formidable opponent with the sinister ability to bewitch fishermen. On the seventeenth of June 1977, for example, several men were hauling in a seine in front of Itacoatiara when mãe de peixe struck. The fishermen had netted what promised to be an exceptionally large catch of jaraqui when they felt an irresistible tug on the seine. The men were obliged to let go of the net or be pulled into the swirling current. Some attributed the disappearance of the expensive, thirty-five meter net to the suction of an eddy, but others affirmed that cobra grande liberated the catch.

Fishermen believe that the mother of fish is sent by God to serve as a guardian angel over her flock. She protects fish by scaring away fishermen with loud noises, stealing their nets, and robbing their souls. Mãe de peixe is particularly vigilant over schools of jaraqui and curimatá during their breeding season when waters are rising. She discharges loud underwater explosions to keep fishermen at bay. Curimatá males produce a vibrating sound by flexing muscles around their air bladders when it is time to mate, but the muted beckoning call of the silvery fish is quite unlike the detonating tremor made by the mother of fish. Mãe de peixe also watches over curimatá as they leave the Amazon floodplain after laying their eggs.

Mother of fish is strongly identified with other fishes important in commerce and for subsistence, such as tambaqui and pirarucu. To discourage fishermen, the mother of fish often assumes the shape of one of her flock. A young fisherman from Itacoatiara recounted a baffling experience he had one day with the fleeting mother of fish. João had spotted an unusually large pirarucu, so he hurled his harpoon at it, but he missed. Undaunted, João pulled in the lance and tried several more times. Even though the pink and silver-gray fish cruised by quite close, his efforts to spear it were futile. João then put his harpoon in the canoe and paddled away. Mãe de peixe was playing games with him. In a similar case, a fisherman reported that he repeatedly threw his harpoon into a tightly packed school of tambaqui, but to no avail. Ajenor finally desisted, concluding that the fruit-eating fish were being protected by the mother of fish. One person suggested that each fish species has its own mother protector, but only those fish that are eaten seem to find a place in the regional lore.

Mother of fish may slip into other guises to ward off people. One day, two fishermen were setting out trotlines in the flooded forest surrounding Lago de Cucui along the Rio Preto de Maués when they heard a voice commanding them not to fish there. At first, the men thought it must be another fisherman trying selfishly to secure the area for himself, so they made a search. Then the booming voice repeated the instruction to leave; it came from a towering miritinga tree. Mother of fish was speaking from the moraceous giant. The men promptly fled, leaving their trotlines behind.

Sometimes mother of fish intervenes in human form. A fifty-four-year-old fisherman who has lived his entire live in the vicinity of Itacoatiara recalled a visit that the mother of fish paid to a friend of his one night. The friend, who lives on Ilha do Risco near Itacoatiara, had spent many consecutive evenings in lakes and channels spearing fish. Catches had been plentiful, and the man anticipated another good night. But as he twisted in his canoe to tug a fish off his gig, he saw a woman sitting on the back bench. She was dark skinned, had long, flowing black hair, and wore a deep red dress. The uninvited passenger returned the man's amazed glance, said nothing, and vanished. The fisherman immediately felt unwell and paddled home. He soon developed a high fever, became delirious, and kept trying to leap into the water. He was taken to a pajé who contacted a spirit of light. The medium told the fisherman that the mother of fish had taken his shadow because he had been fishing excessively. The spirit of light contacted by the pajé is the soul of a person who lived a decent, charitable life on earth. Such souls are called upon by mediums to advise and to recommend treatments.

A host of other humanoid waifs occasionally appear along rivers and around lakes, and most of them are potentially dangerous. The black man of the waters (*negro d'água*) is no taller than one meter and lives in the Tocantins and Araguaia Rivers. The midget has a bald, shiny black head like the polished calabash gourd used to serve *tacacá*, a hot soup sold by street vendors in some Amazonian towns. The black man of the waters is shy and normally retreats in the presence of people. Negro d'água wanders along sandy beaches, but when a canoe or boat approaches, it runs into the water.

Farther up the Tocantins in the state of Goiás, negro d'água is reputedly less benign. There, it is accused of occasionally tipping over canoes. In Goiás, the waif is described as a humanoid with a bald head and webbed hands and feet. In the savanna part of the Tocantins watershed, negro d'água usually appears around rocks in the late afternoon and on moonlight nights. Its tough hide reportedly repels bullets. Along the Parnaíba River in the dry, northeastern state of Piauí, a similar creature, called gourd head (*cabeça de cuia*), is active at high water and attacks boys and girls. Gourd head reportedly eats girls called Maria every seven years. Gourd head allegedly arose when a mother cursed her son because he had been mistreating her.

Mermaids (*sereias*) are also reported from the Araguaia. Dona Ruth, a fifty-year-old housewife who now resides in Marabá, recalled a day in her childhood when she came close to a sereia. Ruth was fifteen years old when she was swimming one morning in front of Araguatins, her native village on the right bank of the Araguaia. In those days, the river flowed relatively clear. Nowadays, the water is cloudier because widespread deforestation and gold mining have accelerated soil erosion. Ruth was diving in shoulder-deep water to collect colorful pebbles when a mermaid glided by only two meters away. Ruth was struck by the siren's stunning beauty. She had blond, translucent hair trailing behind as she swam and sparkling blue eyes set in a pink face. Ruth knew the woman was a mermaid because the bottom half of her trim body was covered with fish scales. Although Ruth admired the sumptuous appearance of the siren, she grew scared and swam ashore.

Sereias are reported to sit upright on roots jutting into the water where they sing in the late afternoon. Sereias show the influence of European mythology; fish-women have evidently found a niche in the regional lore, where they mirror indigenous concepts of female water spirits. Mermaids are not the only nymphs to grace Amazonian waters. In contrast to sereias, *yaras* are not half-fish; rather, they are beautiful women who live in the water. Sometimes, though, yaras spend part of their lives as snakes.

An informant who has spent most of his life farming and fishing on the Amazon floodplain downstream from Itacoatiara explained the dual personality of an enchanting yara. A man was fishing one day in a lake on the Amazon floodplain near the boundary between Amazonas and Pará when he noticed a commotion in the water. The churning of the water grew more intense and waves started to build, thus disturbing the otherwise smooth lake. A graceful woman suddenly emerged from the embroiled surface. She had silky blond hair that tumbled down her back and sides. The fisherman was startled and wanted to flee. "Don't be afraid," the exquisite yara cried out. "Do you have the courage," she continued, "to go and fetch some milk from a black cow?" The fisherman remained transfixed and speechless. "If you do, then bring a glass to the edge of this lake and I will return." The yara left explicit instructions to toss the milk into her mouth when she appeared. While she swallowed the offering, he was to swipe her head with an ax in order to break the spell. If the milk or ax missed its mark, she warned, he would perish.

Some time later, the fisherman returned to the lake and stood at the margin holding a cup of milk. The water soon stirred in front of him, but to his amazement out popped a loathsome snake, rather than the becoming, Godiva-like lady whom he had met on the lake. He flung the milk at the serpent's gaping mouth and followed through with an ax blow to its broad, scaly head. As the keen blade struck the creature's forehead, the repulsive apparition turned into the gorgeous yara for whom the fisherman had developed a yearning. She walked out of the water and returned home with the bachelor. The yara explained that she had been enchanted (*encantado*) and was forced to live as a snake on the lake bottom. European influences—the appearance of a blond woman and the cow—are evident in the story. Milk is a fertility symbol and signifies a new beginning; the cow is not native to the Amazon. Indigenous people did not raise animals for meat, and they did not drink milk. Black is the color of evil. Passion, desire, and danger clearly underlie the above tale, as they do with most of the stores about enchanted beings.

Yaras are legendary throughout Amazonia. In the vicinity of Belém, for example, yara is a green-eyed, golden-haired beauty who appears in certain streams and sings with an enchanting voice. She only appears before bachelors, and young men about to marry are particularly susceptible to her charms. If they hear yara's enticing voice and linger to catch a glimpse of her, they later become ill. The spellbound bachelors lose interest in their fiancées and try to throw themselves into the water to join yara. Similar symptoms appear when the mother of fish assumes the shape of a woman to bewitch fishermen.

Another yara is reported to haunt the once-spectacular Tarumã Falls on the outskirts of Manaus. In the nineteenth century, the yara of Tarumã Falls was a golden-haired maiden who could enrapture anyone setting eyes on her. No one has apparently reported any sightings of the beguiling yara of Tarumã for many years. The extensive cutting of trees and removal of large quantities of pink and white sandstone rocks just above the falls for construction purposes, such as bedding material for the main runway at the Manaus international airport, are undoubtedly involved in the disappearance of the nymph of Tarumã Falls. In the Peruvian Amazon, a white, attractive female spirit with blond hair sings from the top of tall lupuna trees in the forest. The Cocama claim that it is fatal for young men to try to find her.

Ghosts of varying sizes and shapes also drift into the world of the caboclo. People normally steer well clear of the suspected haunts of phantasms (*visões*). For example, a fisherman was working one night in Lake Castanhal Grande, which is connected to the Rio Preto de Maués in Amazonas, when he saw the faint outline of a human floating across the lake surface. The *visão* soon dissipated, but he nevertheless left the lake. Later he felt unwell and remained sick for a month. A pajé explained to the fisherman that the specter had made him ill, and he warned him never to fish there again.

Sometimes ghosts are mischievous rather than malevolent. A fisherman was paddling across Lake Poocoo in the vicinity of Itacoatiara one evening when the back of his canoe was lifted out of the water. The man, sitting at the front of the craft as is customary, was almost tipped out. The *visagem* then released the canoe and the fisherman paddled home in a hurry. Ghosts are generally attributed to the souls of those who have not found peace.

A childlike apparition is reported to accompany people for a short distance along the Tocantins near the village of Ipixunas. According to local lore, Maria Joana Alves was dumped into the broad river by her mother in 1958. The child did not know how to swim, so she sank after a brief struggle. Unlike some babies who allegedly turn into giant snakes when they are deliberately drowned in rivers, Maria's soul lodged in a large rock that partly emerges at low water. This visagem does not interfere with people, but at night helmsmen pick a course well away from the boulder. Maria speaks through mediums along the Tocantins and tells audiences that her mother still suffers spiritually because of her heinous act.

Unnatural death can give rise to another type of ghost that is far more dangerous. *Pisadeiras*, literally, "footsteps," form when someone is murdered and their blood spills into water. Footstep ghosts coax you to sleep and render you dumb. Their reported haunts, such as parts of Lago de Vassoura in the Canaçari complex northeast of Itacoatiara and Lago de Fatura near Urucurituba, are shunned accordingly. The scarecrow ghost, *marmota,* is the spirit of a man that wanders along the shores of certain lakes, particularly Lake Aricuru in the Amazonas municipality of Itapiranga. Marmota alarms fishermen by shouting extremely loudly. It is not safe to tarry if one is alone and hears a marmota yell.

Matin is another nocturnal ghost that scares fishermen and rural folk in upland areas. Known variously as *matinta-perera, matintaperera,* or *matin-tapirera,* the apparition can assume various forms, but the most common guise is a black bird that calls with a high-pitched whistle. A fisherman heard it one night in a floodplain forest along the Amazon some fifteen kilometers downstream from Itacoatiara, and he quickly left the area. The unmistakable, piercing call of matin is considered an evil omen. A little farther downstream near Itapiranga, a couple of fishermen were sleeping in their canoes on a lake waiting for fish to swim into their gillnets when a black, round shape flew overhead singing "tin-tin-tin." The startled men promptly paddled home.

Matin also persecutes fishermen on land. Raimundo Nonato remembered a particularly scary experience he had with the nocturnal spirit a few years ago. It was already nightfall when Raimundo and his brother were returning home from a day's fishing on the Tapucara River, an affluent of the Tapajós. The fishermen were walking along a twisting forest path when they noticed what appeared to be a man lurking in the deep shadow of a massive tree. Both men stopped abruptly. The region was sparsely settled: who could it be? Raimundo's brother called out, but instead of returning the greeting, the figure let out a shrill whistle. The brother immediately fired in the direction of the matin, and it vanished. The apprehensive fishermen continued their journey home, and the plaintive whistle of matin followed them. Raimundo remembered goose bumps erupting all over his body each time he heard the phantom's eerie call.

Even after the men arrived safely home, the matin still hovered in the vicinity. Around ten o'clock, when all were lying down, Raimundo's brother was tossed out of his hammock on to the floor of the hut. Something invisible then tore up the mosquito net draped around the hammock and rolled up the suspended bed. The matin subsequently drifted outside and hurled one of the dogs against a wall of the home. Soon all of the dogs were yelping in pain, but no one ventured outside to see what was happening.

Matin crops up in a greater variety of places than any other ghost or monster inhabiting the minds of rural folk. Matin disturbs folk on lakes, along rivers and streams, and in villages. The ghost is feared throughout Amazonia, where it performs a number of roles. Along the Madeira, for example, matin-taperera patrols the shores of islands and persecutes people who disturb nesting turtles. In aboriginal cultures, the mother of turtles assumes other shapes. The idea of a supernatural protector of turtles seems to be widespread. In Micronesia, for example, the Palauans believe that the god inhabiting Ngerur watches over green and hawksbill turtles when they lay eggs on the island's sandy beaches. Such beliefs at least codify the fragility of economically important species during crucial stages in their life cycles in regional cultures, even if they do not always effectively deter people from overexploiting resources.

Matin is a creation of indigenous people in Amazonia and is often attributed to the transformation of human souls. The Mundurucú of the upper Tapajós believe that matin-tapirera is the spirit of a deceased member of the tribe that descends from the night sky to hunt. It resembles a bird and sings in an irregular fashion, calling its own name. One of the last members of the Manáos tribe claimed that *matin-tapêrê* is a shaman who plays a flute in order to fly. Approximately one thousand kilometers to the southeast, the Carajá believe that shamans have a soul that adopts the guise of a bird so that they can fly to a place from which they derive their power. Cashibo shamans are allegedly able to change into birds so that they can reach their victims and toss poison at night. Jívaro shamans dispatch spirit birds, *wakani,* to terrorize people.

The idea of a person turning into a bird crops up in a number of other aboriginal myths. The Jurúna talk of a baby girl who transforms into a bird. A Witoto myth relates how a boy is abandoned in the forest by his parents and is turned into a bird by a culture hero. The bird-boy sings on moonlight nights. Among the Tapirapé, a nocturnal bird arose when a woman died from wounds suffered while her face was being cut for ritual scarring. The Kayapó of the Rio Fresco have two myths that mention humans turning into birds. In one tale, the daughter of rain flies up into the sky to fetch sweet potato and sweet manioc to feed hungry tribesmen on earth; in the other, a boy is tossed into the air and becomes a bird. The Xikrín relate how, in the distant past, a shaman became a fowl. In the neighboring Orinoco basin, a couple of Makiritataré myths describe how humans turn into birds; in one case, the bird-man shrieks at night. Such transformations are rarely benign. A Shipibo myth, for example, recounts how a boy turns into a squirrel cuckoo, and today it is considered an ominous sign if the cinnamon-colored bird ventures close to a village. The Amahuaca believe that a night bird that sings "chieu-chieu" is an evil omen. And the Kayapó who live in the Rio Fresco watershed dread the horrible call of the bird spirit *bekãre.*

As in the case of hunters, fishermen encounter strange lights while working at night. The color of incandescent balls varies, and so do the reactions of the persons observing them. Along the Paraná do Silves near Itapiranga, for example, fishermen regularly see a fiery globe glowing underwater, but they are not alarmed even when the burning orb rises above the surface and follows them. The shifting red balloon seems to have a will of its own and is only seen on Friday nights. A blue light is sometimes noticed along Paraná Arariá some five hours upstream by canoe from Maués. The blue glow materializes over the site of a long-abandoned village as evidenced by the dark earth full of pottery pieces. Antonio Pereira recalled paddling by the black earth site one evening when he noted the cool, phosphorescent light. He quickened his paddling. An orange-yellow luminescence frightened two fishermen in Lake Miwá one night. The man had just killed three caimans when the underwater blob approached them. They retreated to a bank and waited until daybreak before returning home.

Lore has also grown up around animals that exist in nature. Two species of dolphin ply the waters of Amazonia, and people along all the region's major rivers can recount a sizable stock of tales about them. Unlike some parts of the world, dolphins are not eaten in the Amazon basin, although they contain plenty of meat. Meat of the Amazonian dolphins is shunned because it is considered excessively oily and because the animals can be helpful. Furthermore, ill fortune may befall the killer of one of the beasts. Stories are told of the gray dolphin, called tucuxi in the Brazilian Amazon, saving people from drowning by nudging them ashore. On the lower Machado River, an affluent of the Madeira, both the gray and pink (boto) dolphin alert fishermen to the presence of migrating schools of jatuarana. Another symbiotic relationship between dolphins and man has developed in the vicinity of São Luis on the Tapajós. At night, gig fishermen work the shores of the clear-water river and scare some fish to deeper water, where they are intercepted by the pink dolphin. Pink dolphins snap up some of the fleeing fish and chase others back to shallow water, where they are within striking range of gig fishermen.

The pink and gray dolphins are generally respected, particularly the former, because of its supernatural power. The pink dolphin is reputed to assume the shape of a human, and both dolphins carry a strong sexual connotation. Women who are menstruating are particularly attractive to pink dolphins and must carry some garlic if they travel by canoe to keep the dolphins at bay. The connection between humans, dolphins, and sex may have its roots in indigenous cultures, but dolphin tales have been enriched over the centuries by peasant society. A Jurúna myth, for example, recounts how an unfaithful wife and her lover are turned into dolphins by the woman's irate husband. Peasants have introduced the concept of dolphins that transform into humans to some Indian groups, such as the Mundurucú. The potent sexuality of the pink dolphin is legendary among peasants throughout the basin, including Peru.

Male botos allegedly turn into handsome men at night and join festivities in order to seduce young ladies. Pink dolphins thus provide convenient scapegoats when unexpected pregnancies occur. A doctor in Tucuruí told me about a pregnant teenager he attended in 1970. The mother-to-be insisted that she was not to blame for her premature condition; a boto climbed through her bedroom window one night and took advantage of her.

The sexual appetite of pink dolphins sometimes incurs the wrath of rural folk. After spending a day visiting the farm and one of the fishing grounds of a caboclo along Surubim-Açu near Santarém, the captain of the boat I was traveling on gossiped to me in a low voice that the farm's owner, Vicente, killed a pink dolphin because he suspected it was attempting to have an affair with his wife, Dona Maria. Vicente was returning home one night in 1993 from a fishing trip when he heard a boto whistle on land. Vicente is the proud father of nine children and has a reputation for being feisty (*valente*). Irate that a dolphin would attempt to take advantage of his absences from home, Vicente waited at the "port" of his home along Surubim-Açu, and when the boto surfaced, he shot it.

Female botos excite the sexual interest of fishermen, and coitus with them is apparently so enjoyable that it can lead to physical exhaustion, mental derangement, and even death. Fishermen come into contact with live dolphins when they occasionally become entangled in seine nets; some individuals reportedly succumb to their unnatural desires at that time. Female pink dolphins reputedly seek out bachelors or married men to have affairs with them.

A tale told by a middle-aged farmer and fisherman who has spent his entire life on Ilha Grande, near Obidos, attests to the dangers of such encounters. The interview was conducted one night in June 1994 in a wooden-plank house completed surrounded by water on Big Island. The storyteller, Romão Lopes de Oliveira, recounts an uncanny experience he witnessed one evening in 1985. He was sitting in a friend's house at the tip of Ilha Grande closest to Obidos. Ten people were engaged in conversation when small pieces of earth and wood suddenly began striking the little kerosene lamp. The debris was being tossed through an open window. When the startled people went outside to investigate, nothing unusual was to be seen. This happened three nights in a row. So the owner sought the advice of a curandeira, Dona Ondinha. The curer explained that it was the mischievous workings of a pink dolphin. She prescribed some ritual baths and smokings for the afflicted person, and these remedies took care of the problem.

When the storyteller was pressed as to why the dolphin was persecuting that individual, he seemed a little embarrassed. Romão explained that I had a strong spirit and such things would not happen to me. While I took that as a compliment, I was still interested in his explanation as to why his friend had been bothered by a pink dolphin. His eyes look down and he fiddled with his fingers. Romão did not want to be specific, but evidently there had been some "goings on" with the pesky dolphin. I got the impression that the victim had undertaken some sexual acts with a female dolphin and that he was being punished for his transgression.

Genitalia and the eyes of the pink dolphin are sold as charms in certain stores and street stalls to improve the "love-life" of customers. Individuals rub the preserved genitalia of the pink dolphin on their private parts to enhance their sexual allure. When the eye of a pink dolphin is pointed at a desired partner, all resistance to the consummation of a relationship crumbles. In Itacoatiara, the story is told of a fisherman who noticed a pretty maiden on a boat journey down the Amazon. He decided to employ an eye from a pink dolphin to help him in his conquest. Unfortunately, at the precise moment when he lined up the shy teenager in the boto's eye, the captain stepped in the way. For the rest of the trip, the fisherman had to discourage the amorous intentions of the burly skipper.

Botos are also involved in the formation of lugares encantados. Along the Madeira, a pink dolphin came out of the water one evening, turned into a man, and joined the party. He soon made friends with a flirtatious lass, led her away from the *festa,* and made love to her. When he awoke, it was already daylight, so he took the cluster of houses and their inhabitants into the river with him. The spot where the festa took place is called Canta Galo (cock crow), and today one can reportedly hear music and cocks crowing from the depths of the light brown Madeira.

Another fisherman interviewed in the vicinity of Itacoatiara insisted that Canta Galo arose because of the exploits of a cobra grande rather than a pink dolphin. In the snake version, Norado participated in a festa as a man, then took all the houses with him when he slithered back to the river as a snake. In a further example of an enchanted place caused by the giant serpent, Manduca, a fisherman in his mid-fifties who has spent most of his life along the Madeira, explained the genesis of Sapucaia along his native river. Sapucaia lies within the municipality of Borba and is characterized by underwater music, the clucking of chickens, and the lowing of cattle. Women are sometimes spotted on a nearby beach at low water; when people approach, however, they scurry into the river.

The origins of Sapucaia, named after a delicious wild nut, extend back to the amorous encounter of a woman with an enchanted man. The lady subsequently gave birth to two small snakes. The male one she named Norato, the female, Maria. The twins were kept in a clay pot and were fed milk squeezed from their mother's breasts. Upon the recommendation of a pajé, the twins were baptized by a priest. The snakes were then taken to the shore of the Madeira, where they were released. The pajé left strict instructions that no one was to watch the twins enter the river. Only the splashing of their entry could be heard.

Some time later, a six-day festival commemorating Saint Thomas was held at a small village. Norato left the water, metamorphosed into a handsome young man, and strode into the festivities. He shortly endeared himself to a lady and spent the night with her. When he awoke, the sun was already up and the village was stirring. He became a snake again and slithered into the water, taking the settlement and land with him. To this day, strange underwater voices, turkey gobbles, cock crows, and goat bleats mark the spot where the village slid into the water.

Still a third storyteller suggested that Canta Galo situated at Sapucaia-roca is the result of the adventures of a couple of fair-skinned men of unknown origin. During a prolonged festival, the two men, dressed crisply in white, suddenly appeared at the dance. Little attention was paid to the newcomers because everyone was having a good time. The strangers grew displeased because of the wanton dancing and drinking, so they took the settlement and land into the Madeira. Today the site is dangerous to navigation because of the strong upwelling currents and treacherous whirlpools. One can still hear guitar melodies, the rattle of tambourines, and the insistent crowing of cocks emanating from the depths of the turbulent water. The party goes on, even though the people drowned. Another festa continues underwater along the Amazon near Urucurituba. At a site called Terra Preta de Limão, a large chunk of land slipped into the restless Amazon one night, carrying with it people engaged in celebration. Dog barks, the fussing of chickens, and muffled conversations mark the spot where the settlement disappeared below the river surface.

The story of Canta Galo and some other tales of enchanted places incorporate a number of elements from aboriginal lore that have been influenced by Christianity. The enchanted snake-twins are blessed by a priest, upon the instructions of a pajé. Disapproval of uninhibited dancing and excessive drinking echoes in part Christian ideas on sinful behavior.

Canta Galo stories are caboclo versions of a Mura Indian legend. Sapucaia-oroco, a Mura village along the Madeira, was holding a festival in honor of the god Tupan. The villagers danced lasciviously, sang impure songs, and reveled in debauchery. *Angaturámos,* spirit protectors of the village, became anguished. Tupan was displeased: he shook the earth and the village fell into the water. Angaturámos crow below was a warning that the wicked are punished.

The notion of people living underwater is found in a number of Amerindian myths. A culture hero of the Kamayurá who gave the tribe manioc, for example, lives in a large underwater house. And the Kayapó of the Rio Fresco recount a myth in which twin boys live in a wooden underwater home.

The emergence of cobra grande in one version of the Canta Galo story also highlights the tie such concepts have to aboriginal cosmologies. The giant serpent and its formidable sexual powers weave through several tales, ranging from copulation with women to the birth of snakes. Such ideas can be found among widely separated Indian groups. It is told among the Kayapó, for example, that a husband took a bath in an enchanted stream and became a snake-man; his wife subsequently delivered snakes. Among the Waiwai of the Mapuerá and upper Essequibo Rivers, the anaconda symbolizes rivers and fertility. A myth tells of anaconda-people attempting to abduct an adolescent girl for a bride. A Desana myth portrays a seven-headed snake that tries to seduce a pubescent girl. The Arapaço of the lower Uaupés consider themselves grandchildren of an anaconda that transformed into a man when he saw a woman bathing and lay with her. The Xikrín who live along the Cateté, a tributary of the Itacaiúnas southwest of Marabá, recount a tale in which a woman has intercourse with a snake under cover of the forest, and a Shipibo myth relates how a woman makes love with the tail of an anaconda in a lake. A colorful tale of the Cubeo relates how land boas rape women in manioc gardens and the latter subsequently give birth to snakes. Male snakes are not always the culprits. A myth of the Sharanahua of the upper Purus describes how a man falls for the charms of a snake-woman, then joins the serpent in her lacustrine abode.

Lugares encantados are the underwater residences of various spirits and the souls of people who have drowned, or are sites where graves have tumbled into water, a not uncommon occurrence along the banks of meandering rivers. In the case of enchanted places that are due to the loss of life in water, dolphin-men and snakes are not always responsible. An enchanted spot called Poção das Cruvina at the confluence of the Tocantins and Cajazeiras is the result of a tragic accident. A fifty-one-year-old farmer who has spent his entire life along the Tocantins recounted a sad incident that happened to a cousin of his, Francisco. The latter was paddling down the Tocantins with a companion one morning in 1943 when the canoe struck a rock. Francisco was sitting on the front bench and was thrown into the choppy water. He never surfaced.

A short time later in Jacundá, a village on the right bank of the Tocantins some forty kilometers downstream from the scene of the accident, a well-known pajé, João Torneiro, was holding a spiritualist session when the deceased cousin spoke to the people present. Francisco said that he wanted to make sure that his sister would be taken care of. He added that he was fine and that friends and relatives should not worry about him because he was living in a world just like the one on earth, except that it was underwater. Francisco was not lonely because others were with him in the benthic underworld.

Before a large stretch of the middle Tocantins was tamed by the Tucurui reservoir that has flooded two thousand square kilometers of forest, submerged rocks and rapids were a hazard for boats. As the Tocantins has carved into the Brazilian shield, some granitic boulders have resisted the erosive power of the river for millions of years. Treacherous rapids along the middle Tocantins were the main reason a railroad was built in the first part of the twentieth century between Jatobal and Tucuruí (then Alcobaça). The railroad transported Brazil nuts and other goods around a series of rapids that have claimed many lives. Now all is quiet for more than a hundred kilometers of the Tocantins, and several enchanted places have been drowned by the reservoir. One enchanted place submerged by the placid Tucuruí reservoir is Canal de Inferno. Many boats are reputed to have foundered on boulders, thereby spilling occupants into the swift current.

Other enchanted places with spirits of the departed are found scattered along the rivers and lakes of Amazonia. In the vicinity of Itacoatiara along the Amazon, for example, people live at the bottom of parts of lakes Canaçari and Arari. Such ideas are not confined to fresh water, but probably extend along much of the coast of Brazil. On the Atlantic shore of Pará near Salinas, a prominent rock called Castelo is exposed at low tide. Fishermen who live near Salinas, now a popular weekend retreat for Belém's middle and upper classes, claim that music from tambourines and flutes drifts from the boulder at night and enchanted people live there. Folk come from as far as Belém to lay gifts and to light candles at Castle Rock, and mediums hold sessions on a stone slab there. A shipwreck is implicated in the origin of this enchanted place. At the mouth of the Gurupi River, 150 kilometers east of Castelo, another lugar encantado remains above high tides even though it is 8 kilometers offshore. The rock contains a small cave that shelters shipwrecked crews. On clear nights with calm seas and a full moon, fishermen hear music played with unfamiliar instruments coming from the rock. People habitually avoid the enchanted spot after twilight.

According to caboclo lore, the souls of drowned people do not reach heaven. Instead, they proceed with their afterlife in a watery world, as people, dolphins, or snakes. The theme of those who have lost their lives in water and thus cannot attain the sky crops up in several tales of riverine folk. Such a predicament can arise due to an accident, the criminal act of tossing a child into the water, or the supernatural force of a cobra grande or a pink dolphin. Although inhabitants of enchanted places do not appear to be so fortunate as those who share a life with the Lord in heaven, lugares encantados do not correspond to Christian concepts of hell. Peasants who pass by enchanted places do not hear the roar of an inferno, the gnashing of teeth, or the wailing of tortured souls. Life seems to be fairly pleasant below water, because it includes festivities. Some enchanted people are able to escape their limbolike existence by, for example, persuading someone to gash them on their heads or having their reptilian coils burned while they attend parties.

Many enchanted places are associated with collapsing banks and powerful whirlpools, so it is just as well that people generally steer away from such places. A fear of the supernatural is nevertheless the primary motivation for avoiding lugares encantados, especially after dusk. Two enchanted places are shunned because objects allegedly disappear in them. In a section of Paraná Sumidor about half an hour by motorboat downstream from Itapiranga, a village on the banks of the middle Amazon, a lugar encantado apparently swallows large floating mats of vegetation. A cattle ranch operates underwater. The mooing of cows, the clucking of chickens, and people's voices indicate that life is just as busy below as it is on land. A similar spot is reported along Furo Jaboti, a small channel that can be reached within an hour's motorboat journey from Itapiranga. It is especially unwise to fall asleep near an enchanted place. A young man who lives on Ilha do Risco near Itacoatiara asserted that he fishes near a lugar encantado in Lake Jurupari, but only during the day. And he makes sure that he does not doze off during the midday heat while near the enchanted spot.

One reason that enchanted places are respected is that they can siphon off a person's shadow. A gold miner who was born in Pará but was based in Aripuanã in northern Mato Grosso at the time of our conversation in 1978 recalled an incident that took place at an enchanted place called Com Vento. Com Vento, a cavern leading in from a smooth rock face that juts into the river, is found along the upper Cupari, an affluent of the Tapajós. A breeze blows gently from the dark interior of the cave, hence the name of the place: "with wind." The entrance to the cavern looks like a regular doorway and faces a deep, sluggish portion of the river that flows off the northern rim of the Brazilian shield. Attractive women are sometimes seen sitting at the entrance to the cave while music and cock crows emanate from the cool, dark interior.

One day a priest was traveling up the Cupari to minister to some folk in the headwaters. When the father came abreast of Com Vento, he remarked on its unusual appearance and felt the refreshing breath of air coming from the entrance to the grotto. Against the advice of the crew of the tiny boat, the priest decided to stop and inspect the cave. The crew declined to enter and waited apprehensively outside. After a while, the father emerged looking dazed. He clutched his head as if suffering from severe pain but did not utter a word. The father had obviously taken a turn for the worse, so the party returned to base at Aveiro on the right bank of the Tapajós. The distressed priest never spoke of what had befallen him. His condition deteriorated, so he was transferred to a hospital in Belém, where he expired.

Another treacherous lugar encantado reportedly exists among the rapids near Belo Monte on the lower Xingu between Vitória and Altamira. A Transamazon colonist who has lived in the Xingu region since birth remarked that voices beckon people who travel that dangerous stretch of the river as it tumbles off the Brazilian shield. If a person gets too close to the point where the underwater voices are coming from, he or she can be mesmerized and die. A large snake (cobrão) apparently guards some precious minerals at the enchanted place, a further deterrent to the curious.

The supernatural can also strike a fisherman if he does not respect holy days. One tale recounts the demise of a young man at the hands of a mapinguary because he chose to hunt on a Sunday, and it has been noted that the father of game plays tricks on some hunters on days that commemorate saints. Fishermen may also suffer misfortune if they do not respect religious holy days.

Caboclos generally consider Sunday a day of rest. Apart from sleeping, fishermen mend nets, play soccer, visit friends and relatives, and patronize taverns. A substantial portion of the week's earnings is often spent on quick-acting sugarcane alcohol and beer as well as on sexual affairs. A limited amount of fishing in the morning for the day's needs is not considered too disrespectful, provided that the trip is short and the catch modest. Some fishermen pay no heed to such religious taboos and fish Sunday night so that they can sell their catch on Monday morning in town and village markets, when there is often a scarcity of fresh fish. Seventh-day Adventists fish on Sunday with a clear conscience because Saturday is their day of rest.

Whereas evangelical Christians are stricter in keeping Sunday as a day of repose and worship, they do not recognize Catholic holy days. Saint Peter (São Pedro), for example, is the patron saint of fishermen and is honored on the twenty-ninth of June with firecrackers, rockets, and a parade of boats decorated with brightly colored streamers in front of most Amazonian towns. Bishops and priests huddle with other dignitaries on the bridges of the lead boats and bless crowds gathered on Saint Peter's day. Disrespect for São Pedro is especially ill advised because he is called upon in the event that a boat is having difficulties in a storm or when a fisherman is in distress while fishing alone. Portraits of Saint Peter are sometimes hung close to the helm of boats for added protection.

In the vicinity of Itacoatiara, the story is told of a fisherman who "doubted" Saint Peter's day and went fishing. On his return journey to Itacoatiara in the late afternoon, he was paddling across the Amazon when a violent squall suddenly swept over the expansive river and swamped his canoe. The hapless fisherman lost all his gear and catch and struggled in the wave-tossed water for several hours until he managed to reach the shore of Ilha do Risco, some fifteen kilometers downstream from Itacoatiara. The storm was construed as a punishment and a warning.

Easter is also deemed an inappropriate time to fish. According to some rural folk, the devil is loose during that week and it is better not to venture out onto lakes and rivers to work in case one should meet him in some form. A man reportedly went fishing in a lake near Itacoatiara one Good Friday, and while he was pulling a fish off a hook attached to a trotline, a black caiman suddenly reared out of the water and clamped on his arm (figure 5.5). The fisherman managed to escape, but the caiman sheared off one of his arms.

Few fishermen work on Christmas Day. All sizable urban centers along the Amazon have major festivals honoring the Virgin Mary, known locally as *cirio*. The cirios of Terra Santa and Juriti, for example, fall in June, and many fishermen refrain from working on those days. Other religious holiday, such as the nineteenth of January (Saint Sebastian), the eleventh of February (Saint Lazarus), the thirteenth of June (Saint Anthony), the twenty-fourth of June (Saint John), the twenty-fourth of August (Saint Bartholomew), the fourth of October (Saint Francis), the first of November (All Saints' Day), the eighth of December (Our Lady of Immaculate Conception), and the thirteenth of December (Saint Lucia), are not respected by all. Catholics may make vows to some, but rarely all, of the saints. A plea is made to a saint for deliverance from illness or misfortune with the promise that if the prayer is answered, the person will pay homage on his or her day. Thus in 1977, some fishermen in Itacoatiara participated in the procession honoring Saint Francis while others were busy fishing. Some of those who joined the column snaking through Itacoatiara

Figure 5.5. "There was a great head which emerged." A caiman surprises fishermen in a floodplain forest along the Madeira River in 1910. From H. M. Tomlinson, *The Sea and the Jungle* (London: Duckworth, 1930), 268.

wore habits, imitating the simple attire of Saint Francis; others walked barefoot over the hot asphalt and concrete streets. A few fishermen even pressed heavy rocks against their necks as a sign of piety.

A fisherman was operating the diesel motor of a fishing boat on Saint Anthony's day in 1977 when he accidentally jammed his thumb between the drive belt and a wheel. I witnessed the injury, which happened while he was attending to a mechanical problem with the engine. Fortunately, the injury was not serious, but a throbbing pain persisted for the rest of the day. The fisherman vowed to respect Saint Anthony's day in the future.

In addition to religious holidays, fishermen recognize other days when it is considered disrespectful to fish. Such days include the seventh of September

(Brazil's independence day), when children march through the dusty streets of Amazon towns to the loud and incessant beat of enthusiastic drummers, and the second of November, when people are in a more somber mood to commemorate the day of the dead. On that day, cemeteries are festooned with flowers, usually plastic ones, and candles are lighted by tombs. Families and individuals tarry at grave sites to contemplate the departed and pray for their souls.

A native of Pará state who now works as a gold miner in northern Mato Grosso recalled the misfortune of a man who scorned his companions for not fishing on the day of the dead and set off across the Amazon. He had not been fishing long when he felt a strong tug on his handline. Excited by the prospect of a large catch, the fisherman eagerly pulled in the line. But instead of hauling up a sizable fish, a human skeleton surfaced. The fisherman was immediately assombrado.

The first Monday of August is another day off for many fishermen because it is considered potentially dangerous. Violent storms are more likely. Most fishermen are unsure why that particular day is so perilous, but some suggest that it commemorates a day recounted in the Old Testament when Cain slew Abel.[1] That murder is placed in the context of the third chapter of Genesis, which deals with the fall of man. From that point on, not only was the vertical partnership with God offended but the horizontal relationship between man and nature was also disrupted. Thus, the first Monday in August is symbolic of disharmony between man and his environment. The forces of nature are unleashed and ominous.

Clear parallels can be drawn between the lores surrounding hunting and fishing. Both realms have spirit protectors charged with overseeing wild animals important for subsistence and commerce and with punishing the greedy. The mother of fish fulfills a role similar to that of the father of game. Mãe de peixe steals the shadows of fishermen, while curupira chastises those who kill more than five peccaries. The haunts of the giant snake and enchanted places are shunned by fishermen, just as hunters avoid the territories of forest ogres and enchanted springs.

The fact that certain parts of lakes and rivers are left alone by fishermen because of reported encounters with the supernatural helps to preserve the productivity of fisheries. Some fish are left unmolested to feed and breed. These supernatural reserves are not permanent fixtures of the landscape, nor are their borders precisely defined. If no more huge serpents are reported from a lake, for example, men eventually resume fishing there on the assumption that the giant snake has moved on. When a new sighting is reported, another no-man's-land is created. Some reserves are thus lost, but new ones are constantly being formed.

Areas prohibited for fishing are more permanent with some of the remaining indigenous groups in Amazonia. One village of the Arapaço along the Uaupés, for example, has set aside seventeen of twenty-nine streams in its territory because of guardian spirits. In such areas, which account for 62 percent of the combined lengths of all streams in the territory of the Arapaço, fishing is either restricted or prohibited.

Respect for religious holidays illustrates the notion that fear of punishment, rather than a conscious desire to conserve fish and game stocks, is the reason caboclos refrain from fishing at times. Observance of certain holy days may also benefit fisheries. Breaks in fishing activities increase the chance that fish will be able to lay their eggs before capture. The fact that a relatively large number of holidays fall in December (Christmas), January (New Year's Day, Saint Sebastian's day), February (Carnival, Saint Lazarus's day), and April (Easter) is particularly relevant because many fish species breed during those months as the water levels of the Amazon and its southern tributaries rise. Much of the lore surrounding Amazonian waters serves to conserve resources, but it does not stem from a desire to preserve the lives of other creatures or to avoid protein malnutrition. Fear of supernatural reprisal, rather than notions about living in harmony with nature, curb the harvesting of renewable resources.

Fishermen's tales reveal many yearnings, needs, and moral concerns. Some of the lore is surely born of a desire to entertain. In a world in which few people read and fewer still watch television, lively storytelling is much appreciated. Some of the stories of fishermen and hunters were invented to dispel boredom. An abiding interest in sex surfaces in several tales of haunted waters. Copulation with snakes is a common theme, and so is punishment for excessive drinking and unruly dancing. Pink dolphins impregnate young girls but also take villages into the water when parties become undisciplined. And the fact that water nymphs and mermaids are usually light skinned and blond indicates the prestige whites enjoy among caboclos. Few peasants are blond, hence the fascination and heightened desire with which fair-haired individuals are regarded. The rich tapestry of caboclo lore is thus colored with a generous palette of hues, reflecting many cultural values and serving multiple purposes. The extraordinary biological diversity of Amazonian waters is mirrored in the exuberance of legends among river folk.

A Hex on Hunters and Fishermen

In addition to an assortment of monsters, ghosts, sudden storms, and unusual "accidents" because of disrespect for sacred days, hunters and fishermen must contend with panema, a hex that prevents people from catching fish or killing game. Panema is far more serious than just a temporary bout of bad luck. Unless properly treated, a person can remain *empanemado* indefinitely. Given the importance of fish and game to the regional diet, and as a source of income in the case of fishing, rural folk are understandably concerned about avoiding panema. Fortunately, a number of precautions can be taken to avoid this condition. No matter how careful one is, however, panema can still strike.

Even if a hunter behaves himself in the forest, ill fortune can befall him upon his return home. If a menstruating woman should step on a kill, or if a pregnant person should eat some of the animal, the hunter may become empanemado. A panema-afflicted man cannot bring down any more game. A hunter who is empanemado stalks the forest but does not come across any sizable creature, or if he shoots at some game, he consistently misses. The concept of panema thus implies far more than just bad luck. The victim of the baneful influence fails to bring home any game even after repeated forays into the forest. It is as if his skill had been paralyzed.

Pregnant women are one of the most common causes of panema. Mothers-to-be can trigger panema in the person who killed the animal when they eat some of the carcass or step on a piece of the flesh, hide, or bone of the slain animal. Women pregnant for the first time and those with child during the first three months are especially likely to change the fortunes of a hunter. A case of panema will be particularly severe if the lady who caused it likes to sleep in late. Fortunately, a man's wife is not normally responsible for the emasculation of his hunting prowess. The origin of the idea that pregnant women can adversely affect the performance of hunters lies in aboriginal culture. The Urubu of the Gurupi River, for example, do not allow bitches that have recently delivered puppies to accompany hunters, nor are the female dogs allowed to eat any part of the kill for fear they may provoke panema among the men.

Women in menses can also tarnish the reputation of hunters if they step on kills. The notion that menstruating women can interfere with the luck of hunters is clearly tied to Indian cultures. The Desana of northwest Amazonia consider menstrual blood impure, and women who are in that phase of the monthly ovulation cycle should avoid contact with masculine objects, such as bows. This prohibition placed on menstruating women in Desana culture is related to a myth in which the sun has an incestuous relationship with his daughter and thereby causes her to have periods. A similar prohibition is found among the Yuquí of the Bolivian Amazon.

The idea that females in menses are "dangerous" is ancient and can be found in other regions. The Eskimos believe that menstruating women upset the master of animals when they break certain taboos. The Bisa of Gambia forbid menstruating or pregnant women to touch guns, otherwise they might malfunction. Such taboos probably arose during the early evolution of human society, well before agriculture came on the scene, and serve to maintain the division of labor between the sexes.

Females are not the only culprits when it comes to casting panema. Both sexes can *empanemar* a hunter if they deliberately or inadvertently mistreat his kill. Defecating or urinating on any part of the carcass is a sure way to precipitate panema in the individual who dispatched the animal. Even taking care of physiological necessities on top of stakes used to stretch the hide of a quarry can prevent the hunter from being successful again. A hunter's ability to locate and kill game can also be impaired if someone places a chunk of meat in the fire below the pot. Care must be taken with the discarded parts of the kill to reduce the risk of catching panema. No bones from the kill should enter the fire, nor should they be tossed over the shoulder. Respect for unwanted parts of butchered game is not confined to caboclos. The skin and viscera of game animals killed by the Wayãpí should not be discarded in the river, and the bones of game are carefully collected up by the women and stashed in the forks of trees near the villages to prevent dogs from eating them. If these strictures are not followed, Wayãpí can be afflicted with *pane* (panema). And farther afield, the Micmac of eastern Canada took pains to ensure that bones of esteemed game, such as beaver, moose, and bear, were not burned or eaten by dogs.

The various causes of panema are well known among rural folk, and such knowledge is employed by those who bear a grudge against a hunter. A person may upset a neighbor, for example, if he kills a fully grown deer and refuses to share the meat. The disgruntled neighbor might secure the discarded hooves and urinate on them or place them under a stove. Deer's feet and jealousy were allegedly involved in a stubborn case of panema endured by a Transamazon colonist who lives along a side road of the highway some twenty kilometers northeast of Altamira. Izake has lived his entire life in the Xingu region and enjoys a reputation as a good hunter. One day, the informant carried home a large deer he had killed in the forest near his home. A neighbor came by and requested a section of the carcass. Izake readily obliged, reasoning that his family would benefit one day when the neighbor also killed a large animal. The neighbor in turn was approached by a man who lived close by with a request for the hooves of the deer. The man explained that he needed the feet to prepare some remedy, and his request was granted. Shortly thereafter, Izake lost his usual facility for bringing down game. He figured that the man had really used the hooves to do some mischief (*besteira*).

A spiteful person can provoke panema even if he is given some game. He cannot always be placated with a section of the carcass if he bears a grudge against the hunter. It is thus important to maintain good relationships with all your neighbors.

Francisco, a settler who lives along the Transamazon near Itaituba, described how he became empanemado. A friend asked for the hindquarter of a white-collared peccary he had just killed, and his request was promptly granted. But two days later, while hunting in the forest, the informant became lost. He managed to return home, but Francisco resolved to try his luck closer to his hut next time. A few days later, he set up a platform near a tree with falling flowers and waited as the sun went down. Before darkness descended, a large deer stepped into view. The buck was unusually tall and muscular and it dragged its full testicles on the ground as it walked. Francisco remembered being scared. He released eight volleys toward the head of the virile stag, but the creature just stared at him in defiance. Something was amiss. Francisco reached into his pouch and pulled out a bird's nest that he always carried with him while in the forest in case of a supernatural encounter. He stuffed part of the nest and some tobacco down the barrel of his shotgun and fired again. This time the shot hit its mark and blood spurted from a gaping wound in the deer's broad chest. The bleeding buck nevertheless continued to glare at Francisco. Then instead of collapsing from what seemed like a mortal wound, the jinxed deer walked nonchalantly away.

Francisco vowed never to hunt again. He felt that he had been permanently empanemado by the man to whom he had given the section of white-collared peccary. Francisco's "friend" must have been upset with him and was responsible for his getting lost as well as for his inability to kill the stag. Francisco suggested that his friend had turned into the deer to taunt and punish him. Such witchcraft is too powerful for ordinary panema treatments.

Much of the lore surrounding panema thus serves to encourage neighborly relationships. A hunter who shares large kills and gets along well with people is a less likely target for panema than a person who frequently refuses to distribute portions of his kills or who argues regularly with colleagues. Broken taboos do not cause any inconvenience to the person who infringes the rules. A menstruating woman who touches a rifle may thwart the aim of the weapon's owner, but she will not suffer any consequences for her action. A hunter must therefore be sensitive to people around him as well as remain alert for supernatural dangers while in the forest.

Two other methods of provoking panema do not seem to be involved in promoting social harmony or maintaining the gender division of labor. For example, game is sometimes cut up into chunks, skewered with a slender stake, then cooked over an open fire. The wooden skewer is jabbed into the ground at an angle so that the pieces of meat are suspended over the flames. Panema can ensue if the top of the stake used to pierce the meat is poked into the ground. Furthermore, it is inadvisable to carve meat on a wooden mortar used to dehusk rice.

Sexuality and panema surface again in these two examples. The act of skewering meat has phallic overtones. The prohibition of slicing game on wooden mortars is also rooted in sex; women usually pound cereals, and they might be pregnant or menstruating when they work. The hollowed-out shape of a mortar symbolizes a womb. The sexual connotation of some panema lore is especially evident in the story recounted by Francisco. The buck's testicles are so pendulous they drag on the floor.

Some causes of panema can be traced to a horror of corpses rather than a concern for sex. A twenty-six-year-old pioneer who migrated to the Trans-amazon from Rio Grande do Sul recalled a morbid experience he had in the forest in the early 1970s that resulted in a case of panema. Bencail and a companion were hunting some seven kilometers from the Nova Fronteira settlement along the Altamira-Itaituba stretch of the highway when they startled a deer and gave chase. Shortly they came upon a stream where the companion noticed some bones. Both of the men approached to investigate: it was a badly decomposed cadaver, still partly clothed, lying on its back on a bank with skull and shoulder submerged in the clear water. Bencail bumped the corpse with his foot but did not think much of the incident at the time. The men retrieved a plastic bag containing documents near the deceased and left to report their gruesome find.

Detectives from Altamira visited the death scene and found no evidence of foul play. The deceased was related to Altamira's police chief and had apparently been dead for two or three months. The dead man was known to be mentally disturbed and may have wandered into the forest and become lost. For six months following the discovery of the corpse, Bencail was unable to kill any game. He attributed his stubborn case of panema to his inadvertent touching of the cadaver.

Death is involved in another cause of panema. Peasants consider it inadvisable to kill giant armadillo, even though the heavily clawed mammal can weigh up to sixty kilograms. Smaller armadillos, such as the nine-banded, render a sweet, fatty meat that is relished by caboclos. Giant armadillo is shunned because it reportedly burrows into graveyards and thereby brushes against corpses. Giant armadillos reputedly eat cadavers, although they more likely feast on maggots that feed on decomposing bodies. Termites and colonial ants appear to be the mainstay of the giant armadillo's diet. The observation that giant armadillos forage around the remains of the departed is an ancient one. A myth of the Barasana who inhabit northwest Amazonia relates how the moon becomes an armadillo and eats bones in a grave excavated below a house. A hunter who shoots a giant armadillo allegedly contracts a severe case of panema.

Panema instigated by a pregnant woman is also especially difficult to cure. If the panema victim tries to rid himself of the curse by resorting to one of the

Figure 6.1. Paxiúba palm with characteristic stilt roots, approximately the height of an adult man in this case. Paxiúba is involved in some curing rituals to treat *panema,* and the thorn-studded roots are cut to serve as kitchen graters. The trunks also make durable flooring. Combu Island, Amazon estuary, near Belém, Pará, 15 December 1994.

remedies, he is likely to provoke a miscarriage in the woman responsible for the affliction. The safest recourse, caboclos insist, is to be patient and wait until the baby is born before commencing treatment. If the hunter is not prepared to wait for several months, he may undertake a mild form of treatment to reduce the chances of triggering the loss of an embryo or fetus.

Men incapacitated by panema resort to a wide variety of remedies and rituals to shed the spell's vicelike grip. Several treatments involve baths, normally taken during the early hours on a Friday morning. It is important to refrain from talking to anyone after rising until the treatment is completed. A clear forest stream with stilt-rooted paxiúba (figure 6.1) is the preferred location for performing the cleansing ritual that includes swimming between the thorn-studded roots of the palm. The significance of paxiúba is not clear, because other moisture-loving palms, such as açaí, adorn the banks of streams in Amazonia. But at least one tribe in the region, the Barasana, ascribe special importance to the slender-boled tree. According to Barasana mythology, paxiúba sprang from the ashes of a culture hero.

If no paxiúba palms are growing nearby, a panema victim can plunge into a stream in which manioc roots have been laid down to soften (figure 6.2). After the tubers have soaked for a few days, they are easily mashed and placed in a press prior to making manioc flour (*farinha puba*). If the roots are not soaked, they must be grated; the resulting flour, called *farinha seca*, has a different texture and is not as popular in Pará as farinha puba. A hunter may also get rid of panema by swimming under the smooth board used by his wife to wash clothes. In the latter ritual, the curse is transferred to the woman, but that does not matter because she does not hunt.

Figure 6.2. Manioc tubers that have been soaking in a stream to soften them prior to making flour. Near the community of Lastancia, municipality of Itupiranga, Pará, 11 November 1992.

Other bathing ceremonies to treat panema do not require submergence in water. Typically, a pot containing an infusion of herbs is carried into the jungle before dawn on a Friday or Monday. Not a word is uttered to anyone before departing alone. Once inside the forest, the hunter undresses and pours the chilly solution over his entire body. In one ritual bath (*banho*), a specimen of João Burundi, an understory plant, is pounded in a bowl together with some hot chili peppers. Water is then added and the concoction is left to steep for six days. Another ritual bath is prepared by crushing a section of cipó caçador, a jungle vine, in a pot. Water is then poured on the mashed liana and left to soak for three days so that the solution becomes more potent. In Acre, hunters reportedly prepare purifying baths with the roots of paxiúba palm.

Hunters in Amazonia have employed banhos for purification purposes for thousands of years. Ritual baths are used by many tribes in the basin, such as the Kamayurá of the upper Xingu, the Kayapó of the Xingu-Tocantins interfluve, and the Amahuaca of the Peruvian Amazon. A Barasana myth mentions a purification bath for girls entering puberty that is made from the bark of a tree. The use of cleansing solutions to improve one's hunting luck is not confined to the Amazon. The Ndembu of Zambia, for example, prepare baths using various plants in order to improve the fortune of hunters.

Smoke from certain plant and animal concoctions also allegedly benefits panema sufferers. The use of smoke for curing the sick is a widespread practice among indigenous people in the region, such as the Kamayurá. The custom of ceremonial smokings (*defumações*) has continued in peasant culture. At least three defumações employed by peasants require red chili peppers to be effective. In one version, shiny fruits of the condiment, known locally as *pimenta malagueta,* are mixed with hair from a game animal and resin from canaraú,[1] beijuí, or crajiru; the combination is then heated in a pan. The hunter fans the ensuing smoke over himself, his gun, and his protesting dog. Hunters in Acre prepare a ritual smoking with crajiru and the nest of the caurê hawk.[2] Smoke is thought to drive away the evil spirit.

The idea of using chili peppers to treat panema is an aboriginal contribution. Chili peppers were domesticated in the American tropics to deal with the supernatural world. Their use as a food flavorant, or perhaps a cover-up for food that is on the verge of going off in the days before refrigerators, has come much later. Chili peppers are now widely used in cuisine, particularly in Mexico, the southwestern United States, and parts of Southeast Asia. Few people who relish hot Thai food realize that their joy can be traced to shamans in the

Neotropics. The Barasana, Cubeo, Maracá, and Amahuaca employ chili peppers in fumigations to ward off evil. In neighboring Guiana, some indigenous peoples rub their eyes with red chili peppers to make themselves "invisible" to water spirits that dwell by prominent rocks.

In another defumação using chili peppers, the hot spice is placed in a tin along with hair from a prehensile-tailed porcupine. The can is then put on a fire and the hunter stands, grasping his struggling dog, over the acrid smoke. Care is taken to ensure that the gun is also fully exposed to the pungent fumes. In a third remedy employing red chili peppers and smoke, the short, slender fruits are burned together with some game hair, João Burundi, and cipó curimbó, a forest liana. A less noxious ritual smoking is prepared by collecting the copious cobweb of a certain forest spider, taking a bone from a game animal, and placing them on a bed of dry leaves. The hunter then ignites the mound of animal and plant ingredients and allows the rising smoke to waft over his body. If none of the above items is readily at hand, packages for ritual smokings can be purchased in umbanda stores, or the ingredients can be bought in a market.

If any of the more conventional treatments for panema fail, a man so afflicted may try some unorthodox rituals in a desperate attempt to regain his hunting ability. In one remedy, a tree with fresh, new leaves is selected. The hunter then walks around the tree with spouting foliage three times, taking care to complete the third circle at the point where he began the ritual march. The new growth of leaves symbolizes a fresh beginning, and walking around the tree thrice invokes the Trinity. A more humiliating ritual requires that the hunter lie on his back at sunrise in front of the entrance to a chicken coop. The door to the chicken house is then lifted and the birds file out across the man's chest and stomach.

Chickens are not the only Old World ingredient in panema cures. The influence of Christianity is evident in the case of the man who walked three times around a tree invoking the Father, the Son, and the Holy Ghost. Garlic, used by caboclos to ward off forest goblins, is also employed to shield people against evil in the Old World. One Transamazon colonist who has spent most of his life in the Tocantins valley asserted that he always carries a tooth of garlic with him while hunting to reduce his chances of contracting panema.

Ideas related to the proper conduct of hunters do not stem from a need to conserve sources of dietary protein. In the case of panema, concern for the division of labor underlies much of the lore dealing with bad luck on the hunt.

Several writers have postulated that protein is in short supply in upland areas of Amazonia, and thus the size of aboriginal groups has been limited. The rich diversity of game taboos among native groups has also been tied to a supposed scarcity of high-quality protein in the region. Although some adherents to the "protein deficiency" school have backed down somewhat from previous positions, the limited productivity of game is still envisaged as a major constraint on the size of villages. But a convincing case has yet to be made that folklore of either indigenous peoples or peasants in Amazonia is a cultural response to a shortage of protein in the regional diet.

The rain forest is rich in animal and vegetable sources of protein, and no scarcity of this dietary item, or the paucity of faunal resources, has limited the size of indigenous populations. Besides, humans can thrive on a very modest supply of amino acids. An adult requires no more than fifty grams of high quality protein a day in order to maintain good health, and a good deal of protein comes from vegetable matter, particularly beans.

Protein malnutrition is not now, and probably has never been, a significant public health problem in Amazonia. In addition to game animals, plenty of foods rich in protein, such as insects, certain fungi, and nuts, can be gathered in the forest and second growth. Grasshoppers, beetle grubs, and ants are significant items in the diets of several aboriginal groups in Amazonia. In Western society, insects are not food, but food is of course a cultural term.

An indigenous group may shift the location of a village because of game depletion, but that does not mean that protein is lacking in the environment. An aboriginal community may move because its favorite game animals are becoming scarce, not because the diverse habitats of the forest and rivers cannot sustain them. The fact that no animals were domesticated for food in the Amazon basin suggests that protein is plentiful.

The current small size of Amazonian tribes is not an accurate reflection of the environment's potential for supporting humans. Over four hundred years of the ravages of introduced diseases and often violent confrontations with whites have decimated the region's indigenous population. Before the arrival of Europeans, populations were often dense, especially along rivers. Even the interfluves, thought to have been sparsely settled, were inhabited by sizable and permanent groups.

Links between protein supplies and beliefs in supernatural protectors of game are even more tenuous in peasant culture. Caboclo communities do not move because game yields decline; they rely increasingly on domestic animals, crops, and purchased food. Unlike precontact Indians, peasants keep several domesticated animals for food, particularly chickens and pigs. It seems unlikely that peasants would limit themselves to a take of five peccaries each because of a need to maintain a diet rich in high quality protein. Chickens, eggs, beans, and fish caught in streams and artificial ponds take care of the amino-acid requirements of most caboclos. Several animals appear prominently in the lore of hunters, especially deer, peccaries, and paca; these are among the prized game. A preoccupation with the supply of esteemed game animals, rather than a protein shortfall, underlies the lore of hunters.

As in the case of hunters, fishermen are also prone to panema, and the notion is widely held among fisherfolk of Brazil. For example, Ipanema, one of Rio de Janeiro's most enticing beaches and about which a famous song that started the bossa nova craze was written, means the place where there are no fish. Few people who enjoy the lilting rhythm of *The Girl from Ipanema*, written by Tom Jobim in 1963, realize that the title incorporates Brazilian folklore. Fishermen and hunters share many ideas about panema. Women who are pregnant or in menses can trigger panema in both hunters and fishermen. Some fishermen take special care with the disposal of fish remains in order to prevent panema, just as hunters pay attention to the destiny of discarded bones of game animals. Fishermen also employ baths and smoke to dispel panema, though the ingredients in the treatments often differ from those used by hunters.

A menstruating woman can inflict panema on a fisherman if she touches any of his gear, walks over it, or treads on the scales, bones, or viscera of his catch. Fear of panema is the major reason women never accompany men on fishing trips, and this prohibition has been acquired from aboriginal cultures. The Indian roots of prohibitions surrounding menstruating women were explored in the discussion on hunters, but a few examples related to fishing in aboriginal societies will serve to illustrate the ancient origins of this caboclo belief. According to the Kamayurá, the mother of fish can detect the smell of those who have touched a woman during her period, and a fisherman who has had contact with a female in this condition is more prone to attack by caimans, stingrays, and piranhas. Kamayurá in menses are forbidden to touch or even look at fish. The Tapirapé affirm that a trap loses its ability to capture fish if a menstruating woman eats quarry caught in it. And menstruating Sharanahua may not join in communal fish poisoning expeditions, the only fishing event in which women are otherwise permitted to participate.

Pregnant women may provoke panema if they eat a man's catch, although it is rare for a fisherman's wife to be responsible. Fishermen who live in towns often sell some of their catch in public markets, so they cannot be sure of the ultimate destination of commercialized fish. Many pregnant women thus eat fish without triggering panema. In a tribal setting, it is easier to control the distribution of the catch. According to fishermen in the vicinity of Itacoatiara, expectant wives of neighbors are particularly likely to empanemar a fisherman. If the woman is lazy, the case is likely to be especially difficult to cure. As in the case of hunters infected with panema, fishermen suffering from the same misfortune try to find out who is responsible so that treatment does not induce a miscarriage.

An angry or jealous person can cast panema on a fisherman. To perform the spell, he may stick a bone or scale from one of the fisherman's catches into a termite nest. The same result can be obtained by urinating or defecating on the bones or scales. Someone can scorn (*judiar*) a fisherman and bring him panema by throwing a bone from the fisherman's catch three times over either shoulder.

Pirarucu fishermen are particularly prone to catching panema. Special care is taken to dispose of the viscera, bones, skin, and scales of the air-breathing fish in case they should fall into the hands of a sorcerer or be eaten by black vultures, turkey vultures, lesser yellow-headed vultures, dogs, or pigs (figure 6.3). Pirarucu heads are usually taken home because they are the most important part of the fish's anatomy to guard against mistreatment and because the brain is relished. It is not surprising that pirarucu figures so prominently in panema lore because the pink and virtually boneless flesh of the giant fish is held in such high esteem. The lofty price that pirarucu fetches in markets is another reason fishermen are concerned about their catches of this valuable fish. A similar preoccupation for the supply of prized animals lies behind the care hunters take in disposing of deer and peccary parts.

The diverse panema treatments are generally prepared by women, usually the victim's wife, or the person deemed responsible for the affliction. Bathing solutions made from various plants are commonly used to treat panema. One variety of ritual bath is prepared by scraping the thin bark of catauari, a medium-sized tree of floodplain forests that is occasionally planted in home gardens because its fruits are useful as fish bait. Shredded catauari bark, and sometimes the leaves, are mixed in a water-filled gourd, and the solution is splashed over the body. The small tuberous roots of cipó-taia, an upland vine, are grated

Figure 6.3. Skin of a pirarucu hung on a branch so that it is not stepped on or fed on by vultures or domestic animals. Disrespect for the remains of the highly prized fish can lead to a case of *panema* for the fishermen. Harpoons and a float for catching pirarucu are on the upper branch. Igarapé Jari, near Arapixuna, Pará, 31 August 1993.

into water to make another kind of bath. The infusion is poured over the affected person's body, canoe, and fishing gear. A banho is also made from a mixture of alcohol and the roots of mumbaca, an understory palm of upland forest. The various solutions are concocted to soak away panema.

Bathing solutions for expelling panema are also prepared from domesticated plants and from a combination of cultivated and wild species. The roots of the house-yard palm bacabinha are pounded in a mortar and mixed with alcohol. Another kind of banho is made by mixing red chili peppers with the leaves of pião roxo and vindika, all cultivated plants. The frequent use of alcohol, purchased in one-liter plastic bottles, is due probably to its disinfectant properties. A modern product has thus acquired some value in the regional pharmacopoeia devoted to the treatment of supernatural ailments. Red chili peppers are normally used to enhance the flavor of various foods and condiments, but they also have medicinal uses.

The grated roots of vai-vem, leaves of mucura-cáa, and gaivotinha are mixed together in water to make another bathing solution to cure panema. The tuberous roots of vai-vem, which is cultivated in yards, must be scraped toward the body to be effective. Housewives bathe with vai-vem to bring back unfaithful husbands. Vai-vem translates as "go-come" and refers to the comings and goings of a spouse as he pursues extramarital affairs. The plant is also deemed effective in capturing back a man's fishing skills. The root gratings of vai-vem are mixed with either alcohol or tucupi in other versions of the purification bath. Tucupi is the juice that collects when manioc is squeezed. After boiling, the savory yellow liquid is added to soups and sauces. Tucupi juice mixed with red chili peppers is also considered an effective ritual bath, whereas in other cases, a weak solution of ammonia suffices.

Smoke is occasionally used after a bath to further cleanse the body and gear of panema. Fumigations are made by burning red peppers alone, garlic and peppers, or the bones and scales of pirarucu. Cesar Batista, a thirty-five-year-old farmer and fisherman who lives on the Amazon floodplain along Igarapé Jari near Santarém, claimed that he cured a case of panema once by preparing a ritual smoking with ninety-nine red chili peppers. When I mentioned this recipe to a curer in Macapá, capital of the state of Amapá, she opined that it seemed a little excessive. According to Mãe Dulce, twenty-five to thirty-five peppers are usually enough. The fisherman received his instructions from an old man in the village of Maripa on the Tapajós. Cesar attributed his bout of panema to an unknown pregnant woman living along Igarapé Jari who ate a fish that he had caught.

Dry, barbed twigs of unha de cigana (hoatzin's claw), a leguminous shrub of floodplain forests, are also burned for their purifying smoke. It helps if a piece of dress from the woman responsible for the panema can be secured and burned in the defumação. Fishermen stand next to, or over, the smoldering fire and allow the fumes to pass over them and their gear.

In addition to the use of baths and smoke, panema-afflicted fishermen try to decontaminate themselves and their implements by beating their arms, canoes, and gear with aninga or pião roxo. A fisherman under the influence of panema may insert his arm in a tipití, a sleevelike press designed to extract the liquid from manioc dough (figure 6.4). By pulling the tipití taut, the ill fortune can sometimes be squeezed out. Pirarucu fishermen usually make a special effort to find out who has given them panema, so that if it is a woman, she can be persuaded to bite the giant hooks and harpoon points used to catch the esteemed fish. If no suspect is found, the trotline hooks and harpoon heads are rubbed with red chili peppers.

If none of the home remedies work, a panema-struck fisherman seeks out the help of a spiritualist healer. The curer may prescribe a commercial bathing solution, such as Saúde de Bahia (health from Bahia), Gaivotinha (small tern), Descarga de Pescador (fisherman's catharsis), Chama (beckon), Limpa Corpo (body cleanser), or Espanta Azar (scare away ill fortune). These banhos are mostly made in Belém and can be purchased in main-street stores, market stalls,

Figure 6.4. A tipití press expressing liquid from manioc dough. The juice dripping into the calabash gourd on the ground is used to make tucupi sauce. People suffering from *panema* sometimes insert an arm in a tipití to "squeeze" out their ill fortune. A manioc flour house (*casa da farinha*) on the Amazon floodplain in the vicinity of Urucurituba, Pará, 20 March 1993.

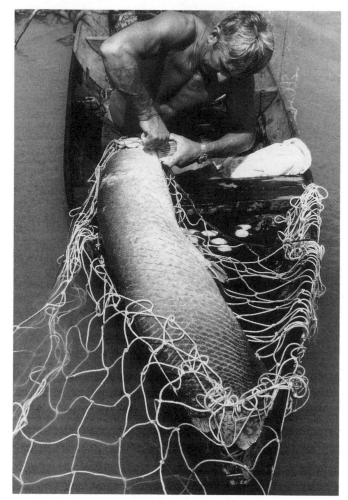

Figure 6.5. Fisherman removing a pirarucu caught in a gillnet in a floodplain lake of the Amazon. Pirarucu is one of the most prized fish in the Amazon and is the subject of considerable lore. Igarapé Açu, Lago Remanso, Surubim-açu, near Santarém, Pará, 2 September 1993.

or from itinerant salesmen. If the fisherman lives far from a town or is hard up, the curer will likely prescribe a bath made from one of the domestic or wild plant concoctions. Panema treatments are always performed on a Friday, preferably at sundown. Hunters usually undertake panema treatments on Fridays as well, but they are performed in the early hours of the morning.

As in the case of hunters, fishermen sometimes carry a talisman with them to ward off panema, monsters, and ghosts. A few leaves of jiboínha, for example, may be stuffed in the prow of a canoe to repel the supernatural. The attractive green and white herb is grown in pots near houses on the Amazon floodplain, usually on elevated platforms to escape the annual surge of water.

In the lower Amazon, rural people sometimes carry baskets containing the roots of tajapurá, an aroid, in the bow of their canoes for the same purpose.

Fear of the loss of protein sources has been suggested as the root of the belief in panema. The relevance of this idea has already been discussed with regard to hunting. The notion that panema is linked to a preoccupation with protein is even more tenuous with respect to fishing. Fish have historically abounded on the Amazon floodplain, and even during the months of privation at high water, indigenous people resorted to dried fish, penned turtles, and upland game for supplies of high-quality protein. Although aboriginal populations were dense in precontact times, there is no evidence that fish were exterminated along rivers, or became scarce, as a result of fishing pressure. The fact that pirarucu (figure 6.5) figures so prominently in panema lore suggests that fear of loss of desirable species, rather than a lack of protein in the environment, accounts partly for the concept's endurance. Panema did not originate in postcontact times, when commercial fishing began on a large scale and led to the depletion of fish stocks in some areas. The extensive use of wild and domesticated plants in panema treatments discounts a recent inception of the concept.

The taboo on menstruating women touching fishing gear is a major reason that women are not allowed on fishing excursions. This notion thus serves to reinforce the division of labor. Women stay behind to perform domestic chores, tend to crops, gather firewood, and take produce to market. To avoid angering someone and risk catching panema in retaliation, fishermen generally cooperate with one another, as do hunters. Thus a request to borrow some fishing gear is likely to be granted. Similarly, a fisherman who has been unlucky will normally be given some fish by a colleague for subsistence needs. The main forces behind the notion of panema are therefore a desire to enforce the division of labor, a wish to encourage cooperation, and a concern for the supply of desirable species of fish and game.

Perilous Flesh

The palatability and digestibility of certain fish and game are subjects of a considerable lore. Ideas that have accumulated about the safety of some fish and game flesh influence the behavior of rural folk at the table as well as on the hunt or in their canoes. At first glance, the system of food avoidances may seem nonsensical and even counterproductive. But upon closer examination it will be seen that peasants have learned which animals are more likely to upset one's health when eaten. People in the Brazilian Amazon rank fish and game according to their potential to affect adversely a person's well-being, and some people thus refrain from eating certain fish and mammals when they are ill or convalescing.

Rural and some urban folk in the Brazilian Amazon categorize game and fish according to how *reimoso* they are. Reimoso is derived from the Latin *rheum,* which means "phlegm" or "thick fluid," and is an undesirable property in food for mothers who have recently given birth and for those suffering from illness, especially skin problems. Most game is reimoso to some degree, but peccary, paca, and tapir are particularly offensive (appendix 3). A person who feels unwell is thus likely to abstain from eating tapir flesh, but will usually accept secretive tinamou, partridgelike birds of the forest floor. The reimoso classification of meats is a discretionary affair rather than a strict taboo. If someone is really hungry and is suffering from some skin disorder, he or she is likely to succumb to the pleasure of dining on succulent paca, a fatty rodent.

The idea of avoiding certain game meats can be traced in part to aboriginal cultures. Among the Witoto, for example, tapir flesh is considered to be very strong, particularly for women, and is thus eaten sparingly. The Desana regard tapir, deer, and white-lipped peccary as risky foods for sick people, children, and women who are menstruating, pregnant, or lactating. Another Tukano group, the Barasana, also rank game meat according to its danger to a person's health. Among the Yuquí of the Bolivian Amazon, small children are not supposed to eat peccary, paca, or capybara because of their high fat content. If children ingest these game animals, the greasy coating in their mouths is thought to trigger thrush, a fungal disease. Kayapó women reject tortoise meat because it is thought to inflame the skin. As in the case of caboclos, the Wayãpí consider tinamou a safe meat to eat when feeling unwell.

Although the meat avoidances observed by peasants in Amazonia stem largely from indigenous lore, the food classification system has been influenced by European ideas about the causes of diseases, particularly those found in the ancient works of Hippocrates in which the proper balance of humors in the body is discussed. Caboclos affirm that reimoso meat provokes latent diseases in the blood; upon ingestion of "strong" flesh, painful boils may erupt on the skin. Any chronic illness grows worse when a person eats reimoso game. Meals of armadillo, paca, tapir, and peccary "thicken" the blood and allegedly cause the legs to swell. A wounded person usually avoids reimoso flesh because it inflames lesions and postpones healing. Those afflicted with venereal disease normally make a special effort to resist the temptation of dining on succulent game meat, otherwise they purportedly suffer from a painful orogeny of welts and sores. People on any kind of medication also habitually refrain from eating reimoso flesh for fear of triggering health complications.

Women with menstrual flow are especially prone to sickness if they eat paca, white-collared peccary, armadillo, or any of the turkeylike curassows. At the very least, the lady is likely to break out in a rash of white spots all over her body, similar to those along the sides of a bulldog-sized paca. Or worse, she may die. The connection between humors and blood is particularly evident in this food avoidance. A female on her period is considered to have blood that is already thickened and unwholesome, hence the perception that reimoso meat exacerbates the condition.

Women who have just delivered a child should avoid reimoso meat lest the substance, when it is passed in the maternal milk, offend the baby. The child could suffer gastrointestinal distress as a consequence of drinking milk tainted by a reimoso meal. Some disagreements arise concerning the length of time a mother should avoid eating game. One person asserted that forty days is sufficient, whereas another suggested that three months is more appropriate. In a town on the lower Amazon, forty-five days is apparently enough time for the child to gain strength and allow the mother to consume reimoso meat.

Beef and chicken are the safest meats. Chicken broth is traditionally prescribed throughout Brazil for people who feel unwell. If no chicken or beef are available, or they are too expensive, then guans (figure 7.1), colorful piping-guans, or noisy chachalacas, all pheasantlike birds of forest or tall second growth, are acceptable substitutes. Certain wild birds are also considered safe among the Desana, who regard pigeons, tinamous, and iridescent trumpeters as inoffensive because their flesh is lightly colored. Duck and pork, on the other hand, are inadvisable for individuals who are sick and for those who have recently given birth, because those meats are extremely reimoso. The idea that nonaquatic fowl are safe appears in the writings of Galen, a physician who worked in Rome in the second century A.D. Galen was heavily influenced by Hippocrates, so it is apparent why water birds would be considered potentially unhealthy. Ponds and swamps were perceived as sources of unwholesome vapors that infected animals coming into contact with the miasmas. Galen felt that water birds and pork could cause obstructions in humans because of their thickening properties, resulting in symptoms such as constipation. Rural people in the Brazilian Amazon believe that the potency of reimoso flesh is tempered by skinning the carcass, washing the meat thoroughly in running water, and adding plenty of spices to the pot.

Game animals are generally reimoso because of their catholic diets. Forest fruits in particular are deemed responsible for the reimoso quality of paca, armadillos, peccaries, agouti, and tapir. Many forest fruits are wholesome and are avidly sought by the regional population for tasty treats and to generate income. But some berries are considered venomous, and the poison taints the flesh when eaten. The small, yellow fruits of the cramuri tree are often considered the cause of the reimoso nature of game. One Transamazon colonist ventured the opinion that forest fruits not normally eaten by people contain strange "vitamins"; when they are consumed by game, the vitamins are absorbed into the animal's flesh. The meat is thus strong and can upset a person's health.

Forest fruits are not the only items in the diet of game animals that render their flesh reimoso. Flowers falling from the canopy are an important food for paca, tortoises, and deer; some of the inflorescences also impart reimoso to

Figure 7.1. Young guans hatched from eggs taken from a nest discovered in the forest. The eggs were hatched by a domestic chicken. When the guans are older, they will probably be eaten, because their delicate flesh is considered inoffensive, particularly for those feeling unwell. Comunidade São João Batista, Gleba Cajazeira, municipality of Itupiranga, Pará, 10 November 1992.

game. The ubiquitous agouti is considered reimoso because it nibbles on a wide variety of herbs as well as fallen fruit. Some forest herbs have swollen roots or tubers, and paca and white-collared peccary become reimoso when they dig up and feast on the tubers. Tortoise meat is relished, but it is considered reimoso because the sluggish reptiles scavenge on the ground and all manner of questionable material is thought to be incorporated into their diets.

Insects, worms, lizards, and snakes are also allegedly responsible for the reimoso nature of certain game. Tortoises, armadillos, and peccaries, for example, reportedly eat venomous insects and spiders, thus rendering their meat strong. Paca and peccaries are reputed to carry unusually heavy worm loads, another reason those game animals are characterized as reimoso. Game animals also become reimoso when they eat, or even come close to, snakes. Tortoises, armadillos, and peccaries are said to eat serpents, thereby poisoning their flesh. Paca is tainted with reimoso when it shares its sleeping quarters in a burrow or hollow log with a snake. How the rodent thus becomes infected with rheum is not clear, but the notion illustrates the general loathing people in the region have for snakes.[1]

Whereas food avoidances directed at game animals are relatively widespread among Amazonian tribes, prohibitions against the eating of fish appear to be less common. Nevertheless, the concept of reimoso is just as important among fishermen as it is among hunters. Although fish taboos are not reported so frequently in the ethnographic literature on Amazonia, aboriginal societies are important sources for some of the ideas about classifying the safety of aquatic animals for consumption. Among the Kamayurá, for example, women and their husbands should not eat fish without scales when the wife is pregnant. Kamayurá in menses are not supposed to eat fish of any kind. The Mundurucú believe that smooth-skinned fish cause dysentery in a child if the mother eats that type of fish during pregnancy or for several months after the infant's birth. The Tapirapé do not eat scaly pirarucu or slippery-skinned pirarara. Formerly, the Jurúna of the upper Xingu would not eat piranha because they thought that the carnivorous fish caused people to vomit blood if they ate it. The bony-headed pirarara is rarely eaten by the tribe because it allegedly triggers stomachaches and acts as an emetic. Likewise, the Wayãpí regard pirarara as ill-advised for those feeling unwell.

Among peasants of the Itacoatiara area, reimoso fish are generally avoided by anyone suffering from a wound, especially one inflicted by a stingray, dog, or snake, because the reimoso substance embroils the lesion. The same dietary rule applies to those suffering from tumors, measles, or skin rashes. People with liver or venereal disease should definitely not eat reimoso fish. Such fish can also apparently provoke a relapse of fever and are thought to be capable of exacerbating diarrhea and stomachaches, particularly among children. As in the case of most game animals, women who have recently given birth should not eat reimoso fish because they may pass the offending substance to their babies when they breast feed them.

At least twenty-seven species of fish are considered reimoso in the Itacoatiara area (appendix 4). Dinner-plate-sized pirapitinga and slender matrinchão are cited most frequently as being potentially dangerous to one's health. Although pirapitinga and matrinchão are generally considered to be the most reimoso, catfish such as the spotted surubim, acarí (which looks like a miniature stealth bomber), zebra-striped caparari, innocuous-looking mandí, potbellied jandiá, sharp-toothed piracatinga, laterally compressed piranambu, olive-skinned jaú, and massive piraíba were cited as potentially hazardous by 59 percent of the fishermen interviewed.

This aversion to eating catfish, at least when sick, is an ancient one. For example, piraíba means "bad fish" in the lingua franca of colonial times. Gray, slick-skinned piraíba is still considered inferior in the Brazilian Amazon, where most of the catch of this species is exported. Young specimens, known as filhote, are acceptable food and form the basic ingredient in fish stews served in Belém. Commercial catfisheries in Amazonia are relatively recent, and the enterprises are geared to extraregional markets, particularly to the United States and central and southern Brazil. The only catfish widely appreciated as food in the Brazilian Amazon are surubim, caparari, black cuiu-cuiu, and the armor-plated tamoatá; the latter two species are mostly eaten by the poor. Both piraíba and mapará are rumored to transmit leprosy. Many inhabitants of the Madeira River shun jaú meat because it is considered capable of causing hemorrhoids and miscarriages.

As in the case of game, the diets of reimoso fish are blamed for their unhealthy attributes. Reimoso fish are reputed to have diets that incorporate a variety of creatures, including insects. Matrinchão, pirapitinga, and surubim are reputed to be potentially unhealthy because they are said to eat venomous fish. Handsome oscar, which enters the aquarium trade because of its distinctive red and black "eye" on the tail, is considered reimoso by some fishermen because its diverse prey includes insects, crustaceans, frogs, and fruit. Curimatá is reimoso because it shovels detritus and algae into its rasping mouth. But not all reimoso fish are omnivorous or insectivores. For example, pirarucu and most species of piranha are primarily carnivorous.

Safe fish include the mouth-brooding arawana, which also enters the international aquarium trade, sardinha, and small tambaqui. Their flesh is considered safe because it is "weak." Other innocuous fish include branquinha, ferocious traíra, cará branca, and the cigar-shaped cubiu. Some people feel that meals of surubim and aracu are benign, yet others assert that they can be harmful. Silvery arawana is the dish of preference for those feeling unwell, and it is an acceptable substitute for chicken soup. Although arawana is deemed a safe fish, the surface feeder's broad spectrum diet includes small fish, crustacea, frogs, insects, and spiders.

Reimoso fish are generally regarded as excessively oily with strong-tasting flesh. Many of the catfish, especially the larger species, do have abundant fat reserves. In the nineteenth century, grease from the river-dwelling piraíba, for example, was boiled down to provide oil for cooking and lighting. The fat content of Amazonian fish varies considerably. Some species fatten during high water, when they disperse into floodplain forests to feed on fruits and nuts. Sardinha and pacu are considered safe by some fishermen, but at low water they nevertheless register fat contents of 25 and 22 percent, respectively. The fruit-eating species accumulate fat after feeding during the high water season; by the end of the dry season, though, the fat content of sardinha drops to around 7 percent because food is scarce. Many predators, on the other hand, gain weight at low water because their prey is more concentrated in lakes and shallow channels. Seasonal fluctuations in the fat content of Amazonian fishes partly explain the discrepancies between fishermen as to which species are dangerous to one's well-being.

Information on the fat content of Amazonian fish is scarce, but the available information indicates a reasonably close correlation between fat levels and the reimoso rating of fish. Mapará, a plankton-eating catfish, has registered a grease content of 29 percent. Matrinchão and curimatá contain 23 and 17 percent fat, respectively, and also appear high on the list. Arawana, a safe dish with mild, white meat, contains less than 3 percent fat.

Some of the game animals considered reimoso are also fatty, particularly peccaries, paca, tortoises, and armadillos. The grease of armadillos, for example, is used to fry chunks of the tender meat; crunchy manioc flour is then stirred into the hot pan to make a savory meal called *farofa de tatu*. Along the Transamazon Highway, white-lipped peccaries are shot mostly during the rainy season, when herds feed avidly on fallen fruits. These important game animals, as well as paca and tortoises, most likely gain weight during the wet months because fruits and nuts form the bulk of their diets. The practice of removing the skin of kills to reduce the potent reimoso quality eliminates some of the fat that accumulates in subcutaneous tissue. Two of the domestic animals classified as reimoso, duck and pig, are known to contain generous amounts of fat.

Rural people in the Amazon are preoccupied with the fat content of foods for reasons different from those held by the well-fed middle-class inhabitants of urban areas. In the more sedentary lifestyles of urban folk, excessive consumption of fatty foods often leads to obesity and can exacerbate hardening of the arteries. Stoutness is not a concern of farmers and fisherfolk; indeed, a generous girth is often perceived as a sign of prosperity and well-being. Other health concerns underlie the reimoso classification system in the "interior." Fats are relatively hard to digest and are renowned for causing minor skin problems. They are also detrimental to damaged livers. A low-fat diet is beneficial to a person suffering from impaired liver function. Many rural folk have been infected with malaria several times, and the parasites that provoke the disease tax the liver. Avoidance or reduced consumption of oily fish and game would therefore be a wise policy.

The system of classifying game and fish flesh does not stem from the high cost of procuring such species, as has been suggested for taboo mammals among aboriginal groups in Amazonia. According to the latter view, Indians have prohibited the consumption of some animals because they take too much time to locate. But neither peccaries, tortoises, armadillos, paca, nor tapir—all high on the list of reimoso animals—are especially difficult to capture, nor are they rare. In predominately forested areas of the Transamazon Highway, for example, peccaries, tortoise, armadillos, paca, and tapir accounted for 82 percent by weight of game captured during the course of a year. And in Aripuanã, a village in northern Mato Grosso that in the late 1970s contained six hundred inhabitants, peccaries, armadillos, paca, and tapir were responsible for 90 percent by weight of the game take in the first four months of 1978. The yield of peccaries, tapir, and paca drops dramatically only in highly disturbed habitats with substantial patches of second growth and a long history of settlement. Reimoso fish are also relatively abundant.

The peasant classification of fish and game according to their digestibility thus stems mainly from a desire to protect the health of individuals rather than to conserve energy. This categorization of game with respect to its safety is also found in some indigenous cultures in the Amazon basin. The Barasana rank foods, including game and fish, into a graded series of relative danger to one's health. People who are ill, have been bitten by a snake, are menstruating, or have recently given birth are all highly susceptible to health complications if they eat foods at the risky end of the spectrum. The ranking of fish among the Barasana is based on their grease content, an important criterion in the ordering of reimoso fish in peasant culture. The Desana, another Tukano group, also avoid eating fish or game high in fat during certain periods, such as puberty and when a person is feeling ill.

Evil Eye

Food items, such as reimoso game or fish, are not the only potential threat to people's health in both rural and urban parts of Amazonia. Many people in the region believe in the power of the evil eye, known in the Brazilian Amazon as *mau olhado* or *quebranto*. Young children are especially vulnerable to the evil eye. If a child is the object of a great deal of admiration, for example, he or she may become weak and feverish. A victim of mau olhado is listless and has little or no desire to eat. Attractive infants, especially girls with soft, blond hair, are particularly prone to the sinister power of the evil eye. Adults, especially strangers or visitors, are deemed responsible for the sudden deterioration of the child's health. People who have just returned from a tiring journey or a strenuous day's work in the field and play with a little girl are likely to trigger quebranto. Lavish attention by outsiders toward children is thus not always welcomed by parents. Illicit sexual desire partly underlies the concept of the evil eye. To ward off its harmful influence, women plant pião roxo, pião branco, vassoura, and rue in their yards, especially by the front entrance to the home.

The concept of the evil eye was born in the Old World. In certain parts of India, for example, parents become apprehensive when a stranger praises a child. An attractive baby is especially susceptible to the dangers of the evil eye. In Thadenpally, a predominately Hindu village near Hyderabad in central India, I saw young girls with a black spot painted on their foreheads in June 1981. The dark smudges were placed there by parents to thwart the evil eye. In Tunisia, children are traditionally dressed in shabby clothes to discourage the attention of the evil eye.

It is not surprising, then, that a plant native to the Mediterranean, rue, serves as a shield against the evil eye among Transamazon settlers. In ancient Greece, the shrub was widely acclaimed for its miraculous powers and was cultivated in Southwest Asia by the time of Christ. In addition to treating a wide variety of ailments, the strong odor of rue leaves has long been thought capable of flushing out witches.

Although the notion of the evil eye comes from the Old World, it has been grafted onto aboriginal ideas about spirit-mothers that live in water. A Transamazon colonist who was born in Pará and lives thirteen kilometers northeast of Altamira claimed that the mother of water (*mãe d'água*) can also cast an evil eye. The mother of water lives in streams, and when a child is bathed in a brook, the mãe d'água may look at the baby and make it ill. Symptoms of such a glance include fever and a glazed look in the child's eyes.

A glimpse from the evil eye can also upset the health of pets, livestock, or plants. In the case of crops and animals, jealousy and spite, rather than sexual desire, are motives for triggering mau olhado. A housewife in Itacoatiara lamented over the fate of her pet woolly monkey when I spoke to her in 1979. She had acquired it from a river trader and the velvet-furred creature soon ingratiated itself with the family. Her children frequently played with the affectionate pet on the front doorstep of their house overlooking the Amazon. One day, the children awoke to find the young monkey had died. Its sudden demise was attributed to a covetous person who had cast an evil eye on the household's favorite pet. Woolly monkeys are notoriously difficult to keep in captivity and frequently succumb to diarrhea and dehydration. The end of this particular monkey, which I had seen in 1977, was nevertheless attributed to sinister causes.

A Transamazon colonist who lives near Altamira recounted another unfortunate experience with the evil eye. One day in 1979, all his chicks began to teeter until two dozen had collapsed and died, all within a couple of hours. The hens and cocks remained in robust health, but their recent progeny stumbled and keeled over. A migrant worker (*peão*), whom the colonist had just dismissed over some dispute, was blamed for the alarming mortality of the chicks. Upon leaving, the dissatisfied peon had apparently cursed the settler's chicks by scowling at them. As in the case of humans, only young animals seem to be affected by the evil eye.

The evil eye can also singe some houseyard plants. It is common to see empty eggshells posted on top of stakes by vegetable gardens, particularly near spring onions. Ornamental agaves are also frequently festooned with white eggshells, thereby protecting the house and garden against mau olhado.

Eggs are also important in treating victims of the evil eye in Mexico. An egg is cracked and placed at the head of the bed in which the child suffering from *mal de ojo* is lying. Eggs symbolize the resurrection of Christ, just as Easter eggs do in North America and Europe. Easter eggs represent the boulder that was rolled away from the tomb of Christ; they therefore symbolize rebirth and the power of the Almighty. By invoking the divine, people feel they derive some protection from the capricious and destructive whims of the evil eye. The eggshells also fertilize vegetables with calcium, which leaks during torrential tropical storms.

Trees, Treasure, and Treachery

Rural folk step into the supernatural in virtually every subsistence and commercial activity they pursue. Hunters may be plagued by the father of game or chased by a forest ogre. Fishermen fear the giant snake and avoid enchanted places. Parents watch for signs that the evil eye has scanned their children. The plant kingdom and mineral deposits are also suffused with spirits, some of which serve to protect resources. Animism in caboclo cosmology thus involves the inorganic as well as the living world. As in the case of game and fish, only plants and minerals of economic significance appear in peasant lore.

One spirit with broad responsibilities in the plant world is John of the forest (*João da mata*). According to a man who lives near Aripuanã, John of the forest is an invisible caretaker who tends to plants, especially those that colonize light gaps in the forest caused by tree falls or clearings for fields. John of the forest promotes the growth of sun-loving plants so that forest scars heal. João da mata sows many of the noxious weeds that invade fields, especially those with prominent hooked thorns, such as jurubeba. John of the forest also disseminates sirica, a stiff, climbing grass with sharp blades that slice the limbs of those who venture into the jungle. No rules of conduct have been established to deal with João da mata. This spirit nurseryman serves to remind people that they do not completely dominate nature. He is there to undo that which man tries to accomplish in the forest. People just have to put up with John of the forest.

Most jungle spirits, though, are assigned specific plants over which they keep watch. Rubber, one of the most important trees in the economic history of Amazonia, has attracted a fair number of tales. Rubber trees are guarded by a spirit mother, just as fish and game have their maternal protectors. Rubber trees grow along the banks of black-, white-, and clear-water rivers, sometimes in groves, but more usually spread out in the forest. Where the trees occur in clumps, people have probably had a hand in the bunched arrangement. Rubber seeds are an important source of food for certain species of fish and are used for bait.

During the latter half of the nineteenth century, a rubber boom swept through Amazonia, spurred by the discovery of the vulcanization process in 1836 and the bicycle craze of the 1890s. In the early part of the twentieth century, mass production of automobiles added impetus to the rubber boom. Hundreds of thousands of men poured into the region and soon fanned out along rivers in search of the lucrative trees. Flamboyant mansions and the Manaus opera house with its Italian tile are testament to the fortunes accrued by the lucky few during the boom, which lasted about fifty years. The Amazon rubber boom collapsed in the 1920s, when plantations of "white gold" were established in Southeast Asia.

Prior to the boom, rubber was not particularly important to the regional economy. Much of the lore surrounding rubber trees has grown up in the last one hundred years or so. Indigenous people had limited use for the tree; its olive-sized fruits were used for fish bait, and the Omagua, who once occupied the floodplain of the upper Amazon, made boots and water bottles from rubber. The Cavina and Tumpasa of the Beni also apparently had some use for rubber, for they believe that the trees are inhabited by spirits that punish those who tap the trees without need.

Although the rubber boom is over, a limited amount of latex is still collected along some rivers. Rubber tappers are frequently heavily indebted to their bosses, from whom they purchase supplies at inflated prices. Tappers live in isolated huts strung along water courses, or in small communities, called *colacações,* in the middle of the forest, particularly in Acre. Typically, a rubber tapper rises early in the morning and sets off along a path leading to a few dozen widely spaced trees. The trees are gashed with a special upturned knife so that the milky sap trickles down a groove into a cup secured to the trunk. The rubber tapper makes a second trip through the forest later in the day to fetch the latex that has collected in pots or kerosene cans. Ammonia is added to retard coagulation, and the tapper returns home to prepare a large ball of rubber. To do this, the tapper prepares a smoky fire and erects a rotating spit, much like that used to turn a pig over a fire, and adds latex to the stick a little at a time.

If tappers have been overzealous in draining sap from rubber trees, the mother of rubber trees (*mãe de seringa*) is likely to encourage the men to relax. The mother of rubber trees is seen on trails cut by tappers, especially on Good Friday. The mother of rubber trees is short and has long, dark or fair hair. She can always be distinguished from other spirit-mothers by her bleeding arms and legs, which look as if they been gouged by a rubber tapper's knife. She only appears to those who have been slicing rubber trees too deeply. A rubber tree can withstand a daily cut during the tapping season, but the wound must be light and not too extensive. Each day a fresh, slanting cut is made below and parallel to the previous one; in this manner, the mottled bark has a

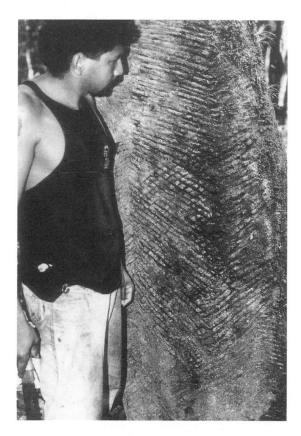

Figure 9.1. Herringbone scar pattern from repeated tappings of an old rubber tree. Combu Island, Amazon estuary, near Belém, Pará, 15 December 1994.

chance to heal. Older rubber trees are thus often adorned with a herringbone pattern of scars (figure 9.1). If the tree is cut more than once a day, or if the gashes are too long and deep, the tree dies. Mãe de seringa becomes upset when people abuse her children, and caboclos take her seriously because she can steal a person's shadow.

The story of a rubber tapper, told by a man in his sixties who lives along the upper Rio Negro, illustrates the power of the mother of rubber trees. Some years ago, a man had set up a temporary camp on Ilha do Silva, a short trip down the Negro from Tapurucuara, for the duration of the four- to six-month rubber-tapping season. As usual, he had been grubstaked by a patron so that he could devote his energies to collecting latex. The tapper had rung up a hefty bill with his boss to stock up on provisions. Unfortunately, though, the trees were not cooperating that year and the patron was growing impatient with the paltry production. Spurred by an admonishment from his patrão, the tapper began inflicting frequent and severe wounds on the rubber trees along his zig-zagging trail in a desperate effort to extract more latex. One day he was gashing the trunk of a rubber tree when something tapped him on the shoulder. He immediately spun around and to his amazement came face to face with an ugly, light-skinned woman. "You are mistreating my daughters, draining away all their blood," observed the hag with fair, unkempt hair. "Stop cutting them," she instructed.

The tapper explained his predicament to the mother of rubber trees. "My patron is pressuring me to come up with more rubber to pay off my debts," he replied, "but the trees seem to be drying up and I am destitute." The mãe de seringa felt compassion and decided to help the beleaguered man. A deal was struck. The mother of rubber trees agreed to leave a large ball of smoked latex in the fire-hut every night from October until March if the tapper would leave her daughters alone. The man was warned never to tell anyone about their accord, otherwise he would remain with her. The tapper thus spent the remainder of the season loafing, hunting, fishing, and making easy money.

During the next tapping cycle, the same arrangement was made with the mother of rubber trees. When the tapper brought the first consignment of rubber balls to the floating warehouse operated by his patrão, the boss and his employees were surprised at the tapper's productivity. The huge load delivered by canoe was much larger than normal, and the men remarked on his change of fortune. Flush with cash, the satisfied tapper immediately bought a bottle of *cachaça*, a cheap, white rum, and started drinking with some of his less fortunate friends who had also arrived to sell their produce. The potent sugarcane alcohol, referred to as fire-water by the initiated, soon took effect. Before long, the exuberant tapper was boasting aloud about the special arrangement he enjoyed with mãe de seringa. Upon returning home, the tapper went into the forest, where he was bitten by a venomous snake and died. A neighbor later found his crumpled body lying by the trail leading to the rubber trees. The tapper's death was attributed to his indiscretion in revealing the nature of his relationship with the mother of rubber trees.

The mother of rubber trees makes appearances in widely scattered locations in the Amazon basin. Along the Xingu River, for example, a sixty-year-old farmer and fisherman recounted an encounter that a friend of his had with mãe de seringa in 1950. The elderly gentleman was interviewed in April 1991 along the waterfront at Altamira as he tied up his canoe to deliver a request (*encomenda*) for yellow mombim fruits. The storyteller's friend was severely cutting rubber trees on Ilha de Farol when an old, thin hag appeared and warned him to be careful with the way he was cutting the trees. The tapper never returned to the island.

The mother of rubber trees is not alone in protecting her children from the abuse of man. Curupira, normally associated with game, sometimes intercedes against tappers if they harm rubber trees. Raimundo Nonato, a middle-aged Transamazon settler who has spent all his life in the vicinity of Itaituba, recalled an experience he had with curupira in the 1940s. Raimundo was hacking a path through the jungle near Rio Tapacurazão to connect some dispersed rubber trees when he heard a loud "hee-hee-hee." A curupira came close, but Raimundo was unable to see it. Raimundo put some tobacco on a fallen log for the waif and left the area. It would be unwise to persist in cutting a path in that section of the forest.

Curupira is not always so lenient toward rubber tappers. Several decades ago, a man who lived along the Tapajós was slashing rubber trees deeply to force them to release their sap more freely. One day as he was slicing the bark of a rubber tree, a small black boy came from behind and whipped him with a length of vine. The bewildered tapper ran home and soon developed a high fever. He lingered on the threshold of a coma in his hammock for two months before he succumbed. The man was only thirty years old and in apparent good health until he rushed into his hut one day mumbling about an encounter with curupira. The sudden onslaught of fever and the tapper's subsequent death were attributed to soul loss.

Amazonian peasants collect a poorer grade of rubber from balata trees that belong to several genera and species, and tales have sprung up about these inferior latex-bearing trees. Balata trees, like most plant species in the forest, are widely scattered, so balata gatherers must trim a winding path through the jungle. Instead of cutting the trunks several times a week, balata trees are wounded every few months or years. If balata trees are gashed more frequently, they usually die. Furthermore, the cuts are more widely spaced, thus requiring a climb up the trunk to make the diagonal slashes. The sap oozes into a metal basin where it thickens. Later it is fashioned into one-centimeter-thick hides. Formerly, a brisk trade developed in balata to supply insulation for cables, for use in medicine, and to manufacture golf balls. With the introduction of synthetic rubber, however, balata prices tumbled, and the latex is now collected sporadically.

In the 1800s and the early part of the twentieth century, balata gathering provided seasonal employment for many caboclos throughout the Amazon. Not surprisingly, then, a colorful lore has accumulated around balata trees. The role of spirit protector of these jungle trees is played by cabokinha, rather than curupira, as in the case of the rubber tree. Cabokinha is similar to curupira, but smaller, and it prefers to live among the trees it protects. One of cabokinha's roles, then, is to serve as the mother of balata trees (*mãe de balateira*). Furthermore, cabokinha can be a boy or girl, whereas curupira is usually masculine. Some people, though, refer to curupira as mother of the forest. Cabokinha makes a long, plaintive whining sound, unlike the abrupt call of curupira, the shrill whistle of a matin, or the deafening roar of the ferocious mapinguary.

One day near the margin of the Rio Branco in Roraima, a man was up a balata trunk collecting latex when he noticed that a cabokinha was cutting the base of the tree. He could see that the sap was hemorrhaging quickly and that the loss was undercutting his efforts, so the enraged *balateiro* slid down to the ground and struck the cabokinha. The response of the mother of balata trees was swift and brutal: the aggressive tapper was punished harshly, although he was much bigger than his foe. The bruised, bleeding, and exhausted man nevertheless managed to escape the incensed mãe de balateira and limp home.

The mother of balata trees can be helpful if tappers treat her with respect and listen to her. An old man who lives along the upper reaches of the Negro recounted a cabokinha story involving another tapper. One day, a man was up a balata tree when a cabokinha appeared at the foot of the tree and made some cuts. Instead of losing his temper, however, the balateiro came down and politely greeted the cabokinha. The balata gatherer urged cabokinha to go ahead with what she was doing. The mother of balata trees was pleased with the man, for he was considerate. "You are a good man," said the spirit-mother. "I am going to give you milk; you are patient." Cabokinha offered to tap the balata trees from Monday until Thursday each week and to deliver the latex to the tapper's hut. In return, the man was asked to bring two bottles of cachaça and some tobacco on Fridays so that she could celebrate. The tapper readily agreed. Under no circumstances, though, was the balateiro to venture into the forest on Fridays other than to deliver the presents. The tapper kept his promise and was thus free to hunt and fish from Monday to Thursday and to relax over the extended weekends.

The importance of Friday in stories about mother of trees and other supernatural entities illustrates again the influence of Christianity. Friday is at least as sacred as Sunday in caboclo lore. An unusual number of supernatural creatures are active on that day. Cabokinha enjoys imbibing on Friday and does not take kindly to intruders. The mother of rubber trees is most likely to appear on Friday of Easter week, which for some parts of Amazonia is during the rubber tapping season. One hunter remarked that he was reluctant to hunt on Fridays because he might upset curupira. Mysterious lights are especially evident in the forest and along the margins of rivers and lakes on Fridays. And panema cures are normally performed on that day. The supernatural creeps close to the surface of everyday reality on Fridays because the day signifies the crucifixion of Christ, a day when the divine was put to death, although He later came back to life. Friday represents a brief period when God seemed to have lost temporarily his power on earth, for Jesus was not rescued from the cross. The appearance of the mother of rubber trees on Passion Friday with her sliced arms and legs is particularly poignant. Christ also suffered considerable abuse that day, including a crown of thorns and a spear thrust into his side.

A spirit protector is associated with another Amazonian tree that enters into the regional commerce. Piaçava palm grows on periodically flooded sand patches in the Rio Negro watershed, where it produces a thicket of dark brown fibers that extend from the base of the fronds down the trunk to the ground. The bulky coat of long bristles is cut by hand, bound into elongated bundles, and sent downriver to Manaus, where the fibers are fashioned into brooms, brushes, doormats, and crude rope. In the last century, considerable quantities of piaçava palm bristles collected from the Rio Negro watershed were exported to Europe and North America via Belém. Richard Spruce, an intrepid Yorkshire botanist who spent more than a decade in the Amazon during the mid-nineteenth century, described a stroll through a grove of piaçava palms thus:

> Nothing that I have seen in Amazonian forests dwells more strongly and pleasantly on my memory than my walk among these strange bearded columns, from whose apex sprang the green interlacing arches which shaded me overhead. . . .To have escaped from the cloud of mosquitos on the bank of the river no doubt enhanced the enjoyment.[1]

Gathering piaçava strands is an unenviable task, however. Ants, spiders, scorpions, and blood-sucking reduviid bugs lurk in the hirsute palm, and the fibers sometimes have to be hauled through extensive swampy forest before they can be loaded onto a canoe or boat. Piaçava gatherers typically beat the bearded palm to dislodge some of unwelcome creatures before the bristles are cut.

An elderly informant from the Rio Negro recalled an unusual experience that happened to his uncle while he was looking for piaçava palm. The uncle had been combing the forest in the vicinity of Rio Preto, an affluent of the Negro about one and a half day's motorboat journey above Barcelos, but he was not having much luck. The groves of piaçava he found had all been recently cut. The uncle grew worried because he was short of cash and his patron was pressuring him for payment. One day, as he walked along a narrow jungle trail, he came upon a woman sitting on a thick branch that had fallen across the path. The woman did not pay him any attention and continued to stroke her thick, coarse hair with a comb made with stiff piaçava bristles. Her hair was long and looked like strands of piaçava, only it was light colored. The uncle halted abruptly. It was most peculiar for a woman to be alone in the forest, especially so far from any settlement. The man's amazement soon turned to curiosity, so he proceeded along the trail. As he did so, however, the woman stopped grooming, got up, and walked down the path away from him. Her cascading hair dragged behind her like a bridal train. Shortly, the silent lady turned off the path, looked back momentarily to make sure that she was still being followed, then vanished into the wall of trees. The uncle hurried to the spot where the intriguing woman had left the trail, but he could not see her. He entered the trackless forest to seek her out, but to no avail. Although he could not find the elusive lady, he soon happened upon a virgin piaçava grove with plenty of mature palms reading for trimming.

That night, after an arduous day of harvesting piaçava, the uncle quickly fell asleep. In a dream, *mãe de piaçava* appeared to him. "I felt sorry for you, that is why I led you to the virgin piaçava grove," she said. "Please cut piaçava properly and do not destroy it," pleaded the mother of piaçava before departing. The nephew asserted that God had sent the mother of piaçava in answer to his uncle's prayers.

Another illustration of the fusion of Catholic and indigenous religions surfaces in a tale involving piaçava gatherers and a curupira. A widowed lady now residing in Tapurucuara on the upper Rio Negro remembered a close call her son had with a curupira while the family was cutting the medium-statured palm in the headwater region of the Rio Parahá. Her son, then nine years old, was enticed away from his parents by a hairy, boylike creature with its feet turned backward. The curupira invited the curious fellow to follow him, which he willingly did. Soon the mother and father noticed that their son was no longer with them, so they called out. When he did not reply, they became anxious. The parents surmised that the mother of the forest (*mãe da mata*) was responsible for their son's disappearance, so they made a cross of sticks and placed it on the trail they had made to some piaçava palms. The parents then prayed, and the spell that held their son captive was broken. The lost son finally responded to their urgent calls. But when they found their son, he was afraid and quite unlike himself. He did not recognize either the informant or his father, nor did he seem relieved to see them. The son behaved oddly, like a zombie. He had clearly been assombrado by the curupira.

The parents escorted their soulless boy home and promptly contacted a folk curer, who treated his transfixed patient with a ritual smoking using the blood-red resin of the caraña tree. The child then regained his sanity. The interviewed lady referred to curupira as mother of the forest, thus underscoring the creature's wider responsibilities in addition to protecting game. The widow asserted that her family never ventured into the headwaters of the Parahá again. Whether spirit-mothers punish people if they abuse trees or scare them away, the result is the same: reduced pressure on natural resources.

The notion of curupira watching over certain trees, such as piaçava, appears to be rooted in indigenous cultures. Indians of the Guinía River, a tributary of the Uaupés in the Colombian Amazon, believe that curupira inhabits piaçava groves at night in the form of a snake. Accordingly, Indians in those remote parts only collect piaçava in groups by day. The idea of spirit protectors of trees is apparently widespread among indigenous cultures in the region. The Aguarana of the Peruvian Amazon, for example, believe that the mente tree is sacred because it is inhabited by forest deities.

Not all encounters with the supernatural while gathering forest products are related to conservation of resources, however. Some spirits are willing to help people make an easy living and are eager to fulfill some of their innermost yearnings. The case of two friends who were collecting latex from sorva illustrates the benevolent nature of an individual who straddled two worlds. The sweet sap of sorva trees is gathered to make an inferior grade of rubber and to stir into porridges. The refreshing taste of sorva latex is widely appreciated; overindulgence, though, is reputed to cause constipation. The following story was recounted by a fisherman in Itapiranga along the middle Amazon.

While a group of sorva gatherers was working the forest along the Uatumã, a left-bank tributary of the middle Amazon River, the two men became firm friends. One was a closet matin. He used to travel to Parintins on Saturdays to join parties. The group of sorva gatherers thought it was odd that on the following day, he recounted events that happened in a town many hours' boat ride away. One day, the matin and his workmate were tapping sorva trees together when the friend remarked on how much he missed his wife and children. The matin revealed his true identity and asked him if he had sufficient courage to fly with him. The matin promised to drop his friend off at home on the way to Parintins. It was Saturday, and they agreed to leave that night. After the group had fallen asleep, the matin appeared at the edge of the large makeshift hut the team had erected and called his friend. When the matin jumped for the third time, his friend leaped on his back and clutched tightly. The pair then took off.

When the matin arrived over his passenger's home, he dropped out of the night sky and let his friend off. The latter was warned not to reveal himself to his family. He could only watch from a distance. The matin then sprang into the air with the promise that he would stop by a few hours later on his way back from Parintins. The passenger felt hot from the journey, so he took off his shirt and left it by the path leading to his home. He made a mental note to don it once again before departure. The man proceeded eagerly to his hut and peered through gaps in the walls. He could see his wife and children asleep, and he wanted to join them. But he held back.

In the early hours of the morning, the matin reappeared and told his friend to hop on. It was only when they had landed at the long hut containing the sleeping sorva tappers that he remembered his shirt. The next morning, his wife was puzzled to find one of her husband's sweaty shirts by the path near their home. She washed it and kept it for his return. When he was through with sorva gathering, the man went home and his wife brought up the incident of finding one of his soaking wet shirts draped by the path near their home. It was then that the man realized he could not have been dreaming when he made the visit.

Diamond seekers, gold miners, hunters, and fishermen encounter ghostly figures and strange lights during the day and at night while they seek food or fortune in forests, lakes, and rivers. Gold and diamonds do not appear to have been mined by Amazonian Indians, although deposits of the metal and the precious stones are extensive in the region. Diamonds are encountered in the watersheds of the Tocantins and Rio Branco, and people pan for gold in widely scattered locations in the Amazon basin.

Gold was important to the Incas and Chibchas of the Andean chain, where it was fashioned into intricate jewelry, but little trade in the precious metal developed among Amazonian tribes, a great disappointment to the early explorers. The Omagua and the Manau were the only tribes in the region that kept appreciable amounts of gold when they were first visited by Europeans in the sixteenth century. The Manau, after whom the capital of Amazonas state in Brazil is named, obtained their gold from the Chibchas of the Colombian Andes either through direct trade by ascending the Caquetá or through intermediaries. The Manau reportedly melted and hammered gold to fashion ornaments for their ears and noses. Most of the lore surrounding gold and diamonds has thus accumulated since the beginning of the colonial period, particularly in the twentieth century. The notion of spirit activity and precious stones and ores is traced in part to medieval European ideas of supernatural beings guarding treasure.

According to a native of Pará state who was based in Aripuanã in 1979, fresh gold fields are often haunted. In Amazonia, gold is not mined in deep shafts because it is encountered in relatively shallow alluvial deposits that require surface digging and the washing of gravel to uncover gold nuggets and particles. The storyteller, a bachelor in his thirties, had spent many years panning for gold in the Tapajós drainage and in Rondônia. Pará recalled seeing ghosts drifting above claims that he had just staked out, always a sure sign that the find would be rewarding. One night, while lounging in his hammock, Pará remembered hearing the clang of shovels and the rattle of gravel. It sounded as though someone was trying to usurp his claim under the cover of darkness, so Pará grabbed his flashlight and shotgun and went to investigate. But no one was to be seen and the ground remained unbroken. As soon as he began work on the find, the apparitions and nocturnal mining sounds promptly ceased. No fear of the unusual sights and sounds associated with the virgin gold field was expressed. "Everything that is admirable has mystery," explained Pará.

Yaras sometimes dwell near mineral deposits and protect them from human greed. Pará recounted the experience of a couple of men with a yara when they were after gold. One afternoon, two miners camped close to a spectacular waterfall on the Rio Urucu, an affluent of the twisting Sucurundi. Hidden gold deposits were rumored to exist under the forest that cloaks the banks of the river, and the men had noticed jaguar and tapir tracks in the vicinity of their camp, a sure sign that people had not tarried there recently. As the men were settling into their hammocks for the night, they noticed a sleek ocelot in the warm glow of their campfire. As the yellow-and-black-spotted cat padded softly by them, the miners jumped up and reached for their guns, for the pelt of a full-grown ocelot fetches a handsome price. But their shotguns were not where they had left them. The guns had unaccountably moved. By the time the men located their weapons, the jungle cat had slipped into the enveloping darkness. The prospectors had scarcely returned to their hammocks when a fair-skinned woman strode into their camp. She was statuesque and pretty, with long blonde hair. The yara warned the miners that they had better leave the river. She explained further that two other men who ignored her advice had vanished. The apparition then disappeared. The men broke camp the following morning and retreated.

Other unusual sightings are reported around suspected mineral deposits. The case of a hunter who shot a deer at night along the Marabá-Altamira stretch of the Transamazon Highway and watched an orange light rise up from the kill has already been mentioned. The incandescent globe wandered about the vicinity of the deer for about half an hour before melting back into the slain animal. Instead of interpreting the glowing ball as the spirit of the deer or a messenger from the father of game, the hunter assumed that some mineral lay beneath the spot where the prey had fallen.

Another Transamazon colonist who lives at kilometer forty-eight of the Marabá-Altamira stretch of the highway attributed the presence of a poltergeist (*assombração*) around his home to minerals somewhere in the vicinity. On some nights, the door and walls of his wooden house are pounded heavily. And one day, while his eight-year-old daughter was bathing in a nearby stream, a stern voice commanded her to leave the water. The terrified child raced home and told her father. When the informant went to the creek to investigate, he noted that a bush rustled, even though no breeze cooled the hot afternoon. He called out and inspected the shrub but could find no trace of an intruder. The site of the informant's home was covered by dense jungle a few years ago, so he doubted the poltergeist could be a human spirit. Metal ore lying underground nearby was deemed responsible for the spirit's antics.

Fishermen and river travelers also come upon supernatural manifestations of mineral deposits. An enchanted place at the Belo Monte rapids along the Xingu is reported to harbor some precious metal that has yet to be discovered. Human voices beckon from below the churning water, and one should not linger. A fearsome giant snake also patrols the enchanted spot. The origin of the enchanted place at Belo Monte is not clear, but it is surely related to people who drowned. The addition of a cobra grande at the scene was interpreted by a farmer who has lived all his life in the environs of Altamira as a sure sign that minerals lie buried in the vicinity.

Precious stones have sparked the creation of some imaginative tales. Diamonds are the only gems mined in Amazonia, and Indians appear never to have placed much value on them. Jadeite and soapstone were held in much higher regard by aborigines, and these semiprecious stones became coveted trade items. The Tapajó and Trombetas, for example, once fashioned ornaments, such as frogs, from gray soapstone and green jadeite. *Garimpeiros* used to pan for diamonds at low water along the sandy and gravelly bed of stretches of the Tocantins, before a substantial stretch was flooded by the Tucuruí reservoir. A limited amount of diamond mining may still occur above the reservoir, but it is no longer a significant activity because the river appears to have been largely picked over. Diamond seekers have been working the Tocantins for at least a century. Diamonds continue to be panned in recent alluvial soils in parts of Roraima. Individuals employ metal basins to swill the river sands, or teams operate from boats equipped with oxygen pumps that permit divers to work below for extended periods. Divers with oxygen masks direct tubes that suck gravel up to the boat, where it is sifted and washed.

Several enchanted places familiar to diamond seekers have arisen along the Tocantins. One famous lugar encantado, called Mineiro, is located on an island in the middle of the broad river. According to an itinerant peasant who used to pan for the clear, hard stones in the dry season and collect Brazil nuts during the rainy months, a blue flame rises from isolated and rocky Mineiro.

When the glow, which resembles a ball of burning gas, reaches tree-top height, it bursts into a blinding flash and disappears. The stretch of river around Mineiro is known for its large diamonds, and the volatile glow is considered confirmation of the area's wealth. The short-lived light does not bother those who keep a respectable distance, but few miners venture on to the island in search of the translucent gems.

Poção das Cruvina, another enchanted place along the Tocantins where the river joins the Cajazeiras, also allegedly keeps diamond miners at bay. The area surrounding the confluence of the rivers became the scene of feverish mining activity in the early 1940s, when the sparkling stones were uncovered in abundance. In 1943, a man drowned at Poção das Cruvina as a result of a canoe accident; thereafter, the place became enchanted. Divers began reporting an enormous underwater snake. The anaconda-like serpent would circle the men as they descended to the river bottom to prospect for diamonds. The creature was clearly not an anaconda, though, because its face constantly changed. One minute a human was grinning at the diver, the next instant a wide-eyed cat stared at him, and then a dog's face appeared on the head of the chameleon snake. The kaleidoscope serpent did not ordinarily attack miners, until one day it cruised so close to a diver that he became scared and struck at the beast with his knife. The weapon only grazed the scaly creature, but the snake turned on its attacker with vengeance, squeezing and nearly killing him. Thereafter, the ever-changing serpent would not allow any more miners to work in the area.

A varied cast of ethereal creatures is thus charged with the protection of some economically important trees and mineral deposits. A theme common to the stories of rubber, balata, and sorva tappers, as well as piaçava gatherers, is that people should be careful with the trees so that they are not unduly harmed and remain productive. The same motif is apparent in much of the lore of hunters and fishermen and also serves to conserve the resources they tap. Another common thread weaving through the tales is the importance of showing kindness and respect. The tapper who is courteous to the mother of balata trees is rewarded with an abundant supply of latex in exchange for modest presents of tobacco and alcohol. If someone strikes a supernatural entity, he or she is likely to be severely punished. The mother of balata trees almost knocked a tapper unconscious when challenged, and a giant snake almost crushed a diamond miner to death when attacked. Spirits of the forest and waters can be helpful, but it is deemed foolish to question their authority.

Haunted Streets

The supernatural in the world view of Amazonian peasants docs not stop at the entrance to villages. Streets and back alleys of settlements can also harbor strange apparitions and startling sounds. For the most part, a new supernatural cast takes over when a person steps into a village or a small town, although some spiritual entities are common to the forest trail and dark sidewalks. The lore of hunters, fishermen, and miners deals primarily with restrained use of natural resources and respectful conduct to others, whereas the ghosts and animal spirits lurking in urban environments touch mainly upon moral and ethical questions. Caboclos are thus not only concerned with a plentiful supply of game, fish, and plant products but are also watchful for behavior that departs from acceptable standards.

Rural folk generally frown upon eccentric or promiscuous conduct, and several tales reflect a desire to warn people of the consequences of licentious acts. Frightening stories are testament to the unhappy fate of those who engage in sex before marriage, bed down with those of the same gender, pursue incestuous relationships, argue incessantly with their mothers, horde wealth, drink heavily, or are loud and boisterous. Many of the supernatural events stirred by deviant behavior occur in and around houses, especially at night.

Homosexuality may be widely tolerated in the larger Brazilian cities, but people generally look askance at such behavior in towns and villages. At least one nocturnal spirit in Amazonia haunts people as a reminder of the potential

Figure 10.1. A street scene in Itupiranga, a village along the Tocantins River, Pará, in 1973. As with many villages in the Amazon, residents have reported seeing or hearing various supernatural apparitions, including *matintaperera* and a giant black sow.

outcome of such sexual appetites. According to a fifty-year-old lady who runs a single-story inn out of her home in Itupiranga (figure 10.1), a small village on the left bank of the Tocantins, matintaperera can be the fate of a woman who has slept with another female. One evening in 1977, Dona Maraquinha recalled hearing the characteristic whistle of a matin flying over her house-cum-hotel around ten o'clock. If a matin buzzes one's home, Dona Maraquinha explained to me in 1979, the best recourse is to say aloud, "I'll give you a piece of tobacco." Then the first person to knock on your door the next morning will be someone mooching a cigarette.

Women who prefer male partners but who succumb to carnal temptations outside the bonds of matrimony are also candidates for becoming a matin. Raimundo Freitas, a fifty-year-old Transamazon colonist who lives eight kilometers from Itupiranga, suspects that an old woman who resides in Itupiranga is responsible for at least some of the reported sightings of a matin in the riverside village. The sloppily dressed female is reported to have had an undiscriminating history of sexual relationships, and she wanders the potholed streets by day mumbling incoherently. At night her appearance and behavior sometimes become even more alarming. She has been seen to exit her hovel at sunset and ply the dimly lit streets with her unkempt hair hiding her face. She occasionally lets out a sharp, unprovoked yell, as if possessed, as well as a loud, prolonged whistle: "feeeet." Raimundo almost bumped into her one night as he turned a dark street corner. "Take these cigarettes and begone," Raimundo ordered, and she went on her way without uttering a word. After her nocturnal sorties, the ugly old matin normally sleeps in late.

A sixty-eight-year-old colonist who lives along the Transamazon sixty kilometers northwest of Marabá remembered hearing the story of a matin in Tucuruí on the left bank of the Tocantins. In 1947, the wife of the mayor of the village, now a bustling town following completion of the Tucuruí dam, heard a matin passing over her home one night, so she called out, "Come by in the morning for some tobacco." Soon after sunrise, an old black lady turned up at the mayor's house. "I've come to pick up what you promised me," she said when the mayor's wife opened the door. The wife then instructed her son to go to a nearby store and purchase some tobacco for the old lady. After receiving her gift, the matin walked away. The old lady was well known in the community; she was a gypsy, reportedly a woman of loose morals who liked to strum the guitar and sing.

Many towns and villages along the Tocantins and other rivers in Amazonia harbor stories of matin. A thirty-six-year-old boatman who works on the Tocantins informed me that a matin lives in Cametá on the lower stretch of the river. José Vasconcellos, who was residing in Tucuruí when interviewed in 1988, asserted that a sure way to identify a suspected matin is to peer into its bedroom at night; a matin will appear headless. According to José, only females can become matintapereras, whereas in other parts of the basin, matin is thought to be male. In the last century, for example, descendants of the Manáos tribe claimed that *matinta perera* is a sorcerer who plays a flute. This Jekyll-and-Hyde-like creature is familiar to Brazilians in other parts of their vast country and has been incorporated into a popular song, *Águas de Março* (Waters of March), by a number of artists, including Elis Regina and Tom Jobim.

José Vasconcellos recounted a personal experience he had with a matin along the Mendaruçu River, an affluent of the Tocantins, when he was younger. José was playing dominoes at his uncle's house along the Mendaruçu when they heard a loud whistle, "fi-fi-fi-tinta-perera." The next morning, a forty-five-year-old lady appeared at the uncle's home requesting some tobacco. The lady was known to the uncle; she lived along a nearby river, the Rio Furtado. The storyteller pointed out that if the matin's request is denied, she will attack one night in a dark place. Tobacco is frequently offered to assuage the supernatural, particularly when people encounter the father of game, spirit-mothers of trees, or a matin. But it is not foolproof. No one, for example, claimed to have tended tobacco to a cobra grande.

Matin is not the only fate of promiscuous women. Some lascivious females turn into giant black pigs that wander through villages at night upsetting dogs and disturbing people. Horace, a Transamazon colonist who once lived in Coco Chato (figure 10.2), near Itupiranga, remembered a startling experience he had around eight o'clock one evening in 1976. He was walking up the hilly entrance to Coco Chato from the Transamazon Highway when an enormous dark sow charged at him from the direction of the general store, which had closed for the day. Luckily, Horace had a shotgun with him, so he fired at the onrushing *porca* and it broke off the attack. Horace speculated that the massive sow is a lass of many sins who probably resides in Itupiranga. He doubted that any ladies in Coco Chato are thus cursed. Caboclo lore is certainly creative; a community of sixty-six houses began to acquire some supernatural tales only five years after it was built by the Brazilian government.

Figure 10.2. Coco Chato twenty years after it was established in forest and old second growth. Km 42 of the Marabá-Altamira stretch of the Transamazon Highway, Pará, 10 November 1992.

Century-old Itupiranga has also been plagued by a boisterous black pig. *Porca de bobi,* so named because it sports hair rollers on its head, is an enormous sow that occasionally prowls the streets at night, especially around the village square. According to Dona Maraquinha, who has lived in Itupiranga for several decades, the restless pig is an unmarried hag whose virtue is open to question. At night, the woman of dubious moral standards attempts to improve her sad appearance by setting her hair with bobby pins that accompany her as she turns into a sow and bounds out of her bedroom window.

The big black pig is not confined to villages of the Tocantins valley. Informants have mentioned its capers in towns up the Amazon as far as Itapiranga in Amazonas and along the Xingu in Pará. A Transamazon colonist who has lived most of his life in the vicinity of Altamira mentioned the case of *porca velha* that used to appear around the Hotel Altamira on certain nights in the 1970s. The porca was exceptionally tall and had a jet-black hide covering a heavy body. A friend of the informant was walking along a street near the hotel with a lady of the evening late one night in 1975 when a pig lunged at them. The man bolted and was saved by some dogs that chased the pugnacious sow away. "It is people who have this destiny," explained the highway settler. Ambushes by the mischievous pig continued for some time, until finally a man stabbed the creature as it rushed him. The next day, an old black woman was found with a deep puncture wound in her arm. Before time robbed the woman of her nubile beauty, she had allegedly earned her living as a prostitute.

The legendary big black pig arose in postcontact times. The pig was domesticated in Asia and only introduced to the New World in colonial times. Where the first big pig story arose is unclear, but it was probably in northern or central Brazil. Many years ago in Belém, a large pig used to rush along the 28th of September Street in the Reduto district every night at ten o'clock. It always followed the same course, from Magalhães square to the stream of souls. The pig apparently had no owner, and some suspected that an old lady who came from the area of the stream every morning and spent the day in Magalhães Square had something to do with the pig. Residents of the afflicted street resolved to kill the ownerless pig and eventually were able to club and stone the elusive animal to death. The next morning, some residents of the 28th of September Street returned to the scene of the fatal encounter and instead of finding the dead pig, came upon an old woman, battered and deceased. In Cuiabá, the capital of Mato Grosso, pregnant women who conduct extramarital affairs reputedly turn into large, nocturnal sows. The porca of Cuiabá is followed by a string of piglets representing the souls of her aborted children. Stories of the big black pig thus incorporate Roman Catholic concerns about fidelity in marriage and the sanctity of human life.

Bizarre punishments for transgressing rules of sexual behavior are not meted out to women alone. Fathers who make love to their daughters may also transform into strange nocturnal beasts. Along the Rio Negro, for example, a type of cow sometimes grazes around houses, especially old ones. The creature, referred to as *lobizoni* by a lady in Tapurucuara, is no ordinary cow. It feeds at night, walks on three legs, and has a multicolored hide of reds, yellows, and browns. Lobizoni lows like a cow, but its eyes glow with a blue light, similar to that described as coming from the eyes of the giant water serpent. People should avoid staring into the eyes of a lobizoni at all costs; otherwise they will be immobilized and lose their souls. According to the storyteller of Indian extraction, lobizonis are men who did not "respect" their daughters.

Double standards, so prevalent in society, are thus reflected in lore. Only men who commit incest are prone to supernatural punishment. Young lads are almost encouraged to explore their sexual prowess, and the maintenance of "mistresses" is a widespread custom for married men in Brazil and many other parts of Latin America. As long as a husband is a good provider and tends to his family needs, dalliances with other women are usually tolerated, and even condoned. Such ideas are losing their hold, however, as more strict Protestant sects gain more adherents and women strive for a more even playing field in society.

The designation of lobizoni for the three-legged cow demonstrates the influence of European culture. Lobizoni is probably a corruption of *lobishomem*, or "wolf-man." Werewolves are strictly an Old World invention; no tales in Amazonia are told of people turning into wolves. Werewolf stories are confined to books and films in Brazil, mainly for consumption by the middle and upper classes in urban areas. Cattle were introduced to Amazonia in colonial times, a further illustration of the creative blend of folkloric traditions in the region.

Immoderate consumption of alcohol can also trigger unexpected and potentially dangerous supernatural repercussions. Apart from the obvious propensity of people who have imbibed too much to exaggerate events, tales involving alcohol have an underlying message: excessive drinking is unwise. Coffins with wills of their own, dog-spirits, human ghosts, and some enchanted places are all poised to scare those who allow themselves to become inebriated.

A seventy-eight-year-old gentleman who lives in Itupiranga and has spent most of his life in the Tocantins valley collecting Brazil nuts, panning for diamonds, and farming recalled a startling event that happened to him in 1922. It was late, close to midnight, when he gulped down his last shot of cachaça and left the small riverfront bar in Itupiranga for home. Bernardino was about halfway to his house when an uneasy feeling crept over him. Something was wrong, and his heartbeat quickened. In the shadow of a building in front of him a shape seemed to be waiting for him. It had no legs or smell, but when Bernardino drew close, it growled and leapt at him. Although the alcohol Bernardino had been drinking had doubtless taken its toll, he was able to dodge the coffin-shaped box. Bernardino pulled a knife and turned around to face his opponent. The coffin charged again, stirring up a dust cloud. When the nimble box was almost upon him, Bernardino tried to stab it, but in vain. The coffin was much too agile. It was as much as he could do to avoid getting knocked down.

After several more narrow escapes and futile attempts to wound the coffin, Bernardino realized that the encounter was reaching a climax. Something had to give. During a brief pause in the melee, Bernardino steeled himself for the final onslaught. With knife raised, he raced toward the squat box. This time, the coffin took off down the street and vanished. Bernardino was even more puzzled by its abrupt disappearance, because the moon was shining brightly, and he could see that the box had not taken a side street. The next day Bernardino returned to the scene of his harrowing experience and found the earth considerably disturbed. Although *caixão* never made another appearance, Bernardino, who was then a young lad, recalled curtailing his drinking hours for some time after the incident.

Bernardino, who enjoys telling stories and gossiping in the evenings from his wicker rocking chair placed on the sidewalk in front of his house, remembered meeting another supernatural creature he attributed to excessive drinking by others and murder. A large white dog (*cachorrão*), the size of a fully grown great dane, used to scare people in the older section of Itupiranga near the Catholic church and especially along Beco Maria Joana, a side street. The giant dog only appeared between eight o'clock in the evening and midnight and would alarm people by jumping up on their chests. Although the creature never clamped its sizable jaws on anyone, nor entered homes, it sometimes scratched pedestrians with its sturdy claws. The dog had a shaggy coat, a broad head, and floppy ears about the size of a man's hand.

One Sunday evening the dog irked a pious man who was dressed in his best for mass. The gentleman was walking to church when the creature appeared and immediately reared up, placing its enormous, muddy paws on his clean, white shirt. The dog then vanished, but the man was obliged to return and change into fresh clothes. Another man was surprised by the white dog and slipped; while on the ground he unsheathed a knife and lunged at the beast on top of him. Instead of penetrating the canine attacker, however, the dagger glanced off its tough hide. The terrified man clung to the dog's thick coat until it backed off and evaporated into the darkness. When the man regained his feet, he noticed that he was clutching three hairs, about fifteen centimeters long, in one hand. The beast behaved like a ghost, yet it had a solid, physical appearance. Several individuals tried to shoot the ownerless hound because it set the village dogs barking and howling in unison, thereby keeping people awake at night. But no one could wound the elusive creature.

Bernardino claimed to have seen the giant white dog several decades ago. One night, one of Bernardino's pigs came bolting into the house squealing with fear. This was most unusual behavior because pigs are never allowed in homes and are severely reprimanded if they venture out of bounds. Bernardino decided to go outside and investigate, although his wife urged him to remain in the home and to close all the doors and windows. Bernardino picked up a small lantern and stepped, barefoot, into the night. In the faint glow of his kerosene lamp, Bernardino made out the profile of an enormous snow-white dog sitting on its haunches. The hound looked at him for a moment and then ambled off. Bernardino followed, but when he looked down for an instant to make sure that he was not going to step on anything sharp and then looked up, the dog was gone.

Bernardino suggested that the supernatural canine was the soul of a man who died in a drunken brawl. In the early part of this century, collectors of latex from caucho trees, used to make a poor-grade rubber similar to balata, congregated in Itupiranga to squander their earnings in bars and brothels. Contagious fights often broke out as the evenings wore on, and many *caucheiros* were killed. Another informant, however, asserted that the white dog was the spirit of a Parakanã man who perished when a group of warriors was massacred at the site of Itupiranga toward the end of the nineteenth century. The Parakanã were apparently dislodged into the forest west of the village and have had sporadic and sometimes hostile contact with Brazilian society for much of the twentieth century. The Parakanã now have their own reserve and live in several scattered villages.

The giant white dog stories warn people of the consequences of murder and of abusing alcohol. Alcohol unleashes pent-up passions that can lead to violence. Barbaric death carries the risk of incurring supernatural repercussions in caboclo lore, as evidenced also in the stories of pisadeiras, footstep ghosts that arise when a person's blood escapes into water at death, or when someone falls out of a canoe and drowns. The white dog has not been seen for several decades, ever since the village began to grow rapidly with the arrival of the Transamazon in 1970.

The dangers of imbibing too much liquor are also evident in a couple of stories covered in previous chapters. In one tale, a tapper only breaks his word with the mother of rubber trees not to reveal their special arrangement when he lingers for a few drinks at a bar. The alcohol loosens his tongue and the tapper pays dearly for his indiscretion. And in a story about the enchanted place at Sapucaia-roca along the Madeira, two white men mysteriously turn up at a festival and take the village back with them to the depths of the river when the party degenerates into intemperate drinking and wanton dancing.

Drunken behavior does not appear to have been a problem among unacculturated Indians in Amazonia. Several tribes prepared mildly alcoholic beverages by fermenting manioc or maize with human saliva. Such broths are not nearly as potent as distilled liquor, however. Furthermore, indigenous people generally partake of fermented drinks only during certain ceremonies. Indigenous festivities may last for several days, during which there is usually feasting and ritualized dancing. Vicious brawls and bloodshed appear to be the exception on such occasions, unlike in village taverns, where cachaça is cheap and flows freely.

Loud noises, usually the result of undisciplined consumption of beer, sugarcane alcohol, or coarse Brazilian conhaque, can also incur the wrath of the supernatural. One of the surest ways to stir the anger of the dreaded capé-lobo for example, is to yell in the forest. Such behavior attracts unwanted attention. A ghost that haunts the one-kilometer path connecting the small community of Terra Nova with the village of Itapiranga on the left bank of the middle Amazon River is notorious for teaching inebriated people a lesson. The apparition of a small black man sneaks up on its victims from behind and claps their ears with his hands. The ghost only strikes at night, when a person sings loudly or shouts as he returns home from a bar or party. When the victim attempts to strike back, his fist slices through the apparition as if it were mist. The phantom is reputed to be an enchanted man who lives in a deep hole at the bottom of a nearby creek.

Adilson, a married man in his thirties, came across the specter one evening as he was returning to his home in Terra Nova. A loud bang suddenly exploded in his ears, followed immediately by intense pain and a ringing sound. No one was in front, so the informant spun around and came face to face with the ghost of a dark man. The pair tussled furiously for about a quarter of an hour, but Adilson was unable to hit the waif. Finally, as the exhausted victim was on the verge of collapsing, the apparition broke off the attack and dissipated. Adilson recalled feeling unwell long after his bruises had cleared up. In the world of the caboclo, encounters with the supernatural can injure people, sap their spiritual energy, and kill them.

Daughters who argue constantly with their mothers are also prone to unworldly punishment. The giant pig, already mentioned in connection with promiscuous women, sometimes arises when girls consistently disobey their mothers. The spell descends on the rebellious daughter when her despairing mother falls to her knees and curses her. At night, the cantankerous daughter turns into a pig and roams the streets. Pig-people are dangerous, and one must be fully alert to avoid being bowled over and bitten.

According to a Transamazon colonist who lives near Coco Chato and who has lived most of his life in Pará, one must cut a *porca grande* to break the hex. Raimundo noted further that few individuals summon enough courage to stand their ground and tackle a porca. Most people flee at the sight of a black squealing mass weighing several hundred pounds charging at them. Quarrelsome girls who slip into the guise of a nocturnal sow habitually sleep in late and are often pale and sickly. Their crepuscular forays are physically and spiritually taxing. Stories of the giant black pig are recounted by mothers eager to teach their daughters good manners.

Two incidents that occurred in the relatively quiet village of Itapiranga illustrate the desperate straits of some victims of the giant pig. Around four o'clock one morning in 1955, a fisherman was making his way down deserted and dark Jaquir de Almeida, a street that runs perpendicular to the waterfront. The man was heading toward his canoe for a day of cast-net fishing when an enormous dark pig rushed at him from some shadows. Luckily, the informant was carrying a paddle, so he slammed the wooden implement down hard on

Figure 10.3. Dona Donizette, a storyteller in Itapiranga, Amazonas, with a pet canary-winged parakeet in 1978.

the fat sow's head. At that, the pig ran off into a grove of coffee bushes that have since given way to a row of houses. A year later along the same street, two men were walking home one evening around eleven o'clock when a *porca grande* attacked them. Twelve squeaking piglets trotted in tow and added to the ensuing confusion. The bulky but agile sow almost bit the terrified men on several lunges. Vigorous kicks to the flanks did little to deter the creature. Finally, one of the men located a sturdy piece of wood and struck the persistent pig with all his might; mercifully, the boisterous sow backed away and left them alone. Dona Donizette (figure 10.3), a housewife who resides in Itapiranga and occasionally takes in travelers because there is no hotel in the village, felt that the pig was a wayward soul who had not found pardon with God.

Souls of the departed may not find peace if they hoarded wealth while they were alive instead of distributing at least some of it to the needy. Haunted houses, especially where poltergeists are active, are a sign that a former occupant buried some treasure nearby. Dona Ruth, who lives in Marabá, explained that in former times, people customarily hid their valuables at home or buried them in the yard. Nowadays, they either invest in short-term certificates if they are relatively wealthy or purchase goods, livestock, or real estate to secure their fortune. The spirit feels guilty that he or she did not give sufficient money to charity. This concept is surely a postcontact, Christian influence. A passage in the New Testament beseeches people not to store up treasure on earth where they corrode and where thieves can steal them, but in heaven where the reward will be spiritual.[1] The notion of private property and the conspicuous accumulation of material goods is alien to Indian tribes of Amazonia.

A troublesome ghost (visagem) on the outskirts of Itupiranga illustrates the turmoil and frustration of a greedy soul. *Pinica-pau,* as the ghost was called, used to bother pedestrians at night on the narrow dirt road leading to the old village of Coco Chato some eight kilometers inland. The apparition always materialized in the vicinity of a grove of ancient mango trees, the site of a long-abandoned house. A black couple used to live in the wattle-and-daub home until the wife left and took up residence in Itupiranga. The almost-blind woman was considered crazy and spent much of her time reciting incantations alone in the woods. She is now buried in the weed-choked village cemetery. Her despondent husband, Imidão, continued to live in the house by the trail to Coco Chato until his death. Some people claim to have heard him chopping wood near the tall mango trees, hence the ghost's name: woodpecker. Imidão is rumored to have buried some coins close to his abode, and his soul comes out at night to try to show people where the treasure is hidden so that it can be dug up and given to the poor.

Manuel Santana, a middle-aged Transamazon farmer who used to reside in the old village of Coco Chato, recounted frightening experiences two of his friends had with pinica-pau, or *cicica,* as the ghost was sometimes called. At sundown one day, a colleague was walking home to Itupiranga from his field in the surrounding forest. He was carrying a basket on his back loaded with produce, and when he passed the towering mango trees close to Itupiranga, something heavy climbed on board. The weight was applied so suddenly that it sent the farmer reeling backward, and he almost fell. The bewildered man could not hear or see anything unusual, so he discarded the basket and ran home. By the time he arrived at his hut, he was breathless and felt unwell. His condition soon deteriorated, so a spiritualist healer was called in. The farmer regained his shadow after treatment, but he would not venture alone on the trail leading to Coco Chato for more than a year.

In an incident involving another individual that also happened in the 1950s, a man was walking home to Coco Chato from Itupiranga around ten o'clock one evening when he was intercepted by pinica-pau. As the man reached the stand of old mango trees, he felt a frigid draft from behind, an unusual sensation in a climate where summer never ends. Then he heard footsteps approaching from the direction of the chilly breath of air. Something seemed to be trying to catch up and communicate with him, but he did not linger to find out.

After rushing home, the frightened man shortly ran a high fever that lasted for three days. A curandeiro treated him for soul loss, and the man recovered. But he vowed never to walk that trail again without company.

Pinica-pau has apparently vanished with the sweeping cultural and ecological changes triggered by the arrival of the Transamazon work crews in 1970. The twenty dwellings comprising the community of Coco Chato were razed in 1973 by government bulldozers to encourage people to move into the adjacent planned community called agrovila Castelo Branco, in honor of the first president of the revolutionary government in 1964. Most colonists refer to the orderly settlement as agrovila Coco Chato. In 1970, the dirt road connecting Coco Chato with Itupiranga was used mostly by foot traffic and mules and wove through second growth dominated by babaçu palm. A local name for babaçu is coco, and coco chato means literally the "nuisance palm," because it takes over cleared areas (although it supplies useful fronds for construction and oil-rich nuts). By the mid-1970s, the road had been widened to accommodate trucks and buses and was surfaced with lateritic pebbles. At the time of my last visit in 1992, further changes had taken place. Much of the forest around agrovila Coco Chato had been cut down, and the second growth between Coco Chato and Itupiranga had been replaced by cattle pasture. Itupiranga has grown from a sleepy village to a bustling town, and huts and small stores string out along the road leading to Coco Chato. The old mango trees where the woodpecker ghost used to hang out are long gone.

Pinica-pau served to remind people of the unhappy fate of those who selfishly accumulate wealth and bury it so that no one benefits from their good fortune. Stories about the icy ghost do not suggest that there is anything inherently wrong about becoming rich, just that one should share at least part of the largesse. A parallel can be drawn here between pinica-pau and the snake-woman story recounted earlier. The serpent-lady is disenchanted only when someone is daring enough to smash her on the head with an ax. The soul of Imidão was apparently trying to entice someone to the site where he had buried his treasure. Both supernatural disturbances are the result of evil. In one case a man selfishly hides his wealth; in the other, an unwanted baby girl is tossed into water.

Not all ghosts of streets and houses fall into convenient categories, such as those related to sexual misconduct, parental discipline problems, homicide and drunken behavior, or material greed. Some spirits and supernatural creatures associated with human dwellings are part of the ether, but storytellers are not sure as to the causes of the alarming apparitions. Certain aberrant spirits of villages do not appear to fulfill a particular function in the cosmology of peasants; they are trapped in eddies along the interface between this world and the next. Although the origins and role of some spirits remain an enigma, they are nevertheless associated with evil.

Two storytellers reported tales of pearly stallions that appear after sundown and trot up and down streets. In Itapiranga, an ivory-colored horse appeared occasionally in 1973 and cantered along the narrow streets. The village strays would bark excitedly, but no one ever caught the animal or knew whence it came. At Foz de Aripuanã, a settlement near the marriage of the Madeira and Aripuanã Rivers, a man used to change into a silvery-white steed at night and set off a cacophony of canine howls by galloping along the streets. Inhabitants of Foz de Aripuanã were puzzled because no one kept any horses in the village at that time.

After several consecutive evenings of disturbed sleep, a man resolved to go outside and investigate. When the man found the restless stallion, it reared up and galloped away, so the man gave chase until the frisky animal ducked into the forest. The man decided to wait until the phantom horse emerged from the tree cover so that he might lasso it. Some time passed before he heard the rustle of leaves coming from the woods. The man crouched behind a bush with a coiled rope ready in his hand. But to his amazement, out stepped a villager. "What are you doing out here at this late hour?" inquired the man with the rope. "I have been hunting," came the reply. "Then where is your gun?" asked the man suspiciously. The villager failed to answer and looked downcast. He had been discovered. The next day the horse-man, a bachelor, packed up his few belongings and left for Rondônia.

Cabokinha, a forest waif usually associated with game animals or balata trees, has been reported to wander into villages and raise havoc. José Martins, a Transamazon colonist who has resided in agrovila Tiradentes some eighty kilometers west of Altamira since 1973, recalled seeing what he termed *caboclina* on a couple of occasions in the mid-1970s. The goblin was just over a meter high and extremely ugly. The small black boy wore a dark shirt draped over a powerfully built frame and scruffy trousers that barely reached down to his bulging calves. The goblin's hair was most unusual; it was thick and stuck out behind like a giant anteater's tail. When caboclina strolled across the village square after dark, it promptly stirred up the dogs, which gave chase. The barking dogs always broke off their charge at the last minute, when caboclina emitted a sharp yell.

The noisy waif appeared on the eve of tragic death. The day after it appeared the first time, a man was blasted in the chest at point-blank range with a shotgun while he argued with a neighbor. A feud had been brewing for some time, and ill feelings exploded into violence when a disagreement arose as to the best time to torch two adjacent fields. The evening following caboclina's second visit to Tiradentes, a settler was fatally stabbed outside a party underway in the community center. José was unsure of the origin of caboclina, but he suggested that the banshee lives in the forest in cahoots with Satan.

Another Transamazon settler, a native of Pará who has lived his entire life within the municipality of Altamira, feels that matin has also forged a pact with the devil. He has heard matin fly overhead at night on several occasions. Although matin is usually heard rather than seen, people sometimes glimpse the errant spirit. Some fifteen years ago in Itapiranga, a man was walking down a street around one o'clock in the morning when he heard a long "ting-ting-ting" from overhead. He immediately looked up and saw a huge black bird, much larger than the diurnal vultures, flapping by. The call and enormous size of the bird were distinctive, but what really surprised the onlooker was that the creature was riddled with holes. The perforations in the bird's body and wings were large enough to allow starlight to pass through.

Matin does not always assume the shape of a bird or remain invisible when shocking humans. A matin that plagues the neighboring settlement of Terra Nova is a headless priest who dresses in black and stalks the community's unlit alleyways. The decapitated father intimidates people by chasing them and whistling with a high-pitched "fee-fee-fee." Folk who spot the wayward padre become ill.

Matins of unknown origin can persecute families to the point of despair. Even tobacco does not appear to placate the creature at times. A seventeen-year-old boy interviewed in Altamira in 1978 recalled a terrifying experience his family had with a matin in 1973. The boy was interviewed alone while I was collecting anthropogenic black earth from the yard of his parent's home.

The young storyteller explained that the supernatural bird used to call after dusk with a shrill whistle from the roof of their mud-brick home in Missão, a cluster of homes on the left bank of the Xingu two kilometers upstream from Altamira. At times the piercing call seemed to issue from the air right above their heads. The rudely awakened children used to cry out for their mother who would fall to her knees and pray for deliverance from the invisible affliction. Fortunately, the taunting visits of matin tapered off as Altamira grew with the flood of Transamazon settlers and traders. The bustle and bright lights of busy towns are anathema to most supernatural creatures of the caboclo's world.

Apart from urban growth, a person has recourse to only two methods for getting rid of a matin. Tobacco usually appeases the shadowy bird. Failing that, exposure of the culprit is the only option left. Matins abhor public scorn and habitually flee to another village if they are uncovered. A matin was soaring one evening over Jatobal, a village on the left bank of the Tocantins now flooded by the Tucurui reservoir, when a spiritualist healer heard its call. The medium recited an incantation, and the matin came tumbling out of the black sky and into the home of the pajé. The distraught matin pleaded with the healer to keep his nocturnal personality a secret, for he worked on the now-defunct Jatobal-Tucurui railroad by day and feared ridicule and persecution by his co-workers if they discovered his real identity.

Matins are normally banished when they are identified. For example, an eccentric man appeared in Aripuanã in 1971 and erected a hut by Igarapé Bahia, a meandering stream that skirts the village. According to the informant, a farmer and longtime resident of Aripuanã, the single fellow used to get up during the early hours of the morning to pound maize and rice in his home. Neighbors could hear the rhythmic "thunk" of the wooden mortar and thought it odd that he worked while most people slept.

About the time the restless bachelor took up residence in Aripuanã, a matin started buzzing several houses in the village. The bird's sharp call, "fi-feee," alarmed people, and discussion soon turned to the possible role of the newcomer in these nocturnal escapades. Several villagers decided to watch the bachelor's home closely one night. After midnight, the dull thud of a pestle striking a cereal-laden mortar was heard for some time. When it stopped, a loud whistle came out of the window and sped away. The source of the shrill sound was invisible, but there was little doubt that a matin had just left for a night of mischief making. The next day, several men walked up to the bachelor's hut and challenged him with their observations. The newcomer did not deny the accusation and felt ashamed. He promptly collected his meager belongings and left for the interior to live apart from humans.

The idea that people can transform into animals is widespread among aborigines of the Americas. The rich assortment of myths relating how humans turn into birds has already been mentioned. Many South American tribes recount legends in which shamans adopt the form of a jaguar. In Mexico and Guatemala, *nagualism* refers to the ability of people to turn into wild animals, as well as dogs and chickens. This belief stems from the concept of animal spirit allies. If the animal dies, so does the person. Apparently, the entities were once distinct, but now they have blended so that people allegedly assume animal form. In Ixtepeji, a Zapotec settlement in the Mexican state of Oaxaca, certain individuals (*naguales*) reportedly have the power to assume the guise of coyotes, foxes, cougars, jaguars, bats, or snakes. Naguales usually attack livestock and are motivated by envy. In caboclo lore, some people transform into hairy ogres, giant snakes, dolphins, birds, deer, pigs, three-legged cows, horses, or dogs and bother people in town and country.

The Changing Panorama

A vast array of supernatural characters permeates the world of rural folk in Amazonia. Every conceivable habitat, from village squares and alleyways to placid lakes and the gloomy interior of the forest, is a potential haunt for a spirit, ghost, or monster. Fear of the other world clearly molds the behavior of caboclos. Precautions are taken, such as not fishing on sacred days, and certain procedures are followed, such as the proper disposal of discarded game parts, in order to avoid stirring the wrath of creatures from beyond. This perception of a double-faceted reality in which people inhabit a physical world but are subject to the whims of the supernatural on a daily basis is quite alien to the inhabitants of modern, metropolitan cities.

A middle-class American or Brazilian may profess a religious faith, such as Christianity, but usually conducts his or her daily affairs will little thought to the supernatural. The existence of an afterlife and spirits is often acknowledged, but that is a possibility or certainty that is faced at death. A well-educated North American or European may believe in the concept of the soul but usually does not worry about ghosts or spirits. The roar of jet aircraft, the clatter of train wheels, and the honking of impatient automobile drivers all tend to drown out thoughts of another world. Office buildings, schools, buses, and air-conditioned homes isolate urban dwellers from a feeling of connectedness with the earth. For the most part, urban dwellers rarely enjoy opportunities to appreciate nature and ponder some of its mysteries. City folk do not have to worry as much about the weather as do fishermen and farmers. Television, films, plays, and concerts entertain and replace the need for storytelling over campfires in forests or along lake shores. It is mainly around the coals of dying fires, or the erratic flame of an open kerosene lamp, that people steeped in tradition habitually discuss unusual events and speculate on their possible supernatural causes.

Although cities are shut off from the awe of nature, they are not hermetically sealed from ideas concerning the impact of the supernatural. In the poorer suburbs of Belém and other large towns and cities in the Amazon, African Brazilian cults hold sessions presided over by mediums. Matintapereras, enormous pigs, and headless priests have haunted residents of Belém for a long time. In New York and London, séances are held regularly in some fashionable homes. And some shamans have reportedly set up shop in trendy New York. Millions of Americans and Europeans scan their horoscopes in daily newspapers searching for clues as to the best tack to pursue in business or romantic affairs. The notion that celestial bodies control the destiny of humans is held by many people, including sophisticated Parisians and the well-to-do in the eternal city, Rio de Janeiro.

Visitors to Amazonia may feel that the lore of rural people is fantastic, even ridiculous, but would probably be reluctant to admit that they skirt around a ladder propped up against a wall, or that they flinch if a black cat scurries in front of them. Superstition and belief in the supernatural survive in megalopoli, with their shopping malls and glass-encased office buildings, but such notions pale when compared to the extraordinary variety of Amazonian lore.

The gulf between urban and rural life in Amazonia is widening rapidly as cities expand and the ranks of the middle class grow. At the turn of this century, no Amazonian city had more than 100,000 inhabitants. Today, Belém has close to 1.5 million inhabitants and is still growing. The population of Manaus stood at 50,000 in 1900; by 1982, it had leaped to 600,000, and a decade later had reached 1 million. The third largest city in the Amazon, Santarém, had about 300,000 inhabitants in 1995; in the mid-1850s, it was an overgrown village of 2,000 souls.

The character of regional society is thus changing rapidly. More people are living in towns and cities than before. As recently as 1940, 80 percent of the population of the Brazilian Amazon lived in isolated houses or in villages with less than two thousand inhabitants. In 1970, 41 percent of the regional population lived in urban areas, and a decade later the proportion had reached 52 percent. As cities continue to burgeon, cultural links with the countryside weaken. Inhabitants of Belém and Manaus, for example, increasingly purchase foodstuffs and other supplies in air-conditioned supermarkets instead of open-air markets where gossip and other information is exchanged.

While high-rise apartments and office buildings create an ever-changing urban skyline, a plethora of monsters, goblins, and ghosts haunts the minds of rural folk, some of whom live within earshot of aircraft bringing tourists to Belém, Manaus, and Santarém. The superstitious beliefs of city dwellers do not match the complexity or color of caboclo lore, with its more than two dozen supernatural entities (appendix 5). Many of the spirits of the "interior" play multiple roles. The mother of rubber trees occasionally persecutes hunters, and the father of game sometimes harasses rubber tappers. Some supernatural apparitions are confined to specific habitats, whereas others roam widely from deep forest to shadowy side streets. Diminutive cabokinha, for example, alarms hunters while they track game in the jungle and frightens children playing in the community square. Matin buzzes people as they walk along forest trails, paddle across lakes, or try to sleep at home.

Four main factors account for the richness of rural lore in the Amazon. First, the stock of aboriginal cultures was diverse and numerous. Although the number of indigenous groups has diminished considerably since contact and the cultural integrity of many surviving groups has suffered, aboriginal notions about the supernatural have threaded into the colorful mantle of caboclo lore. A map of the tribes that share supernatural concepts with the mestizo population of today reveals a strong pattern of indigenous groups in headwater regions (figure 1.4). But this pattern is a reflection of the dying out or complete integration of indigenous groups along the main river courses. Second, an overlay of European notions about the other world, particularly Christianity, has added highlights to the regional tales. Third, African ideas on the spirit world have contributed ethereal figures to the already extensive cast of supernatural characters inhabiting the peasant's world. And finally, the immense wilderness, cut off from the mainstream currents of economic development for so long, has provided a fertile setting for the sprouting and flourishing of unusual interpretations and perceptions about land and life.

Remarkably little caboclo lore deals with fields and crops. This barren patch in the otherwise rich folk narratives indicates that rural people, including many indigenous groups, are not particularly concerned with agricultural productivity. Rural folk in other tropical regions hold festivals for gods or saints at planting time in order to promote the germination of seeds and to give thanks for bountiful yields. Maize, for example, figures prominently in the religious life of the Mayans of Central America. In Amazonia, fewer rituals appear to be associated with crops among indigenous people when compared to myths and legends that involve hunting, fishing, and gathering.

Although most Amazonian tribes ascribe supernatural causes for the origin of crops, few creatures have been assigned to protect cultivated plants. The Jívaro, who live in the Ecuadorian Amazon, believe in a chubby and squat earth mother, *nunuí,* who looks after growing crops. Three guardian spirits look after manioc according to the Kamayurá of the upper Xingu. Compared to supernatural concerns related to hunting, fishing, and health, however, fewer legends and myths appear to surround field crops in the Amazon basin.

Cultivated plants are also poorly represented in the regional lore of peasants. Vegetables are the only cultivated plants that figure in tales of rural people in the Brazilian Amazon. Individual families in both rural and urban areas sometimes surround their patches of tomatoes and spring onions with egg shells supported by stakes to protect the tender plants against the glare of the evil eye. Field crops are not the focus of rituals designed to placate spirits or to encourage rewarding harvests. Water surrounding manioc tubers placed in streams is, however, considered an effective treatment for panema. Manioc presses also expel the ill fortune. And although peasant lore seemingly ignores rice fields, mortars used to pound the grains must not be used to cut up game meat.

The major reason that so little lore has germinated around cultivated plants in Amazonia is that the basic staples are root crops, particularly manioc and sweet potato. Tuber crops produce higher yields than cereals and are much more reliable because they are less vulnerable to pests, diseases, dry spells, and storms. Manioc and sweet potato were domesticated in the tropical lowlands of South America and have been cultivated in Amazonia for thousands of years. Amazonians have thus had less to worry about when it comes to their crops than those who rely on cereals for their main food supply. The fact that only vegetables are vulnerable to the evil eye stems from the fact that they are more susceptible to diseases and pests than root crops. In general, farming is a more reliable source of food than hunting and gathering. Much of Amazonia's myth-legends thus focus on "chancier" subsistence and commercial activities, such as fishing, hunting, and gathering of forest products. But the fabric of the region's lore is enriched considerably by stories that relate to social behavior.

Some of the lore dealing with behavior has been stimulated by Christian ethics and is thus relatively recent to the region. Such lore usually focuses on aspects of people's lives that cause the most concern or tension. Numerous stories, for example, reflect an absorbing interest in sex. Aboriginal groups generally have a much more liberal attitude toward extramarital affairs than rural society today.

Other stories reflect disapproval of excessive drinking, dishonesty, greed, laziness, and an uncooperative attitude. Several tales express resentment toward those who horde wealth rather than help others. Even accounts that deal with hunting and gathering often contain moral lessons that pertain to people. The mother of balata trees, for example, rewards the tapper who is kind and patient. A desire to avoid panema helps motivate good neighborly relationships. The fewer enemies one has accumulated, the less likely you are to be the target of a spell arresting your hunting or fishing skills. Rural folk are usually up at dawn, and their impatience for late risers is revealed in stories about giant pigs and in the assertion that lazy women cause particularly stubborn cases of panema. And the unscrupulous woodsman who removes a gold chain from an image of Saint John is only able to find his way out of the forest after he replaces the offering in the forest shrine.

Most of the regional lore deals with natural resources, particularly the productivity of game, fish, and commercially valuable trees. People have hunted, fished, and gathered a lot longer than they have farmed, one of the reasons for the lopsided number of tales related to experiences in the forest and on rivers and lakes. Many supernatural beliefs help to conserve natural resources. More than two dozen supernatural entities either watch over plants and animals or patrol sections of the forest, lakes, or rivers (Appendix 5). At one time, the Amazon floodplain was densely settled, with some chiefdoms extending for more than one hundred kilometers. Although precontact aboriginal populations were dense, they did not trigger massive destruction of natural resources. Cultural checks were evidently in play to prevent abuse of fish, game, and other natural resources.

In precontact times, a constellation of reserves overseen by supernatural forces was complemented along certain stretches of rivers by buffer zones between hostile tribes. Such areas were rarely exploited and were probably as large in some cases as zones considered off limits because of ghosts or monsters. The Orellana expedition down the Amazon in 1542 reported some "gaps" of essentially empty landscape between belligerent groups. The number and location of such buffer zones would vary over time, as in the case of supernatural parks.

Some stretches of the Amazon apparently devoid of people could have been deceptive. Several floodplain islands may have been deserted, but villages may have been abundant farther back from the main river channel along the interface between the uplands and the alluvial soils of the Amazon. Neutral war zones and no-man's-lands because of the threat of supernatural beings would have provided safe havens for wildlife and valuable recruiting grounds to restock surrounding areas with fish and game.

Within a hundred years of contact, many tribes along the Amazon and other major rivers had vanished or were considerably reduced in numbers. Apart from a few select species, such as the South American river turtle, much of the wildlife and plant resources in the region received a respite from human interference. Although buffer zones disappeared, so did millions of people. In the twentieth century, and particularly in the last fifty years, pressure has began to build on the natural-resource base again.

The human population of the Amazon floodplain and tributary rivers is currently less dense than before the arrival of Europeans, but much forest had been destroyed, particularly to raise cattle and water buffalo. Echoes of past cultural checks to overexploitation of natural resources can still be found, but they are probably not as effective as in the past. When powerful chiefdoms held sway over extensive stretches of the Amazon River, cultural checks to overexploitation were likely enforced or respected more rigorously than today.

Some portions of the floodplains of all the region's major rivers are still off limits to fishermen because ghosts or supernatural beasts are rumored to lurk there. The locations of such spots shift with time. Some no-fishing zones are eventually discredited when no more unusual sightings or sounds are reported. But others spring up to take their place. In the jungle, enchanted springs and the imagined territories of curupira and mapinguary are given wide birth. But overall, the influence of folkloric beliefs in mediating relations between people and their environment is probably not as strong as it was in the past.

Herein lies the dilemma. As the human population again increases and more destructive land use systems expand, such as cattle ranching, few mechanisms are in place to help conserve the region's extraordinary biodiversity. In the past, human population densities probably waxed and waned along the major rivers in response to a variety of factors, such as migration. Some civilizations arose in situ and then declined. But when population densities increased, cul-

Figure 11.1. Settler of German descent in the Brazilian Amazon from the southern state of Rio Grande do Sul. The farmer is drinking chimarrão, a customary tealike drink of *gaúchos,* in the late afternoon in a home garden. Settlers from other regions of Brazil sometimes ridicule local "superstitious" beliefs. Comunidade Boa Esperança, km 43 of the road from Santarém to Curuá-una, 2 October 1992.

tural checks were surely in place to help balance demands on resources. I do not wish to imply that indigenous people are always in harmony with nature. Such romantic notions are not congruent with the archaeological record of severe soil erosion in some areas of the American tropics. But the fact remains: the Amazon River was densely settled in the early 1500s, and wildlife was abundant.

As the impetus for development ratchets up, buffer zones no longer exist and supernatural constraints to runaway harvesting of resources are weakening. The loosening grip of rural customs and belief in legendary figures has been noted in the Amazon basin and central Brazil. Settlers from other parts of Brazil (figure 11.1) are bringing new values to the Amazon, and they sometimes ridicule the traditional beliefs of caboclos.

The conservation role of folklore is being diluted by the homogenizing effect of development. In addition to settlers, the media have been at the vanguard of the wave of new values pouring into the region. Many rural folk may not be able to read well, but they glance at magazine pictures and are curious about events in the region and in the outside world. Even the poorest family usually owns a radio. During the day, the household may listen to popular music coming from a nearby town or catch the national news on Radiobras beaming from Brasília. One reason why so many people have acquired radios is because they are relatively cheap and because telephone service is sporadic or nonexistent in the interior. Radio stations serve as clearing houses for messages. Urgent requests are often relayed over the air for someone to send money or to visit a sick relative. At night, Portuguese-language programs of the British Broadcasting Corporation, the Canadian Broadcasting Corporation, the Voice of America, Radio Havana, and Radio Moscow compete for the attention of caboclos.

In recent years, television has further expanded the horizons of rural and urban folk. Most towns in the Brazilian Amazon are now served by at least one television station that broadcasts national and foreign programs. Westerns and often-racy soap operas depicting opulent life-styles in Rio and São Paulo are especially popular. Extravagant variety shows featuring pop singers and scantily clad samba dancers also draw appreciative audiences. In rural areas surrounding towns and cities, many modest homes employ car batteries to operate their television sets. A symphony of crickets and the cascading calls of camouflaged potoos now compete with the fast-paced music of variety shows. Many families will forego the purchase of either an electric or kerosene-powered refrigerator in order to secure a television.

Many peasants have not ventured into large cities to see skyscrapers, department stores, or busy airports, but they have glimpsed such technological achievements on television. On visits to town to buy supplies, it is not unusual for rural folk to linger at shop fronts or at the windows of homes to stare at images of faraway places flickering on television screens. The ever-deeper reach of this communication medium into the lives of peasants is breaking down their cultural isolation and in some cases takes the place of storytelling time.

As the region's cities continue to grow and external markets for Amazonian products increase, so will the pressure on fisheries and other resources. The size of fishing fleets operating from towns and cities along the Amazon grows every year, and they probe ever farther afield as local fisheries are depleted. When strangers fish in areas thought to be dangerous for supernatural reasons and get away with it, local beliefs are shaken. Fewer no-fishing zones are thus left intact.

While traditional conservation is being undermined, modern concepts of protecting the environment are only just penetrating the region. Efforts to implement parks and biological reserves in Amazonia are still in their infancy.

By the early 1990s, approximately 37 million hectares had been set aside in the Brazilian Amazon for parks and reserves, up from 24 million hectares in 1981. The governments of Colombia, Ecuador, Peru, Bolivia, and Venezuela have also been busy designating indigenous territories and setting aside parks and reserves. Colombia has been particularly sensitive to the importance of conservation of rain forests and recognizing the rights of indigenous people, although development pressures in the Colombian Amazon are not as severe as in some other parts of the basin.

As impressive as these gains have been, the region is still in somewhat of a conservation limbo. Parks and reserves only cover a small percentage of the basin; many of them are not respected by loggers, miners, and settlers, and their boundaries are often ignored by fishermen, hunters, and gatherers. Few reserves are found in floodplain environments, so crucial for the productivity of many of the region's fisheries. Efforts to safeguard existing reserves and create more should be redoubled.

Another approach to conservation involves local communities and the private sector. A number of different projects throughout the Amazon basin are encouraging local communities to manage their resources on a more sustainable basis. Although such an approach has merit, reliance on communities alone to maintain the productivity of resources is fraught with difficulties. Not all communities are particularly cohesive, due in part to different religious and cultural backgrounds. As yet, few communities are armed with the technical skills and knowledge to carry out such a task, nor can they coordinate their activities with far-flung villages. Many fish and game animals migrate over large distances, so protection in one area may not work if habitat is being destroyed, or resources overexploited, in another part of the basin. The large scale of the Mamirauá project is particularly interesting in this respect because many communities are involved in participatory research over large stretches of the Amazon floodplain near Tefé. The community approach to resource management is one of several complementary approaches to conservation and sustainable resource management in the Amazon.

Much of the land in the Brazilian Amazon is in the hands of individually owned plots, both large and small. How to involve small farmers, ranchers, plantation owners, and mining operations in conservation efforts is a major task. Some of the larger mining corporations and plantation operations have environmental safeguards in place. It is with the small farmers on their own lots, ranchers, and itinerant miners that the main challenges lie ahead. Little work has been attempted with them to agree on adjacent forest patches for set asides and protection of watersheds. It should be possible for growers' associations to work closely with nongovernmental organizations, government agencies, and other groups to foster the better use of natural resources in the region by employing a nonpolitical approach that incorporates incentives for conservation rather than the threat of punishment.

So where does this leave folklore? One can hardly expect to teach folkloric beliefs as truths in an effort to resuscitate cultural checks to overexploitation of resources. But many of the stories told by caboclos contain themes that dwell on respect for nature and the importance of not being greedy when harvesting fish, game animals, and plants in the wild. Tales of curupira, the mother of fish, and the mother of rubber trees, for example, could be incorporated in the region's textbooks for schoolchildren. Such stories would bring alive texts dealing with the importance of maintaining forest cover and of conserving fish stocks. They would be used to illustrate the traditional concern for the wise management of resources.

A bold effort in this vein was instigated by Warwick Kerr, a Brazilian geneticist and the former director of the National Institute of Amazonian Research (INPA) based in Manaus. INPA's mandate is to purse scientific research on the biology, ecology, and some of the diseases of the region, but under the leadership of Kerr, an attempt was made to reach primary schoolchildren with the results of scientific research. In collaboration with the then-governor of Amazonas, Henoch da Silva Reis, professors and students from the University of Amazonas, and a professor from the University of São Paulo, INPA published a workbook for young school children. Called *Cartilha da Amazônia*, this innovative workbook was full of regional flavor and contained several legends about spirit protectors of natural resources as examples of the importance of conservation. Approximately 300,000 copies were distributed between 1977 and 1983, but unfortunately, the workbook is no longer used.

Such efforts should be revived. Education is a major key to development of the Amazon region and for a more equitable life-style for all. Instead of textbooks portraying temperate-zone living standards, such as blond children eating strawberries while father drives home in a car, teaching materials should reflect regional realities. All that is lacking is political will. Mayors might commission youngsters to paint murals depicting folklore motifs on some public buildings, thereby possibly discouraging the spray painting of walls by youth gangs that is penetrating even small towns in the Brazilian Amazon. Youngsters would enjoy trying out their budding artistic talents painting becoming yaras, pink dolphins transforming into people, or giant snakes scaring fishermen away from a lake. Other ways to promote the conservation message of the region's lore would be through posters and airline menus. Varig, one of Brazil's airlines, depicts some of the region's colorful birds on its menus for international flights.

An important point to remember with regard to the region's lore and its role in conservation efforts is that we are not simply dealing with some quaint anachronism. Although the influence of lore on the daily life of people in Amazonia is surely diminishing, it is by no means dead. Even youngsters in once-small towns now on their way to becoming larger metropolitan areas express an interest in folklore and often recount supernatural tales related to life in the interior. Tales are reinvented with new twists, incorporating more recent perspectives. In pioneer areas of the Amazon, ghosts and goblins soon make their appearance and are kept alive by storytellers, both old and young. Along the Transamazon, for example, we have seen that poltergeists, pugnacious black sows, and tiny but fearsome cabokinha have all made appearances within a few years of settlement. The current gold rush in Amazonia is sure to generate a fresh crop of tales about strange lights hovering over virgin fields and giant snakes patrolling new finds.

Huge expanses of Amazonia have been bypassed by development, particularly in the northwest, and are likely to remain in a relatively undisturbed state for the foreseeable future. Pockets of tradition will persist in little-explored headwaters, thereby helping to maintain the distinctive cultural flavor of the region. The embers of caboclo folklore still ignite the curiosity and engender awe among the region's inhabitants. Let us hope that its conservation message is spread widely for the benefit of people and nature for generations to come.

Checklist of Scientific
and Common Names of Plants

English Name	Local Name	Scientific Name
Açaí palm	Açaí	*Euterpe oleracea*
Aninga	Aninga	*Montrichardia arborescens*
Babaçu	Babaçu	*Attalea speciosa*
Bacabinha	Bacabinha	*Oenocarpus minor*
Brazil nut	Castanheira	*Bertholletia excelsa*
Buriti palm	Buriti	*Mauritia flexuosa*
Caraña	Caraña	Burseraceae, possibly *Protium* sp.
Catauari	Catauari	*Crataeva benthami*
Caucho	Caucho	*Castilla ulei*
Chili pepper	Pimenta	*Capsicum* spp.
Cipó curimbó	Cipó curimbó	*Tanaecium nocturnum*
Cipó-taia	Cipó-taia	*Piper dactylostigmum*
Crajiru	Crajiru	*Arrabidea chica*
Curuá palm	Curuá	*Attalea spectabilis*
Gaivotinha	Gaivotinha	*Croton nervosus*
Gameleira	Gameleira	*Ficus* sp.
Ingá	Ingazeir	*Inga* sp.
Jiboínha	Jiboínha	*Fittonia* sp.
João Burundi	João Burundi	*Piper lanceolatum*
Jurubeba	Jurubeba	*Solanum* spp.
Kapok tree	Sumaúma	*Ceiba pentandra*

English Name	Local Name	Scientific Name
Manioc	Mandhioca	*Manihot esculenta*
Mente	Mente	*Chorisia insignis*
Miritinga	Miritinga	*Olmedia maxima*
Mucura-cáa	Mucura-cáa	*Petiveria alliacea*
Mumbaca	Mumbaca	*Astrocaryum gynacanthum* and *Bactris* spp.
Paxiúba palm	Paxiúba	*Socratea exorrhiza*
Piaçava palm	Piaçava	*Leopoldinia piassaba*
Pião branco	Pião branco	*Jatropha curcas*
Pião roxo	Pião roxo	*Jatropha gossypifolia*
Piquiá	Piquiá	*Caryocar villosum*
Pupunharana	Pupunharana	*Bactris macana*
Rubber	Seringeira	*Hevea brasiliensis*
Rue	Arruda	*Ruta graveolens*
Sorva	Sorva	*Couma macrocarpa*
Sweet potato	Batata doce	*Ipomoea batatas*
Yellow mombim	Taperebá	*Spondias mombim*
Unha de cigana	Unha de cigana	*Machaerium aristatum*
Vai-vem	Vai-vem	*Maranta arundinacea*
Vassoura	Vassoura	*Scoparia dulcis*
Vindika	Vindika	*Alpinia japonica*

Checklist of Scientific and Common Names of Animals

English Name	Brazilian Name(s)	Scientific Name
Mammals		
Agouti	Cutia	*Dasyprocta* sp.
Armadillo	Tatu	Several genera and species
Brocket deer	Veado	*Mazama americana*
Capybara	Capivara	*Hydrochaeris hydrochaeris*
Giant anteater	Tamanduá bandeira	*Myrmecophaga tridactyla*
Giant armadillo	Tatu canastra	*Priodontes maximus*
Giant otter	Ariranha	*Pteronura brasiliensis*
Gray dolphin	Tucuxi	*Sotalia fluviatilis*
Howler monkey	Guariba	*Alouatta* spp.
Jaguar	Onça pintada	*Panthera onca*
Manati	Peixe boi	*Trichechus inunguis*
Margay cat	Maracajá-mirim	*Felis wiedii*
Nine-banded armadillo	Tatu comum	*Dasypus novemcinctus*
Ocelot	Maracajá-açu, Jaguartiça	*Felis pardalis*
Paca	Paca	*Agouti paca*
Pink dolphin	Boto	*Inia geoffrensis*
Prehensile-tailed porcupine	Coandu	*Coendu* sp.
Puma	Onça vermelha	*Felis concolor*
Sloth	Preguiça	*Bradypus* spp., *Choloepus didactylus*

English Name	Brazilian Name(s)	Scientific Name
Tapir	Anta	*Tapirus terrestris*
Tortoise	Jabotí	*Geochelone* spp.
White-collared peccary	Caitetu	*Tayassu tajacu*
Woolly monkey	Barrigud	*Lagotrix lagotricha*
White-lipped peccary	Queixada, porcão	*Tayassu pecari*

Birds

Black vulture	Urubu	*Coragyps atratus*
Canary-winged parakeet	Periquito	*Brotogeris versicolurus*
Chachalaca	Aracuã	*Ortalis* spp.
Curassow	Mutum	Species of *Crax* and *Mitu*
Guan	Jacu	*Penelope* spp.
Lesser yellow-headed vulture	Urubu	*Cathartes burrovianus*
Piping-guan	Cujubim	*Pipile* spp.
Squirrel cuckoo	Alma de gato	*Piaya cayana*
Tinamou	Inhambu, tona	Species of *Tinamus* and *Crypturellus*
Trumpeter	Jacamin	*Psophia* spp.
Turkey vulture	Urubu	*Cathartes aura*

Fish

Acarí	Acarí	Species of *Pterygoplichthys* and *Plecostomus*
Aracu	Aracu	Species of *Leporinus, Rhytiodus,* and *Schizodon*
Arawana	Aruanã	*Osteoglossum bicirrhosum*
Branquinha	Branquinha	Species of *Gasterotomus* and *Potamorhina*
Caparari	Caparari	*Pseudoplatystoma tigrinum*
Cará branca	Cará branca	*Chaetobranchopsis* sp.
Cubiu	Cubiu	*Anodus* sp.
Cuiu-cuiu	Cuiu-cuiu	*Oxydoras niger*
Curimatá	Curimatá	*Prochilodus nigricans*
Electric eel	Poraquê	*Electrophorus electricus*
Jaraqui	Jaraqui	*Semaprochilodus* spp.
Jatuarana	Jatuarana	*Brycon* sp.
Jaú	Jaú	*Paulicea luetkeni*
Mandí	Mandí	*Pimelodus blochii*
Mapará	Mapará	*Hypophthalmus* spp.
Matrinchão	Matrinchão	*Brycon* sp.

English Name	Brazilian Name(s)	Scientific Name
Oscar	Carauaçu	*Astronotus ocellatus*
Pacu	Pacu	Species of *Metynnis*, *Mylossoma*, and *Myleus*
Peacock bass	Tucunaré	*Cichla* spp.
Piraíba	Piraíba	*Brachyplatystoma filamentosum*
Piranha	Piranha	*Serrasalmus* spp.
Pirapitinga	Pirapitinga	*Colossoma bidens*
Pirarara	Pirarara	*Phractocephalus hemiliopterus*
Pirarucu	Pirarucu	*Arapaima gigas*
Sardinha	Sardinha	*Triportheus* spp.
Stingray	Arraia	Several genera and species
Surubim	Surubim	*Pseudoplatystoma fasciatum*
Tambaqui	Tambaqui	*Colossoma macropomum*
Tamoatá	Tamoatá	*Hoplosternum littorale*
Traíra	Traíra	*Hoplias malabaricus*
Reptiles		
Anaconda	Sucuriju	*Eunectes murinus*
Black caiman	Jacaré-Açu	*Melanosuchus niger*
Boa constrictor	Jibóia	*Constrictor constrictor*
Pepéua	Pepéua	*Cyclagras gigas*
South American river turtle	Tartaruga	*Podocnemis expansa*
Surucucu	Surucucu	*Lachesis muta*

Game Considered *Reimoso* by Fifty-nine Colonists along the Transamazon Highway, Brazil, 1978–1979

Common Name	Percentage of Colonists Citing
White-collared peccary	53
Paca	49
Tapir	38
Tortoise	29
Armadillo	29
White-lipped peccary	22
Brocket deer	22
Agouti	18
Trumpeter	9
Curassow	5

Fish Considered *Reimoso* by Fifty-eight
Fishermen in the Vicinity
of Itacoatiara, Amazonas, 1977

Common Name	Percentage of Fishermen Citing
Pirapitinga	84
Matrinchão	67
Curimatá	48
Piranha	33
Oscar	26
Surubim	14
Acarí	12
Jaraqui	12
Pacu	12
Peacock bass	12
Caparari	10
Pirarucu[a]	9
Tambaqui[a]	9
Catfish	7
Aracu	5
Mandí	3
Stingray	3

[a]Large specimens only

Some Supernatural Entities in the Cosmology of Rural People in the Brazilian Amazon, with Their Habitat, Function, and Danger to Humans

Brazilian Name	Habitat	Function	Danger
Assombração	Streams	Protects minerals	Persecutes people
Boto	Rivers, lakes		Impregnates young women, creates enchanted places; female dolphins drive men crazy with lust
Cabokinha	Forest, villages	Protects game and balata trees, harbinger of death	Attacks people and dogs
Cachorrão	Villages		Attacks people
Caixão	Villages		Attacks people
Capé-lobo	Forest	Protects game	Kills people, dogs, goats
Cobra grande	Rivers, channels, lakes	Protects fish	Kills people, impregnates women, creates enchanted places, steals people's shadows
Curupira	Forest	Protects game, rubber trees, piaçava palms	Steals people's shadows, leads them astray
Guariba-boia	Lakes, channels, flooded forest	Protects fish	Kills people

Brazilian Name	Habitat	Function	Danger
João da mata	Forest	Forest caretaker	Plants weeds that cut people
Lobizoni	Near houses	Discourages illicit sex	Steals people's shadows
Lugar encantado	Rivers, lakes, springs, rapids, rock outcrops	Protects game and fish	Steals people's shadows, sometimes associated with treacherous currents
Luzes	Forest, channels, lakes		None
Mãe de peixe	Rivers, lakes, channels, flooded forest	Protects fish	Steals nets and people's shadows
Mãe de piaçava	Forest	Protects piaçava palm	Can steal people's shadows
Mãe de seringa	Forest	Protects rubber trees	Kills people and steals their shadows
Mapinguary	Forest	Protects game	Kills people
Marmota	Lake shores	Protects fish and turtles	Attacks people
Matin	Forest, floodplain forest, lakes, rivers, streams, villages	Protects turtles	Attacks people and dogs, makes people ill
Negro d'água	Rivers		Mesmerizes people
Pai da mata	Forest	Protects game	Leads people astray
Pisadeira	Shores of lakes and banks of rivers	Protects fish	Renders people dumb
Porca	Villages	Discourages illicit sex	Attacks people
Sereia	Rivers		Mesmerizes people
Tai-açu-iara	River channels	Protects fish	Attacks people
Tapirê-iauara	River channels, streams, rivers, swamps, flooded forest	Protects fish	Kills people and steals their shadows
Visagem	Lakes, rivers, roads	Protects fish	Attacks people and steals their shadows
Visão	Lakes	Protects fish	Makes people ill
Yara	Lakes, streams, forest	Protects minerals	Kills people and makes them ill

Chapter 1: Lore and Land in Transition

1. When known, the scientific and local names of plants are listed in appendix 1.

Chapter 2: Forests, Rivers, and Minerals

1. When known, the scientific and local names of animals are listed in appendix 2.

Chapter 4: Goblins, Ghosts, and Hunters

1. Probably an inselberg, a fairly common feature of the upper Rio Negro landscape and certain other parts of the Amazon basin that are underlain by the Guianan or Brazilian shield. Inselbergs are massive mounds of resistant granitic rock that protrude above relatively flat terrain, ancient formations that have survived millions of years of weathering and erosion. Inselbergs are sometimes regarded as sacred, the dwelling places of spirits, and pictographs are occasionally found on their flanks.

2. Tobacco is also left as a present for *negrinho pastoreiro*, a small, black human figure of concern to farmers and ranchers of southern Brazil. Transamazon colonists from Rio Grande do Sul and Paraná explained the antics of negrinho. The mischievous figure ties the manes of horses into tight knots at night then uses the tangled hair as a stirrup for his single leg. The horses are then ridden until exhausted. The intricate knots are virtually impossible to unravel, and the manes usually have to be cut off. To discourage such nocturnal escapades, rural folk in southern Brazil leave cigarettes for negrinho on fence posts. The sprinkling of holy water on corrals by a priest is also helpful.

3. Probably a species of *Protium* belonging to the *Burseraceae*. In the Orinoco drainage, for example, caraña resin from *Protium heptaphyllum* is burned by Warao shamans as an incense. The resin is also rolled into the cigars of shamans for fragrance and as an agent of transformation. Resin from another member of the *Burseraceae*, almécega (*Teragastris trifoliata*), is rubbed on the foreheads of Kayapó children to protect them from evil.

Chapter 5: Submerged Spirits

1. Genesis 4.

Chapter 6: A Hex on Hunters and Fishermen

1. Resin from the canaraú tree is said to collect in cavities in the trunk and branches. One longtime resident of Pará state who lives along the Transamazon Highway some forty kilometers northeast of Altamira asserted that the brittle resin is derived from the saliva of a frog. When the arboreal frog croaks, it allegedly froths profusely at the mouth. The spittle flows into a hole and therein hardens to a dark red lump.
2. The caurê hawk is probably either the pearl kite (*Gampsonyx swainsonii*), bat falcon (*Falco rufigularis*), or aplomado falcon (*Falco femoralis*).

Chapter 7: Perilous Flesh

1. Fear of snakes is a major reason that caboclos are generally fastidious about keeping the earth around their homes bare. A lawn would attract potentially bothersome snakes and insects. Not all snakes are considered enemies, however. I was in the home of a rural family along the Rio Negro in 1972 when a two-meter-long snake crawled up the front steps. Instead of showing alarm, the family members expressed satisfaction because the visitor would soon clean up the irritating rats in the thatch roof.

Chapter 9: Trees, Treasure, and Treachery

1. Richard Spruce, "On Leopoldinia Piassaba, Wallace," *Journal of the Proceedings of the Linnean Society of London, Botany* 4, no. 14 (1859): 58–63.

Chapter 10: Haunted Streets

1. The King James Version of Matthew 7, verses 19 to 21 reads:
   Lay not up for yourselves treasures upon earth, where moth and rust doth corrupt, and where thieves break through and steal: But lay up for yourselves treasures in heaven, where neither moth nor dust doth corrupt, and where thieves do not break through nor steal: For where your treasure is, there will your heart be also.

Campbell, A. T. *To Square with Genesis: Causal Statements and Shamanic Ideas in Wayãpí.* Edinburgh: Edinburgh University Press, 1989.

Chernela, J. *The Wanano Indians of the Brazilian Amazon: A Sense of Space.* Austin: University of Texas Press, 1993.

Cleary, D. *Anatomy of the Amazon Gold Rush.* Iowa City: University of Iowa Press, 1990.

Dean, W. *Brazil and the Struggle for Rubber.* Cambridge: Cambridge University Press, 1987.

Galvão, E. *Santos e Visagens* (Saints and Ghosts). São Paulo: Companhia Editora Nacional, 1955.

Goulding, M. *Amazon: The Flooded Forest.* London: BBC Books, 1989.

Goulding, M., N. J. H. Smith, and D. Mahar. *Floods of Fortune: Ecology and Economy along the Amazon River.* New York: Columbia University Press, 1995.

Hemming, J. *Red Gold: The Conquest of the Brazilian Indians, 1500–1760.* Cambridge: Harvard University Press, 1978.

Leacock, S., and R. Leacock. *Spirits of the Deep: A Study of an Afro-Brazilian Cult.* New York: Anchor Press/Doubleday, 1975.

Monteiro, W. *Visagens e Assombrações de Belém* (Ghosts and Apparitions of Belém). Belém: Edições CEJUP, 1993.

Moran, E. F. *Through Amazonian Eyes.* Iowa City: University of Iowa Press, 1993.

Murphy, R. F. *Mundurucú Religion.* Berkeley and Los Angeles: University of California Press, 1958.

Nimuendajú, C. *The Apinayé.* Washington, D.C.: Catholic University of America Press, 1939.

Plotkin, M. J. *Tales of a Shaman's Apprentice: An Ethnobotanist Searches for New Medicines in the Amazon Rain Forest.* New York: Viking, 1993.

Reichel-Dolmatoff, G. *Amazonian Cosmos: The Sexual and Religious Symbolism of the Tukano Indians.* Chicago: University of Chicago Press, 1974.

Schultes, R. E. *Where the Gods Reign: Plants and People of the Colombian Amazon.* Oracle, Ariz.: Synergetic Press, 1988.

Schultes, R. E., and R. F. Raffauf. *The Healing Forest: Medicinal and Toxic Plants of the Northwest Amazonia.* Portland: Dioscorides Press, 1990.

———. *Vine of the Soul: Medicine Men, their Plants and Rituals in the Colombian Amazonia.* Oracle, Ariz.: Synergetic Press, 1992.

Slater, C. *The Dance of the Dolphin: Transformation and Disenchantment in the Amazonian Imagination.* Chicago: University of Chicago Press, 1994.

Smith, N. J. H. *Man, Fishes, and the Amazon.* New York: Columbia University Press, 1981.

Stewart, D. I. *After the Trees: Living on the Transamazon Highway.* Austin: University of Texas Press, 1994.

Terborgh, J. *Diversity and the Tropical Rain Forest.* New York: Scientific American Library, 1992.

Villas Boas, O., and C. Villas Boas. *Xingu: The Indians, Their Myths.* New York: Farrar, Straus and Giroux, 1973.

Wagley, C. *Amazon Town: A Study of Man in the Tropics.* New York, Knopf, 1967.

———. *Welcome of Tears: The Tapirapé Indians of Central Brazil.* New York: Oxford University Press, 1977.

Wilson, E. O. *The Diversity of Life.* New York: W. W. Norton, 1992.

Yungjohann, J. C. *White Gold: The Diary of a Rubber Cutter in the Amazon, 1906–1916.* Oracle, Ariz.: Synergetic Press, 1989.

assombrar. *See* soul loss
aviamento. *See* patrons

babaçu, 155
bacabinha, 113
balata: dispersion of trees, 134; protected by
    cabokinha, 134; tapping of, 134
bamboo: habitat for tapir nymph, 77
banhos, 108. *See also* bathing
Barasana Indians: origins of paxiúba palm,
    107; food avoidance, 119; food classifica-
    tion, 125; panema, 105; ritual bathing, 108;
    ritual smoking with chili peppers, 109
Barcelos, 33
Barra de Corda, 53
Bartholomew, Saint, 97
bathing: before eating game to placate
    curupira, 50; cleanliness, 56; panema
    treatment, 106; potions used in treating
    panema, 108, 112, 113, 114, 115
Batista (lake): haunts of cobra grande, 71
batuque, 34. *See also* peasants, religious
    beliefs
bauxite, 2, 21
beijuí, 108
bekāre, 88
Belém: founding date, 26; growth of, 161;
    entry point for slaves, 27; haunts of
    supernatural pig, 147; wholesalers of forest
    products, 39
Beni River: spirit protectors of rubber trees,
    130
benzedor, 31
Bernardino (storyteller), 149–50
biodiversity: buffer against diseases and pest
    attack, 14; loss of, 3, 4; richness of, 13, 14,
    17, 42, 63
black caiman: as mother of fish, 81; attacking
    fisherman, 97, *98*
black man of the water. *See* negro d'água
boa constrictor: length of, 63; origin of cobra
    grande, 63; raping women, 93
Bocinha (storyteller), *49*
boi-una: attacking humans, 64; etymology
    of, 64; origins of, 64; *See also* cobra grande
boráro, 55. *See also* mapinguary
boto. *See* pink dolphin
Branco River: diamond mining, 139; haunts
    of cabokinha, 134
branquinha, 123
Brazil nut: dispersion of trees, 13, 16; flowers
    as food for deer, 47; gathering of, 4, 10, 16;
    transportation of, 94

brocket deer. *See* deer
buffer zones, 165, 166
buriti palm: habitat for tapir nymph, 77

caapora. *See* curupira
cabbage: grown on raised beds, *40*
cabeça de cuia, 83
caboclina, 156–57. *See also* cabokinha
caboclos: definition of, 23. *See also* peasants
cabokinha, 52, 53, 134–35, 156. *See also*
    caboclina, curupira
cacao: extraction of, 26; fermenting in vat,
    49
cachaça, 132, 135, 149. *See also* alcohol
cachorrão, 149
caiçara, 41
caimans: attacking people, 111; hunting of,
    88; prey of tapir nymph, 76, 77;
    responding to cobra grande, 68; spirit
    protectors of fish, 81. *See also* black
    caiman
caipira. *See* curupira
caipora. *See* curupira
caixão, 149
Cametá: haunts of matin, 145
Cametá Tapera, 67
Canal de Inferno (enchanted place), 94
canaraú, 108, 182
Canta Galo (enchanted place), 91
caparari, 123
capé-lobo. *See* wolf's cape
Capuchins, 32
capybara: prey of tapir nymph, 77; source of
    protein, 38
cará branca, 123
Carajá Indians: power of shamans, 87;
    supernatural reserves, 52;
Carajás: location of, 2; mineral deposits, 2,
    24
caraña: incense, 182; resin used to treat soul
    loss, 51, 137; resin used to ward off tapir
    nymph, 80
Carmelites, 32
Carolina, 64
Cartilha da Amazônia, 169
Cashibo Indians: power of shamans, 87
cassiterite, 21
Castanhal Grande (lake): haunts of visão, 85
catauari, 112
cattle: introduction to Amazonia, 148;
    ranching, 3, 40; supernatural aggressor, 7,
    148; supernatural lowing of, 91, 95. *See
    also* milk, horn

iron ore, 2, 21
Itacaiúnas River: haunts of boi-una, 64, 65
Itacoatiara: effects of the evil eye, 127; haunts
of mother of fish, 81;
Itaituba: fishing village, 21; gold rush town,
21; rubber port 21
Itapiranga: haunts of ghost, 151–52; haunts of
matin, 157; haunts of supernatural horse,
156
Itupiranga: haunts of matin, 144; 147; haunts
of supernatural coffin, 149; haunts of
supernatural dog, 149–50; haunts of ghost,
154; haunts of supernatural pig, 147; site of
alleged Indian massacre, 150

Jacaré (lake): haunts of cobra grande, 70
jaguar: chasing a hunter, 61; hunting of, 16;
local extinction of, 81; tracks of, 140
jandiá, 123
jaraqui: capture of, 20; protected by mother
of fish, 81
Jatobal: haunts of matin, 158
jatuarana, 88
jaú: capture of, 18; danger to health, 123;
reimoso quality of, 123
Jesuits: arrival in Amazonia, 32; expulsion
from Amazonia, 33; role in protecting
Indians, 33
jibóia. See boa constrictor
jiboínha, 116
Jívaro Indians: anaconda attacks, 73; power
of shamans, 87; spirit protectors of crops,
163
João Burundi (plant), 108, 109
João da mata (forest spirit), 129
João Torneiro (medium), 93
Jobim, Tom, 111, 145
John, Saint: day honored, 97; rescuing a
hunter, 61; shrine for, 61, 164
Juriti, 97
Juruá River, 17
jurubeba, 129
Jurúna Indians: food avoidance, 122; human
transformation into animals, 87, 89

kaapoaré. See curupira
Kamayurá Indians: dangers of menstruation,
111; food avoidance, 122; humans living in
aquatic underworld, 92; mother of fish, 81,
111; ritual bathing, 108; ritual smoking,
108; spirit protectors of manioc, 163

kapok tree: buttress roots as sleeping
quarters for curupira, 43
Kayapó Indians: cobra grande, 72; food
avoidance, 119; humans living in aquatic
underworld, 92; humans transforming
into birds, 88; humans transforming into
snakes, 93; preventive measures against
evil, 182; ritual bathing, 108
Kerr, Warwick, 169

land transformation: cobra grande, 68;
cattle pasture, 3, 16; crop production, 41;
deforestation, 1
Lazarus, Saint, 97
legends: definition of, 6
lianas, 108. See also vines
língua geral: definition of, 24
lights: associated with water, 88; in forest,
58; indicator of mineral deposits, 140,
141–42; possible origins of, 59–60
lobizoni, 148
Lucia, Saint, 97
lugar encantado: associated with diamonds,
141–42; causes of, 91, 93, 94; enchanted
spring, 58; indigenous origin of concept,
57; life in, 95. See also Canta Galo,
Sapucaia, Sapucaia-roca, Terra Preta de
Limão

Macapá: site of African-Brazilian church, 34
Machado River: dolphins helping
fishermen, 88
Madeira, river: enchanted places, 91, 92;
gold rush to, 22; haunts of cobra grande,
70; haunts of matintaperera, 87; haunts of
tapir nymph, 78; preparation of rubber
along, 29
mãe d'água, 127
mãe da mata, 137. See also mother of the
forest, João da mata
mãe de balateira, 134. See also cabokinha
mãe de peixe. See mother of fish
mãe de piaçava. See mother of piaçava
mãe de seringa. See mother of rubber trees
Makiritataré Indians: human transformation into birds, 88
maloca, 24
Mamirauá Project, 168
Manáos Indians: gold, 139; matin-tapêrê, 87,
145
Manau Indians. See Manáos Indians

Manaus: African Brazilian religious
ceremonies, 34; growth of, 161; rubber
boom, 125; wholesalers of forest products,
39
mandí, 123
manganese, 2, 21
mango, 154
manioc: flour, 14, 38, 124; mythical origins of,
88, 92; panema treatment, *107;* spirit
protectors of, 163. *See also* tipití, tucupi
mapará, 123, 124
mapinguary: attacking humans, 54, 55;
defensive measures against, 57; description
of, 54; distribution of, 54; ground sloth as
model for, 56–57. *See also* wolf's cape
Maracá, 36
Maracá Indians: ritual smoking with chili
peppers, 109
Marajó Island, 67
maranaüwa, 51. *See also* curupira
margay: hunting of, 16
Maria: as cobra grande, 91
marmota, 86. *See also* ghosts
maromba, 41
master of animals, 51, 52. *See also* curupira
matin: attacking dogs, 87; attacking humans,
87; call of, 86, 87, 145, 157, 158; description
of, 86, 87, 145, 157; disappearance as a
result of development, 158; fleeing of after
exposure, 158; habitat of, 87; origins of, 87,
144, 145; protector of turtles, 87; sorva
gatherer, 138
matin-tapêrê. *See* matin
matin-tapirera. *See* matin
matinta-perera. *See* matin
matintaperera. *See* matin
matrinchão, 122, 123, 124. *See also* jatuarana
mau olhado *See* evil eye
Mayna Indians: belief in cobra grande, 73
medicinal plants: cure for snake bites, 28;
extractive products, 13; potential of 4
mediums: advisors, 31, 34; conduit for human
spirits, 86; conduit for snake spirits, 64, 65;
conferring with a matin, 158; descriptions
of, 34, 35–36, 65. *See also* curer, pajé
Mehinaku Indians: soul loss, 45; supernatural
reserves, 52
Mendaruçu River: haunts of matin, 145
Mendes, Chico: assassination of, 4
mente, 138
Mercedarians, 32
mermaids, 34, 83–84. *See also* sereia

milk: fertility symbol, 84; treatment of
supernatural afflictions, 64, 84;
Mineiro (enchanted place), 141
miritinga, 82
Missão: haunts of matin, 157–58
missionaries: establishment of missions, 32,
33; protectors of indigenous groups, 33;
role in changing culture of indigenous
groups, 24–25
Miwá (lake): haunts of cobra grande, 72;
haunts of strange light, 88
Miwá Grande (lake): haunts of cobra
grande, 68, 70
mother of balata trees, 164. *See also* mãe de
balateira
mother of fish: description of, 81, 82;
protector of fish, 82; soul loss, 81, 83;
sounds produced by, 81, 82
mother of the forest, 134, 137
mother of piaçava, 137
mother of rubber trees: description of, 131;
protector of rubber trees, 132, 133
mrü-kra-o, 72
mucura-cáa, 114
mumbaca, 113
Mundurucú Indians: food avoidance, 122;
matin-tapirera, 87; spirit protectors of
game, 51; supernatural pink dolphins, 89
myths: definition of, 6

Negro River: aquarium fish, 17; color and
origins, 17; gold rush to, 22; Iemenjá, 34;
indigenous languages, 24; Salesian
missions, 33; haunts of mother of rubber
trees, 132; haunts of supernatural cattle,
148
negro d'água, 83
nine-banded armadillo: as game, 15
noise: as an irritant to curupira, 50
Norado, 91. *See also* Norato
Noratinha: as cobra grande, 67
Norato: as cobra grande, 64, 91
Nova Fronteira: encounter with cabokinha,
53; encounter with forest lights, 58
nunuí, 1630

Obidos: prohibition of seine fishing, 20
ocelot: appearance in camp, 140; hunting of,
16;
odor: association with death, 55; association
with unclean habits, 56; boráro, 55; cobra
grande, 68; piranhas attracting tapir

surubim, 123
Surubim-Açu: haunts of supernatural pink
   dolphin, 89
surucucu, 64

tai-açu-iara, 80. *See also* tapir nymph
tajapurá, 117
tambaqui: capture of, *19, 78*; prey of tapir
   nymph, 78, 79; protected by mother of fish,
   82; safety of, 123
tamoatá, 123
Tapajós River: apparition of Saint John, 61;
   color of, 17; dolphins helping fishermen, 88;
   gold mining, 21–22; haunts of cobra
   grande, 69, 72; haunts of curupira, 133
tapir: call of, 14; danger to health, 118, 119;
   game, 14, 15, 125; weight of, 14; tracks of, 140
tapir nymph: attacking humans, 78–79;
   description of, 76, 77; diet of, 77, 78, 79;
   distribution of, 77; habitat of, 76, 77;
   immobilizing power of, 79; soul loss, 79,
   80; trap for, 79
Tapirapé Indians: food avoidance, 122; human
   transformation into birds, 88; panema, 111
tapirê-iauara. *See* tapir nymph
Tapurucuara, 33, *44*
Tarumã Falls: haunts of yara, 85
Tello obelisk, 81
Tenetehara Indians: spirit protectors of game,
   51
termite nest: burned to repel curupira, 50
Terra Nova: haunts of matin, 157
Terra Preta de Limão (enchanted place), 92
Terra Santa, 97
timakanã, 51. *See also* curupira
tin: mining of, 5. *See also* cassiterite
tinamou, 118, 119, 120
tipití: use in treatment of panema, 114, *115*
tobacco: to placate curupira, 48, 50, 133; to
   placate matin, 144, 145, 158; to placate
   wolf's cape, 53; smoking, 15
Tocantins River: diamond mining, 21, 139, 141;
   enchanted places, 93, 94, 141–42; haunts of
   cobra grande, 64, 67; haunts of ghost, 85;
   haunts of negro d'água, 83; lights, 58;
   rapids, 94; sugarcane plantations, 26. *See
   also* Cametá, Itupiranga, Tucurui
tomato: protective measures against evil eye,
   163
tortoise, 119, 120, 121, 122, 124, 125
trader. *See* patrons
traíra, 123

Transamazon: construction of, 2; credit and
   indebtedness, 39; encounters with
   curupira, 46–48, 52, 53; evil eye, 127;
   haunts of supernatural pig, 146; panema,
   103, 105. *See also* Coco Chato, Nova
   Fronteira
transformation: of land, *see* land transformation; of humans, *see* human
   transformations
Trombetas River, 28
trumpeters (birds), 120
tucupi, 114, *115*
Tucurui: haunts of matin, 145
Tucurui reservoir, 94, 141, 158
tucuxi. *See* gray dolphin
Tukúna Indians: storyteller, 54
Tumpasa Indians, 130
Tupan, 92
Tupinambá, 37
turkey: supernatural calls of, 92

Uatumã River: haunts of cobra grande, 68;
   haunts of matin, 138
umbanda, 34, 37
unha de cigana, 114
urban growth: 24, 161–62. *See also* rural-
   urban migration
Urubu Indians: panema, 102; soul loss 45;
   spirit protectors of game, 51
Urucu River: haunts of yara, 140

vái-bogó, 72. *See also* cobra grande
vái-mahsë, 52. *See also* curupira
vai-vem, 114
Varig, 170
Vassoura (lake): haunts of pisadeira ghost,
   86
Vermelho Stream, 48
vindika, 113
vines: panema treatment, 108, 109, 112; tied
   in ball to deter curupira, 50; whip for
   curupira, 46
Virgin Mary: associated with Iemenjá, 34;
   festivals for, 97; syncretism with
   indigenous beliefs, 32
visagem, 85, 86, 154. *See also* ghosts
visão, 85. *See also* ghosts

Wagley, Charles, 8
Waiwai Indians: belief in anaconda-people,
   93
wakani, 87

water jaguar. *See* tapir nymph

water nymphs, 34. *See also* Iemenjá, mermaids, yara

Wayãpí Indians: food avoidance, 122; food classification, 119; spirit protectors of fish, 81; panema, 103

werewolves, 56

white-collared peccary: diet of, 120, 121, 122; game, 14, 15, 103, 125; seasonal movements of, 16

white-lipped peccary: companion of curupira, 43; danger to health, 119; diet of, 120, 121, 122, 124; game, 14, 15, 124, 125; guise for curupira, 51; mount for curupira, 43; protected by curupira, 43, 51, 52

Witoto Indians: food avoidance, 119; human transformation into birds; 88

wolf's cape: attacking dogs, 54; defensive measures against, 53; description, of, 53; *See also* mapinguary

Xikrín Indians: human transformation into birds, 88; snake copulating with a woman, 93

Xingu River: color of, 18; haunts of curupira, 47; haunts of mother of rubber trees, 133; haunts of supernatural pig, 147; rapids in, 18; sugarcane plantations along, 26; supernatural reserves, 52. *See also* Altamira

Yameo Indians: belief in cobra grande, 72

yara: descriptions of, 84–85, 140; protector of gold deposits, 140

Yuquí Indians: food avoidance, 119; panema, 102

yuraretê, 80